A FINE BODY OF MEN

A FINE BODY OF MEN

THE ORLEANS LIGHT HORSE

LOUISIANA CAVALRY

1861-1865

DONALD PETER MORIARTY II

LIEUTENANT COLONEL, US ARMY (RET.)

THE HISTORIC NEW ORLEANS COLLECTION

NEW ORLEANS, LOUISIANA

2014

The Historic New Orleans Collection is a museum, research center, and publisher dedicated to the study and preservation of the history and culture of New Orleans, the lower Mississippi Valley, and the Gulf South. The Collection is operated by the Kemper and Leila Williams Foundation, a Louisiana nonprofit corporation.

© 2014 The Historic New Orleans Collection
533 Royal Street, New Orleans, Louisiana 70130
www.hnoc.org

First edition. 1,000 copies.
Printed in the United States of America

18 17 16 15 14   1 2 3 4 5

Library of Congress Cataloging-in-Publication Data

Moriarty, Donald Peter, 1935–

    A fine body of men : the Orleans Light Horse, Louisiana Cavalry, 1861–1865 / Donald Peter Moriarty II, Lieutenant Colonel, US Army (Ret.).

       pages cm

    Includes bibliographical references and index.

    Summary: "History of the Orleans Light Horse, an independent light cavalry troop that formed in New Orleans in February 1861, mustered into active service with the Confederate army in March 1862, and participated in the major campaigns of the Civil War's Western Theater"— Provided by publisher.

    ISBN 978-0-917860-67-6 (pbk. : alk. paper) — ISBN 0-917860-67-5 (pbk. : alk. paper)
1. Confederate States of America. Army. Orleans Light Horse. 2. United States—History—Civil War, 1861–1865—Regimental histories. 3. Louisiana—History—Civil War, 1861–1865—Regimental histories. 4. United States—History—Civil War, 1861–1865—Campaigns. 5. New Orleans (La.)—History, Military—19th century. I. Title.
II. Title: Orleans Light Horse, Louisiana Cavalry, 1861–1865.

    E565.6.O75 M67 2014

    973.7'4763—dc23

                    2014025412

Mary Mees Garsaud, *Project Editor*
Jessica Dorman, *Director of Publications*

Book design by Tana Coman
Printed by Garrity Print Solutions, A Harvey Company, New Orleans, Louisiana

---

Page 5: Detail from the constitution of the Orleans Light Horse, between June and October 1861; *The Historic New Orleans Collection, gift of Bonnie Lee Corban, 2014.0271*

Page 6: Invitation to a ball given by the Orleans Light Horse, January 16, 1862; *The Historic New Orleans Collection, gift of an anonymous donor, 2003.0282.2.3*

DEDICATION

This book is dedicated, with respect and admiration, to the memory of the valiant men of the Orleans Light Horse, who first assembled in New Orleans in February of 1861 and gave the full measure of their devotion to the land that they called home.

Brig Genl & Mrs Ruggles

Your company is respectfully solicited at a Ball, to be given by the Orleans Light Horse, for the Benefit of our absent Volunteers, at the Opera House, on Thursday Evening, January 16th, 1862, at 9 o'clock!

LADY PATRONESSES.

Mrs. T. L. LEEDS,	Mrs. G. MILTENBERGER,	Mrs. HENRY SHEPHERD, Jr.
Mrs. J. M. ROUZAN,	Mrs. J. H. STAUFFER,	Mrs. ROBERT URQUHART.
Mrs. M. J. BUJAC,	Mrs. C. H. FLOWER,	Mrs. R. GARDERE,
Mrs. J. M. WISDOM,	Mrs. J. D. HILL,	Mrs. R. W. ADAMS.

COMMITTEE OF INVITATION.

Capt. T. L. LEEDS,	Corp'l A. FRERICHS,	W. A. BELL,
Serg't GEO. FOSTER,	J. NORMAN JACKSON,	THOS. L. CLARKE,
Corp'l JOHN F. POLLOCK,	STANFORD CHAILLE,	B. F. PETERS,
Corp'l W. A. FRERET,	CHAS. ANDW. JOHNSON,	W. C. NICHOLS.

TURN OVER.

CONTENTS

LOCATIONS AND COMMANDS OF THE ORLEANS LIGHT HORSE

PERIOD OF REPORT	STRENGTH	LOCATION	COMMAND
June 1861	32	New Orleans, LA	First Division, Louisiana Militia
Sept. 1861	48	New Orleans, LA	First Division, Louisiana Militia
Nov. 1861	50	New Orleans, LA	First Division, Louisiana Militia
Mar. 1862	85	New Orleans, LA	First Division, Louisiana Militia
Apr.–May 1862	85	Corinth, MS	First Corps, Army of Mississippi
June–July 1862	71	Tupelo, MS	Department No. 2
Aug. 1862	64	Chattanooga, TN	Right Wing, Army of Mississippi
Sept.–Oct. 1862	71	Knoxville, TN	Right Wing, Army of Mississippi
Nov.–Dec. 1862	74	Murfreesboro, TN	Polk's Corps, Army of Tennessee
Jan.–Feb. 1863	76	Shelbyville, TN	Polk's Corps, Army of Tennessee
Mar.–Apr. 1863	72	Shelbyville, TN	Polk's Corps, Army of Tennessee
May–June 1863	73	Shelbyville, TN	Polk's Corps, Army of Tennessee
July–Aug. 1863	72	Chattanooga, TN	Polk's Corps, Army of Tennessee
Sept.–Oct. 1863	97	Chickamauga, GA	Polk's Corps, Army of Tennessee
Nov.–Dec. 1863	94	Meridian, MS	Headquarters, Army of Mississippi
Jan.–Feb. 1864	86	Meridian, MS	Headquarters, Army of Mississippi
Mar.–Apr. 1864	95	Demopolis, AL	Headquarters, Army of Mississippi
May–June 1864	91	Resaca, GA	Headquarters, Army of Mississippi
July–Aug. 1864	64	Atlanta, GA	Stewart's Corps, Army of Tennessee
Sept.–Oct. 1864	62	Tuscumbia, AL	Stewart's Corps, Army of Tennessee
Nov.–Dec. 1864	59	Nashville, TN	Stewart's Corps, Army of Tennessee
Jan.–Feb. 1865	58	Newberry, SC	Headquarters, Army of Tennessee
Mar. 1865	54	Bentonville, NC	Headquarters, Army of Tennessee
Apr. 1865	59	Greensboro, NC	Headquarters, Army of Tennessee

SOURCES: OPERATIONS DISPATCHES, NARA M320, REEL 032; *OR*, SER. 1, VOLS. 4, 10, 16–17, 20, 23, 30–32, 38–39, 44–45, 47, 49, 52; *OR*, SER. 4, VOLS. 1–2.

PREFACE

THE ORLEANS LIGHT HORSE, AN INDEPENDENT CAVALRY TROOP ORGANIZED in New Orleans in February 1861, mustered into active service with the Confederate States Army on March 22, 1862. The troop served as the escort company to Lieutenant General Leonidas Polk, a corps commander in the Army of Mississippi and later in the Army of Tennessee. Upon Polk's death in June 1864, the Light Horse continued as the escort to Polk's successor, Lieutenant General Alexander P. Stewart, until the Army of Tennessee's surrender at Durham Station, North Carolina, in April 1865. During the total period of the Orleans Light Horse's existence (February 1, 1861, to April 26, 1865), some 215 cavalrymen served with the unit.[1] According to the compiled service records, published by the National Archives and Records Administration (NARA), the unit's operating strength varied from a total of 85 at its mustering to a high of 97 in October 1863 to a low of 54 in March 1865.

An integral part of the corps's headquarters, the escort company was responsible for security, reconnaissance, and courier services for the commander and his staff. Additionally, its members were detailed out on a daily basis to various staff departments within the corps and, sometimes, outside the corps. More cohesive units, such as infantry regiments and artillery batteries, operated as organizational entities; they were committed as defined units, each with a clear-cut mission. The men of an escort company were scattered throughout the headquarters and, sometimes, throughout the command. For example, while the headquarters was deployed in Meridian, Mississippi, from November 1863 to May 1864, Private Harvey N. Crumhorn of the Orleans Light Horse was detailed to

Louisiana pelican button from the uniform of Colonel Charles Didier Dreux, the first Confederate officer killed in the Civil War; *courtesy of the Confederate Memorial Hall Museum Collection, 007.004.012*

a government bakery in Marietta, Georgia, and seems to have become somewhat of an expert in the building of ovens and the baking of bread. Similarly, Private Jonathan W. Dowsing, a physician by profession, was detailed to the corps's medical staff, led by Surgeon William D. Lyles, and then was subdelegated, from June to December 1862, as acting surgeon of the Forty-First Georgia Infantry.[2] And while the command was deployed in Georgia, from May to September 1864, Corporal Robert S. Griffith was detailed to duties in the Trans-Mississippi Department, completely outside the command's area of operations. This absence of organizational cohesion has made piecing together a comprehensive picture of the Orleans Light Horse a difficult endeavor and explains why the unit's story has until now gone untold.[3]

Who were the men of the Orleans Light Horse? Where did they come from? How many survived the war? What ultimately became of them? For one hundred fifty years, these questions have been unanswered. Over the past twenty years, I have gathered and digitized records from many sources in an effort to document the company's operations. The findings, published in part 2 of this book, include not only the service records of the individual soldiers but biographical and genealogical data as well. Every effort has been made to account for the comings and goings of these men, both prewar and postwar, but with incomplete success, as can be seen by the unknowns that remain, particularly in part 2. With hope, the day will come when all 215 members of the Orleans Light Horse will once again be accounted for in the historical record.

In all the research associated with the retelling of this story, particularly with the fleshing out of the lives and families of its cast of characters, every effort has been made to adhere to professional standards of genealogical proofs and to draw correct and supportable inferences from the evidence available. In the event of any shortcomings or failures of that process, I bear the sole responsibility.

I would like to extend my sincere appreciation to all of the individuals who assisted me in bringing this book to fruition. Henry O. Robertson, PhD, chair of the history department at Louisiana College, offered his encouragement and support throughout the process. Elizabeth E. Wheeler and Bonnie Lee (Hunnicutt) Corban, direct descendants of Captains Thomas L. Leeds and J. Leeds Greenleaf, respectively, wholeheartedly embraced this project, opening up their family archives and providing access to photographs, letters, and artifacts belonging to these two officers. Mark Cave, Goldie Lanaux, and Pamela Arceneaux of The Historic New Orleans Collection made the inclusion of these materials in the book possible. The research staff of the James C. Bolton Library at Louisiana State University at Alexandria and Mary Pezzetti of the Villa Park Library in California were invaluable to my research efforts, as were the staff of the Williams Research Center at The Historic New Orleans Collection, particularly Daniel Hammer, John Magill, and Robert Ticknor.

Illustrations for *A Fine Body of Men* were made possible thanks to the photographers at The Historic New Orleans Collection, Keely Merritt, Melissa Carrier, and Tere Kirkland, who photographed and scanned the majority of the book's visuals. Patricia and Joseph Ricci of the Confederate Memorial Hall Museum in New Orleans gave generously of their time, sharing stories about the Civil War experience as well as materials from their collection. Additionally, the Louisiana State Museum, the Library of Congress Prints and Photographs Division, and the State Archives of North Carolina provided images from their holdings.

Thanks also to book designer Tana Coman and to the publications department at The Historic New Orleans Collection. Jessica Dorman, PhD, director of publications, believed in the product of this effort from the beginning. Mary Mees Garsaud was a most patient, incisive, and endlessly supportive editor. And the research assistance of Cathy Hughes and editorial expertise of Sarah Doerries and Dorothy Ball were invaluable to the finished product.

Donald Peter Moriarty II

NOTES

1 The Orleans Light Horse's constitution and bylaws (appendix A), printed between June and October 1861, lists ten additional members, who had resigned from the unit before November 1861 and are not found in NARA's compiled service records for the unit. Therefore, they are not included in the company's 215 members.

2 It appears that Dr. Lyles neglected to inform the Light Horse leadership of this subdelegation because during this period Private Dowsing was carried as AWOL and nearly classified as a deserter.

3 After the war, Joseph A. Chalaron, former lieutenant of the Fifth Company of the Washington Artillery of New Orleans, observed that "no reports can be found of [the Orleans Light Horse's] actions." Notes on the Louisiana troops at the Battle of Chickamauga, box 5, folder 4, p. 10, J. A. Chalaron Papers, 1842–1909, Louisiana Historical Association Collection, Manuscripts Collection 55-F, Louisiana Research Collection, Tulane University (hereafter Chalaron Papers, Tulane).

❊ 1 ❊

THE OPENING SCENE

SECESSION

ON DECEMBER 20, 1860, THE SAME DAY THAT SOUTH CAROLINA ENACTED a resolution of secession, the Louisiana Legislature called for a special convention to decide the secession question for that state. Delegates to the convention were chosen in a statewide election held on Monday, January 7, 1861. When pro-secession candidates were elected in an overwhelming majority, it was apparent what the course of the convention would be. Within days of the election, the US Army's Baton Rouge barracks and arsenal, as well as Forts Jackson and St. Philip—located on the Mississippi River below New Orleans and responsible for the city's defense—were surrendered to state authorities. Subsequently, Louisiana's ordinance of secession was enacted on January 26, by which time Mississippi, Florida, Alabama, and Georgia had followed South Carolina's lead. In a convention held in Montgomery, Alabama, in February 1861, Louisiana pledged its association with the other newly independent states to form the Confederate States of America.[1] Almost immediately, armed confrontations between agents of this new government and the US government occurred in numerous cities around the Confederate states, culminating in the Confederacy's capture of Fort Sumter in Charleston on April 13. As armies formed across the continent, the call to the colors sounded, and volunteer groups began to assemble. One such unit formed in New Orleans was an independent light cavalry troop whose members chose the name Orleans Light Horse.

John McDonald Taylor, first captain of the Orleans Light Horse, by François Bernard, ca. 1864; *courtesy of the Collections of the Louisiana State Museum*

THE FUNCTION OF LIGHT CAVALRY

In the early to mid-nineteenth century, European and American armies normally had three types of mounted soldiers—heavy cavalry, light cavalry, and dragoons—each structured and equipped for a unique operational mission. In the landmark treatise *Cavalry: Its History and Tactics* (1853), Captain Louis Nolan, a British cavalry officer, described the various types of cavalry and their uses on the battlefields of that era, defining the function of the light cavalry as follows:

> The service required of these is the most important in the field. They are called upon to watch over the safety of the army, and they are constantly hovering in advance, on the flanks, and in the rear of the columns, to prevent all possibility of surprise on the part of the enemy. In enclosed countries they are supported by light infantry: in the open country the light cavalry push on and keep the enemy at a proper distance from the army; they are constantly employed in cutting off the enemy's supplies and communications, in reconnoitering, etc. This varied and often impromptu work requires a combination of numerous qualities in officers and men. And in addition to all these duties, peculiarly their own, they often have to perform also those expected of the heavy cavalry.[2]

Within the Confederate States Army, the Orleans Light Horse was a troop—a company-sized element—organized, trained, and equipped to accomplish activities of this nature.

BEGINNINGS OF THE ORLEANS LIGHT HORSE

Assembling in early February 1861, the Orleans Light Horse established its headquarters and riding hall at 99 and 101 Circus (now South Rampart) Street in New Orleans, initiating monthly meetings and drill sessions there. The founding members of the unit elected John McDonald Taylor, a partner in a local firm of commission merchants, as its captain and called upon Lieutenant William Alexander Gordon, a practicing attorney, to draw up a constitution and bylaws (see appendix A). Simultaneously, the unit was accepted and assimilated into the Louisiana Militia.[3]

Louisiana's Militia Act of 1853 recognized both volunteer and enrolled units. The volunteer militia consisted of specialized units (artillery, cavalry, riflemen, etc.), uniformed and equipped at individual expense. There were five militia divisions across the state. The First Division in New Orleans was composed entirely of volunteer units, such as the Orleans Light Horse. In addition to supplying their own uniforms and equipment, members of volunteer units were required to pay initiation fees and monthly dues. For those who could afford these costs, volunteer units had a number of clear-cut advantages. Friends, relatives, and neighbors could

CONSTITUTION.

OF THE

ORLEANS LIGHT HORSE.

ARTICLE 1.

SECTION 1. In conformity to the Articles of War, or Military Regulations, the Company or Troop shall be composed of one Captain, one Lieutenant, two Sergeants, two Corporals and at least thirty members.

SEC. 2. In the event of the Company increasing its members to the number of sixty privates, then and in that case, in conformity with the above mentioned laws for the regulation of the militia of Louisiana, there shall be elected one First Lieutenant, two Sergeants and two Corporals, in addition to the officers and non-commissioned officers elected or appointed for the first thirty members.

The Company may have two trumpeters, but for the present, one will suffice.

Constitution of the Orleans Light Horse, between June and October 1861;
The Historic New Orleans Collection, gift of Bonnie Lee Corban, 2014.0271

be assured of serving in the same unit. Volunteer units maintained their own organizational structure—selecting members, electing officers, and establishing disciplinary practices—thereby controlling their own destiny to a significant extent. And the fees and dues provided a certain degree of financial independence. These units essentially operated in the manner of private clubs, although under military oversight.[4]

The Orleans Light Horse's governance documents, developed in accordance with military regulations, prescribed the basic structure and method of operation of the company, which comprised one captain, one lieutenant, two sergeants, two corporals, and at least thirty members. When the unit's membership increased to sixty members, a first lieutenant and two additional sergeants and corporals were elected.

Each member of the Light Horse was required to provide his own uniform, horse ("at least fifteen hands high"), riding equipment, and light cavalry saber. The uniform of the Light Horse included a short single-breasted dark-blue frock coat with the pelican buttons of the Louisiana Militia, sky-blue trousers with two-inch-wide dark-blue stripes down the outside seams, a sky-blue kepi (a popular visored cap) with a dark-blue cloth band, and knee-length enameled leather boots. The state was responsible for furnishing each member of the unit with one or two pistols. The $10 initiation fee, $3 monthly dues, and equipment costs represented a substantial financial commitment for the individual soldier.

Almost immediately after commencing operations, the Light Horse attracted attention and was invited to participate in a parade in honor of George Washington's birthday, on February 22, 1861. The *New Orleans Daily Picayune* described the Light Horse as "A fine body of men all splendidly mounted: dress, dark blue coats trimmed with light blue, kepis and cavalry boots."[5]

Less than a month later, on March 6, 1861, the Light Horse participated in an assembly and parade held in honor of Major General David E. Twiggs. Former commander of the US Army's Department of Texas, Twiggs had surrendered the department to the state of Texas some three weeks earlier and accepted a major general's commission in the Confederate army. He would go on to command the army's Department No. 1, which encompassed Louisiana and the southern portions of Mississippi and Alabama.[6] The *Daily Picayune* reported the event as follows:

> The whole force being on the ground, Capt Taylor's company of Light Horse Guards formed into line on the outer edge of New Levee [present-day South Peters] Street, and a guard was detached to clear and keep free the large vacant space [along Canal Street] from the levee to Tchoupitoulas Street. This being accomplished, the Light Horse Guards started at a trot, headed by the Grand Marshal and Aides, being detached as an escort of honor to meet and accompany the General. . . . [E]scorted by the Light Horse Guards, the veteran soldier appeared in an open carriage drawn by four horses. He was accompanied by Major General Braxton Bragg of the Army of Louisiana.[7]

With all this activity, and after only four monthly drill sessions, Captain Taylor found leadership of the Light Horse more time consuming than he had anticipated; he resigned effective June 1, 1861. First Lieutenant Thomas L. Leeds, a partner in the New Orleans foundry Leeds and Company, was elected to replace Taylor as captain. For the next several months, the drill sessions were intensified significantly.[8]

On October 6, 1861, a large number of Union prisoners of war captured at the First Battle of Manassas were brought into New Orleans en route to the place of their incarceration, and the men of the Light Horse acted as guards during their arrival. The *Richmond Daily Dispatch* reported that "the entrance of the Yankee prisoners into New Orleans was greeted with a display that would have done credit to a Fourth of July celebration. . . . A little before twelve o'clock the special train arrived, and the troops cleared a space around it as speedily as possible, for the prisoners to get out of the cars and form by fours. The regiment of Orleans Guards were detailed as the guard, with the Orleans Light Horse in advance to clear an avenue for them through the dense crowds that even closed up the middle of the streets. All was now perfect silence and decorum."[9]

On November 23, 1861, a general review of the First Division of the Louisiana Militia, under the command of Major General John L. Lewis, was held. The troops assembled on Canal Street and were reviewed by Governor Thomas O. Moore and Major General Mansfield Lovell, commanding general of the Confederate army's Department No. 1. The force numbered some twenty-five thousand men. The Light Horse participated in this review with forty of its fifty men present.[10] The leaders of the troop at that time were Thomas L. Leeds, captain; William A. Gordon, second lieutenant; Patrick B. O'Brien, cornet (or third lieutenant); William C. Nichols, surgeon; Leon R. Delrieu, veterinary surgeon; William A. Bell, George Foster, and J. Leeds Greenleaf, sergeants; and Ephraim K. Converse, Charles D. Lallande, and John F. Pollock, corporals.[11] Shortly after the military review, three of the unit's fifty members were released: Stanford E. Chaillé was appointed assistant surgeon general of Louisiana, and Patrick B. O'Brien and Andrew J. Watt accepted commissions in another unit.

The unit relaxed somewhat during the Christmas holidays, and then, on Wednesday, January 8, 1862, the Light Horse was assembled at the drill hall for an inspection by Major General Lewis to verify the unit's progress in its training program.[12]

The following week, on Thursday, January 16, the company hosted a formal ball, "for the benefit of our absent Volunteers," at the Opera House.[13] The "Lady Patronesses" of the event included the wives of unit members of all ranks, supported by additional women from well-known families throughout the city. Invited guests included general officers serving in the New Orleans area and a wide range of prominent citizenry of the city. The cost of the evening was significant, $5 for single gentlemen and $10 for gentlemen accompanying one or more women.[14] The proceeds from this event would have been an invaluable resource to a unit making every effort to fill its ranks with fully clothed and equipped cavalrymen, ready to meet the severe demands of duty in the field.

As the conflict between Confederate and US authorities intensified, and reports of skirmishing in Missouri and western Virginia reached New Orleans, the likelihood of the Light Horse being called to active duty increased, leading to a heightened sense of urgency among the members of the unit. During January and February, the unit's meetings were increased to two per month as various units were called and deployed to the scene of active combat operations in Virginia and Kentucky.[15]

PERSONNEL ACCOUNTABILITY

In an effort to account for the comings and goings of the members of the Orleans Light Horse over time, two tables have been included at the end of each section. The first table tallies the total number of accountable personnel. This figure, derived from enlistments and losses, is broken down into categories detailing duty statuses as recorded in NARA's compiled service records (M320) and explained more fully in the individual data sets in part 2. One category requires a comment: Detailed to Duty. It was common in the Confederate army for soldiers to be sent on work details away from their assigned units. In the case of the escort company in a corps headquarters, these details were often with various elements of the staff as well as with support units. An individual so detailed would not be available for the primary functions of the escort company. The first lieutenant and duty sergeants were charged with managing those present for duty so that the mission requirements of the unit were covered despite these absences. The second table lists the names of individuals joining and leaving the Orleans Light Horse during each period.

ORLEANS LIGHT HORSE PERSONNEL ACCOUNTABILITY
GENERAL MILITARY REVIEW, NOV. 23, 1861, NEW ORLEANS

GAINS	51
LOSSES	1
Discharged	1
ACCOUNTABLE	50
Present	40
Absent—leave	3
Absent—sick	1
Absent—w/o leave	6

FEB. 1–NOV. 23, 1861

GAINS   Bell, W. A.; Blanc, J. A.; Boisblanc, E.; Broadwell, C. B.; Broadwell, J. P.; Carré, W. W.; Chaillé, S. E.; Clarke, T. L.; Clauden, E.; Converse, E. K.; Delrieu, L. R.; De Mahy, H. J.; Denis, H. W.; Duncan, S. P.; Fleitas, J. B.; Foster, G.; Freret, W. A.; Frerichs, A.; Gallier, J.; Gordon, W. A.; Greenleaf, J. L.; Griswold, A. B.; Gubernator, J. L.; Hobart, E.; Hopkins, A. R.; Huntington, B. W.; Jackson, J. N.; Johnson, C. A.; Lallande, C. D.; Lallande, J. B.; Leeds, T. L.; Lonsdale, F.; Nichols, W. C.; O'Brien, P. B.; Peters, B. F.; Pollock, J. F.; Pressprich, O. H. J.; Robelot, E. L.; Robelot, H. N.; Robelot, J. N.; Robinson, E. T.; Saunders, R. W.; Scott, S. R.; Shepherd, H. H.; Simmons, J. W.; St. Phar, A. H.; Taylor, J. M.; Thornhill, H. M.; Watt, A. J.; Woodlief, P. W.; Woods, A. V.

LOSSES   Taylor, J. M.

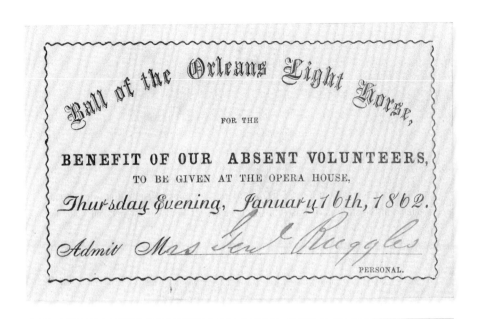

Ticket to a ball given by the Orleans Light Horse, January 16, 1862;
The Historic New Orleans Collection, gift of an anonymous donor, 2003.0282.2.3

CALL AND RESPONSE

On February 28, in Jackson, Tennessee, General P. G. T. Beauregard, who was preparing to take command of the Confederate army's Department No. 2, issued a general call for reinforcements.[16] His statement was published in all the New Orleans daily newspapers on March 1: "Will accept all good equipped troops under the act of 21st August that will offer, and for ninety days. Let the people of Louisiana understand that here is the proper place to defend Louisiana." The act cited was an appropriations act of the Confederate States Congress, providing for the force structure of the Confederate States Army. At this early stage of the confrontation, both armies, confident that any conflict would be short and decisive, were willing to accept enlistments of only ninety days. When General Beauregard stated, "here is the proper place to defend Louisiana," he was referring to western Tennessee, where he was situated. His message was in line with the general feeling that the South's line of defense needed to be through western Tennessee (or Kentucky, if that could be arranged), and every effort was being made to establish forces in that area.[17]

The Light Horse reacted immediately to General Beauregard's call. The following announcement appeared in the *Daily Picayune* on Tuesday, March 4, and ran daily until the unit's muster on March 22: "The Orleans Light Horse, having resolved to go into active service under the call of Gen. Beauregard, will receive applications from parties desirous of joining the troop. Apply daily, from 11 a.m. to 2 p.m. at 118 Common Street." The unit's headquarters and riding hall had been relocated from Circus Street to Common Street most likely at the beginning of March. Although it is not specified in the record, it appears that most applicants, regardless of age, were being accepted. The atmosphere of expectation and patriotic fervor continued to escalate and, in an apparent effort to fill out the ranks of the unit, an additional advertisement began to appear in the daily newspapers on March 9: "HEADQRS, ORLEANS LIGHT HORSE: Horse and equipments furnished, in certain cases. Parties wishing to join the Troop will make application from 11 a.m. to 2 p.m. daily, at 118 Common Street."[18]

DEMOGRAPHICS OF THE UNIT

The members of the Orleans Light Horse were described in contemporary accounts as being "from the first families of Louisiana" and "the flower" of the youth of New Orleans.[19] However, as part 2 of this volume reveals, occupation and social class, place of origin, and age varied widely among the cavalrymen.

The leaders of the Orleans Light Horse seem to have made every effort to chart a more balanced recruiting path than other local volunteer units, such as the flamboyantly uniformed Chasseurs-à-Pied and the ethnically exclusive Chasseurs d'Orleans, Lützen Jägers, and Cazadores Espagnoles. While the founders of the Light Horse gave every indication of being men of means—able to appear well uniformed, well mounted, and well drilled only two weeks after the unit's founding— subsequent recruiting efforts reflect a deliberate intent to cast a wide net, seeking capable and dependable cavalrymen rather than men of a certain ethnic, social, or economic class. The latter point is attested to in the range of occupations laid out below and in the newspaper advertisements that ran throughout March of 1862, announcing "horse and equipments furnished, in certain cases." The language suggests that the Orleans Light Horse would invest its resources in subsidies, if necessary.

The occupations of the cavalrymen ranged from attorney and physician—the second-most-common occupation listed, after farmer—to riverboat crewman and teamster.[20] There were cotton merchants, retail merchants, and teachers, as well as clerks and farm laborers. The Orleans Light Horse was representative of the socioeconomic life of the great port city that its members called home.

GENERAL LABORERS UNSKILLED AND JOURNEYMAN	TRADESMEN MASTER AND SELF-EMPLOYED	PROFESSIONALS
clerk (5)	farmer (24)	physician (10)
teamster/drayman (4)	cotton factor/merchant (8)	attorney (6)
farm laborer (2)	accountant/bookkeeper (5)	corporate executive (3)
railroad agent (2)	merchant, retail (5)	teacher (3)
riverboat crewman (2)	commercial broker (4)	architect (2)
wood and coal dealer (2)	grocer, retail (4)	engineer (2)
constable	cotton inspector (3)	clergyman
conveyance clerk	stockbroker (3)	investor
cotton brokerage clerk	carpenter (2)	newspaper publisher
facilities custodian	grocer, wholesale (2)	pharmacist
grocery clerk	insurance agent (2)	plantation owner
oil mill worker	merchant, dry goods (2)	veterinarian
oyster fisherman	merchant, lumber (2)	
purser	merchant, wholesale (2)	
quirer/builder	real estate agent (2)	
rail splitter	sugar broker (2)	
streetcar driver	assayer at US Mint	
telegraph operator	butcher	
	fire captain	
	harness maker	
	jeweler	
	livestock broker	
	machinist	
	merchant, collections agent	
	merchant, furniture	
	merchant, hardware	
	mortgage broker	
	newspaper printer	
	plantation overseer	
	portrait painter	
	printer	
	riverboat captain	
	riverboat pilot	
	sawmill owner/merchant	
	sugar refinery manager	
	surveyor	
	transportation contractor	

A survey of the places of origin of Orleans Light Horse members demonstrates that for a large segment of the cavalrymen, Louisiana was their adopted home.

PLACE OF BIRTH	NUMBER	PERCENTAGE
New Orleans, LA	36	17%
Other cities in Louisiana	37	17%
Other US states	73	34%
Outside the US	20	9%
Unknown	49	23%

The other states of origin include nine in the Confederacy and eleven outside the Confederacy. Other countries of origin include Ireland, France, Germany, Scotland, Canada, England, Haiti, Switzerland, and Jamaica.

Of the 215 cavalrymen, the dates of birth of 36 (17 percent) have not been found. An analysis of the ages of the remaining 83 percent demonstrates that in the unit's early days, the age range of its members was quite wide. It was not until April 1864 that the age range reflected the youthful description of the account quoted on page 20. For the first few months of 1861, the eldest member, Captain John McDonald Taylor, was sixty-three, and the youngest was sixteen. Taylor's age was far in excess of any age standard for a unit such as the Light Horse. Research suggests that Taylor, a native of Inverness, Scotland, was elected as the troop's first commander despite his advanced age because he had prior experience in the Household Cavalry units of the British army. The Light Horse's early use of the rank of cornet (or third lieutenant), a unique custom of the Household Division in London, reflects the influence of Taylor's earlier military career. Having gotten the Light Horse off to a good start, Taylor resigned in fairly short order, and a younger commander was elected.

By the time of the unit's muster, upon being called to active duty in March 1862, the age range had narrowed slightly to between seventeen and fifty-nine. A number of the younger men, who may have had young children at home, declined enlistment, preferring to remain in the militia and therefore closer to home. Of those who accepted enlistment, a number of older men (over forty-five years of age) and two very young men (both seventeen) were discharged soon after deployment to northern Mississippi, in conformance with army regulations; with that, the unit's active-duty age range began to moderate toward that of the April 1864 period (ages between seventeen and forty-four), which was more in line with the norm for tactical units on active duty.

SNAPSHOT	MEDIAN AGE	MIN./MAX. AGES	AGE RANGE OF 90 PERCENT
Nov. 1861 (militia)	33	16/63	21–47
Mar. 1862 (muster) declined enlistment	33	16/63	20–53
Mar. 1862 (muster) accepted enlistment	38	17/59	18–43
Apr. 1864 (peak)	26	17/44	18–42
Overall average	33	16/63	18–40

MUSTER AND DEPLOYMENT

The Orleans Light Horse's decision to accept active service with the Confederate States Army resulted in significant changes in the unit. Twenty-six men declined enlistment and were released. The remaining twenty-one members, joined by sixty-four new recruits, took the oath of enlistment for a ninety-day term of service. Thus, on Saturday, March 22, 1862, eighty-five members of the Orleans Light Horse were formally mustered into active service of the Confederate States Army as an independent troop of light cavalry.

Despite the many changes, the unit's leadership managed to retain its most experienced members. After the muster, the leadership consisted of Thomas L. Leeds, captain; William A. Gordon, first lieutenant; George Foster, second lieutenant; J. Leeds Greenleaf, junior second lieutenant; William C. Nichols, surgeon; William A. Bell, Ephraim K. Converse, Frederick G. Freret, Charles D. Lallande, John F. Pollock, and Henry Thornhill, sergeants; and William A. Freret II, Aristide R. Hopkins, Philip M. Kenner, and Jules N. Robelot, corporals. Only Patrick B. O'Brien (cornet) and Leon R. Delrieu (veterinary surgeon) had been lost. Five of the leadership (Foster, Greenleaf, Converse, Lallande, and Pollock) had been promoted. One of the new recruits (Frederick G. Freret) was promoted to sergeant almost immediately. The other members of the leadership cadre remained in their respective places.[21]

The unit was ordered to deploy to the Army of Mississippi, a major element of Department No. 2, then operating in the vicinity of Corinth, in the northeast corner of Mississippi. The men of the Light Horse were given one week to get their personal affairs in order. The following Saturday, March 29, the *Daily Picayune* published this notice: "Light Horse.—This troop of cavalry will assemble at the riding hall today, at 2½ o'clock, fully equipped, effects packed, ready for departure." The unit would travel by steamer to Memphis and then by train to Corinth. The paper followed up with a report the next day: "The Orleans Light Horse, Capt. Leeds, one of the crack cavalry troops of the State, left yesterday evening on board

Steamer *General Quitman*, pictured left, docked in New Orleans, 1860s;
The Historic New Orleans Collection, 1977.296.18

the steamer Gen. Quitman. They were 74 strong, all in very good spirits, and seemed longing for the fray. At the same time, the Fisk [Twenty-Fifth Infantry] Regiment, to which we alluded yesterday, left on board the steamer Mary Keene. These two corps were escorted to the steamboat landing by a large military force and several thousand of their friends, who cheered them enthusiastically when the boats left the wharf."[22]

If the newspaper account is correct that "they were 74 strong," eleven members of the Light Horse appear to have missed movement. There is no further record to explain this discrepancy, but eighty-five members reported for duty in Corinth, suggesting that the eleven absentees traveled separately or the newspaper account was inaccurate.

Although not reported in the newspaper on March 30, the rousing send-off on Saturday, March 29, quickly came to a halt when the *General Quitman* collided with another vessel shortly after entering river traffic. The steamer and several of the wagons of the Light Horse on board were damaged. Returning to the dock for immediate repairs, the *General Quitman* did not actually get under way until the following morning, Sunday, March 30.[23]

ORLEANS LIGHT HORSE PERSONNEL ACCOUNTABILITY
UNIT MUSTER (CSA SERVICE), MARCH 22, 1862, NEW ORLEANS

GAINS	64
LOSSES	26
Discharged	26*
ACCOUNTABLE	85
Present	85

*MILITIA MEMBERS WHO DECLINED ENLISTMENT

GAINS

Adam, ——; Adams, J.; Armstrong, C. D.; Beauregard, C. T.; Belknap, M. S.; Bonfanti, H. T.; Branham, W. H.; Bryan, C. A.; Bryan, W. H.; Bryan, T.; Buord, L. A.; Byrne, T. K.; Campbell, M. G.; Carey, H. S.; Christian, P. J.; Claiborne, A. J.; Clough, J. A.; Crain, R. A.; Crumhorn, H. N.; Davis, R. H.; Dowsing, J. W.; Eberle, G.; Fazende, L. J.; Foley, T. W. P.; Freret, F. G.; Gallwey, C.; Gardner, L. H.; Griffith, R. S.; Gunnison, A. B.; Haney, M.; Hardin, J. O.; Harrison, F. W.; Hearn, E. O.; Hildreth, C. A.; Hite, C. M.; Kennedy, J. M.; Kenner, P. M.; Landreaux, P. F.; Lange, L.; May, T. P.; McKnight, J. H.; Mitchell, C. C.; Mitchell, W. C.; Monty, F. P.; Moreau, J. T.; Moriarty, W. A.; Morse, E. M.; Murphy, C.; Opdenweyer, W. C.; Parsons, J. W.; Patrick, J. C.; Riley, B.; Rountree, A. W.; Seiler, F. W.; Shally, C. E.; Shaw, W. N.; Smith, E.; Sprigg, H. S.; Stewart, J. J.; Trepagnier, F. E.; Urquhart, R. P.; Viavant, A.; Walker, J. C.; Williams, T. H.

LOSSES (DECLINED ENLISTMENT)

Blanc, J. A.; Broadwell, C. B.; Broadwell, J. P.; Carré, W. W.; Clarke, T. L.; Clauden, E.; Delrieu, L. R.; De Mahy, H. J.; Denis, H. W.; Duncan, S. P.; Frerichs, A.; Gallier, J.; Griswold, A. B.; Gubernator, J. L.; Huntington, B. W.; Johnson, C. A.; Lallande, J. B.; Lonsdale, F.; Pressprich, O. H. J.; Robelot, E. L.; Robelot, H. N.; Saunders, R. W.; Scott, S. R.; Shepherd, H. H.; Woodlief, P. W.; Woods, A. V.

RE-ENLISTED FOR NINETY DAYS

Bell, W. A.; Boisblanc, E.; Converse, E. K.; Fleitas, J. B.; Foster, G.; Freret, W. A.; Gordon, W. A.; Greenleaf, J. L.; Hobart, E.; Hopkins, A. R.; Jackson, J. N.; Lallande, C. D.; Leeds, T. L.; Nichols, W. C.; Peters, B. F.; Pollock, J. F.; Robelot, J. N.; Robinson, E. T.; Simmons, J. W.; St. Phar, A. H.; Thornhill, H. M.

INTO THE FRAY

After the eventful departure, the remainder of the voyage to Memphis went as planned. Captain Leeds scheduled regular drills, superintended by his lieutenants, on the roof of the boat every morning. The weather was seasonable and the men were well cared for. The voyage served as an almost idyllic retreat for the cavalrymen in advance of the tumultuous future that awaited them.[24]

On Friday, April 4, 1862, after a five-day passage from New Orleans, the *General Quitman* arrived in Memphis, where Captain Leeds telegraphed General P. G. T. Beauregard for further orders, reporting that "two or three days will be required to recruit horses and repair wagons damaged on board." Completing these tasks in short order, the unit boarded trains bound for Corinth, Mississippi, on Sunday, April 6.[25]

The Orleans Light Horse arrived in Corinth early on the morning of Monday, April 7, and was led to its designated campsite, where the members occupied the remainder of that day unpacking and readying themselves and their animals and equipment for operational service.[26] The Army of Mississippi was fighting the second day of the Battle of Shiloh on the Tennessee River in southwestern Tennessee. The army's commander, General Albert Sidney Johnston, had died of wounds received in action the previous day, and General P. G. T. Beauregard had succeeded him to command. General Beauregard was faced not only with Major General Ulysses S. Grant's force, which had been seriously battered by the Confederates the day before, but also with Major General Don Carlos Buell's force, which had arrived overnight from Bowling Green, Kentucky, and Nashville to reinforce Grant. By the afternoon of April 7, General Beauregard had made the decision to withdraw southward from Shiloh toward Corinth.[27]

Early on Tuesday morning, April 8, a courier delivered the first order to Captain Leeds. The Light Horse was to move north from Corinth to meet the artillery of Major General Braxton Bragg and assist them in their move into the post at Corinth. Rainy weather during the withdrawal of forces from the Shiloh battlefield had reduced the surrounding countryside into a mass of mud. The horses of the artillery became bogged down on roads that were barely passable.[28] After the Light Horse completed this mission, the tasks assigned to the unit came thick and fast: prisoners taken during the battle had to be moved with the relocating forces and kept under guard; stragglers needed to be rounded up and returned to their units; a reconnaissance of various routes to Corinth had to be made; and, all the while, a watchful eye on the locations of enemy units and pickets needed to be maintained. The Light Horse was in its element: a well-equipped unit, fresh in the field, not assigned to any major command, and available to be of service to all.[29]

P. G. T. Beauregard by William Watson Washburn, photographer, 1865;
The Historic New Orleans Collection, gift of William W. Cook, 1981.374.15

The unit's command was the next item of focus for Captain Leeds. After numerous conversations with the generals of the Army of Mississippi, Leeds secured a permanent assignment for the Light Horse: escort to Major General Leonidas Polk, commander of the First Corps of the Army of Mississippi.[30]

An 1827 graduate of the US Military Academy, Leonidas Polk resigned his military commission shortly after graduation to become a priest in the Episcopal Church. In 1841 he became bishop of the Episcopal Diocese of Louisiana. When the war began, Polk accepted a commission as major general in the Confederate States Army, and in July 1861 he took command of Department No. 2, a position he held until March 1862, when he was replaced by Beauregard, who also took command of the Army of Mississippi. Polk then assumed command of the First Corps of the Army of Mississippi. During his years as bishop in New Orleans, Polk would have been well acquainted with Captain Leeds's family, which was very prominent in the city and in the Episcopal diocese. This entrée was of considerable assistance to Captain Leeds in securing the Orleans Light Horse's assignment as escort to Polk. The arrangement was made official on April 14, 1862, when the Army of Mississippi published a special order directing that "Leeds's company of Louisiana cavalry will report to Major-General Polk for special service."[31]

THE ARMY AND CORPS

GENERALIZED STRUCTURE OF CONFEDERATE STATES ARMY UNITS

UNIT NAME	COMPOSITION	NOMINAL STRENGTH	COMMANDED BY
Company	Basic unit	100 men	Captain
Regiment	Ten companies	1,000 men	Colonel
Brigade	Four regiments	4,000 men	Brigadier General
Division	Two or more brigades	8,000+ men	Major General
Corps	Two or more divisions	16,000+ men	Lieutenant General
Army	Two or more corps	32,000+ men	General

NOTE: THE COMPOSITION AND NOMINAL STRENGTH NUMBERS SHOWN WERE FOR POLICY OR PLANNING GUIDELINES ONLY AND WERE SELDOM FOUND TO EXIST IN REALITY.

The Army of Mississippi consisted of four corps: the First Corps, Polk's Corps; the Second Corps, commanded by Major General Braxton Bragg; the Third Corps, commanded by Major General William J. Hardee; and the Reserve Corps, commanded by Brigadier General John C. Breckinridge.[32] Each of the corps consisted of two or more divisions with additional artillery and cavalry units. The army commander and corps commanders were also provided one or more escort companies—cavalry companies who were the eyes and ears of

Eng^d by H.B.Halls Sons,New York

Leonidas Polk, from William Mecklenburg Polk, *Leonidas Polk, Bishop and General*, 1893;
The Historic New Orleans Collection, gift of General L. Kemper Williams, 69-20-L.47

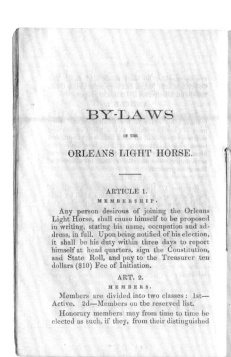

BY-LAWS

OF THE

ORLEANS LIGHT HORSE.

ARTICLE 1.

MEMBERSHIP.

Any person desirous of joining the Orleans Light Horse, shall cause himself to be proposed in writing, stating his name, occupation and address, in full. Upon being notified of his election, it shall be his duty within three days to report himself at head quarters, sign the Constitution, and State Roll, and pay to the Treasurer ten dollars ($10) Fee of Initiation.

ART. 2.

MEMBERS.

Members are divided into two classes: 1st—Active. 2d—Members on the reserved list.

Honorary members may from time to time be elected as such, if they, from their distinguished services to the Company or the State, be deemed worthy of the honor.

ART. 3.

RESERVED LIST.

Such members as from ill health, press of business or occupations incompatible with their constant attendance at drill, may, when they are considered as competent by the Captain to perform their duties effectually when on active service, on application to the Committee on Discipline and Administration, be transferred to the reserved list.

It shall be the duty of members on the reserved list, to keep their arms and equipments at all times ready for active service; to turn out at all full dress parades, and whenever especially ordered by the Captain. It shall be their right to attend all drills and meetings of the Company and vote at the same, but they shall be exempt from fines for non-attendance at ordinary drills, etc., except when, as before stated, they may be especially ordered by the Captain.

They shall pay their dues semi-annually, in advance.

ART. 4.

CAPTAIN.

The duty of the Captain, besides the ordinary duties of his office, and those prescribed by the Constitution, shall be to call together the Committee on discipline and Administration at least

Bylaws of the Orleans Light Horse, between June and October 1861;
The Historic New Orleans Collection, gift of Bonnie Lee Corban, 2014.0271

the commander, providing reconnaissance, security, and courier services to the commander and his staff.

The corps headquarters was the agency through which the commander received and analyzed information affecting his command, and through which he planned and implemented his response to that information. Within the headquarters, the staff assisted the commander in the myriad activities involved in providing support to his own force and in combating the enemy.

The headquarters was divided into two elements: the field headquarters, which moved in close proximity to the deployed divisions, controlling primarily the tactical operations, intelligence, and support to the force; and the base, or main, headquarters, which remained farther behind, often in a nearby town, and focused on legal issues, pay matters, administrative duties, and record keeping. It was the primary function of the chief of staff to ensure that the field and base headquarters acted in concert, without confusion or contradiction. He, along with the judge advocate, paymaster, and other such special staff members, normally would not move with the force but would remain in the base location, with courier pouches being exchanged daily with the field location.

Commanders in both armies, Confederate and Union, varied widely in their ability to organize and maintain control of their respective staffs, proving to be adept or inadequate at this essential duty—to the benefit or detriment of their command as a whole. Polk's track record in this regard was relatively good, a factor of his personality and his tenure in command. He organized well, delegated matters as appropriate, and was universally respected and admired by those who worked for him.[33]

THE STAFF

The operations functions of the headquarters were accomplished by one or more assistant adjutants general, assistant inspectors general, a provost marshal, and the commanding general's aides-de-camp. These staff officers were responsible for helping their commander see the battlefield and understand the significance of what he was seeing. In particular, the assistant adjutant general prepared written orders and reports in the name of the commander, transmitting them to their destination by telegraph (for higher echelons) or by courier (within the corps). Couriers were normally the aides or troopers of an escort company. Inspectors general kept an eye on the status and condition of a command, monitoring the health and welfare of personnel, the condition of weapons and equipment, and, therefore, the combat potential of the organization. A major difference between modern-day practice and that of the Confederate and Union armies is that the nineteenth-century staff did not include an intelligence officer.[34] Rather, the provost marshal was responsible for law enforcement and intelligence activities; in Polk's Corps, J. Leeds Greenleaf, captain of the Orleans Light Horse from November 1862 until the war's end, served as provost marshal and escort company commander. As a matter of policy, the aide-de-camp was on the personal staff of the commanding general; when a general moved, his aides frequently moved with him. All other staff officers were considered to be assigned to the organization and were intended to remain in their positions as generals came and went.[35]

Logistics functions were the responsibility of the quartermaster, commissary, and chief of ordnance. The assistant adjutant general also participated in these functions through management of replacement personnel activities. The quartermaster was responsible for the procurement and distribution of all nonfood supplies (except weapons and ammunition), such as clothing, tentage, and tools. He also oversaw an organization's transportation system, procuring wagons and draft animals and coordinating the transportation of men and materiel. The chief commissary of subsistence procured rations from army depots or from the local economy (depending on current operating conditions), coordinated with the quartermaster to transport rations, and distributed them to subordinate units. The commissary also provided for pasturage and butchering of livestock. The ordnance officer had oversight of weapons (small arms and artillery), ammunition, and peculiar support equipment (caissons, gun carriages, etc.).[36]

The technical staff included a signals officer, engineer, and chief of artillery. They provided technical expertise and operational advice in their respective fields to the commander and other staff members. The signal officer focused on maintaining communications within the command, especially via telegraph, when that service was available. The engineer focused on planning and oversight of field fortifications, roads, and bridges, as well as maps and field surveys. When the command went into camp, the engineer provided advice on the organization and layout of the encampment. The chief of artillery provided advice and oversight of artillery assets, including readiness of men, equipment, harnesses, and horses.[37]

The special staff included a judge advocate, paymaster, and medical director. The primary function of the judge advocate was to preside at courts martial and to provide legal advice to the commander. The paymaster obtained monetary assets and, through assistants, provided payment to soldiers based on unit muster rolls. The medical director provided technical advice to the commander and was a liaison between the corps and the medical staffs and hospitals within the region.[38]

THE ESCORT COMPANY

As an escort company, the Orleans Light Horse had a variety of duties. Its members provided security and courier services for the commanding general and his staff. They were responsible for the security of the headquarters and its surroundings, including verifying the condition of planned positions and fixing the locations of enemy forces and pickets. During troop movements, the Light Horse cavalrymen verified the condition of roads, bridges, and fords; confirmed the movements and locations of subordinate units; located and verified intermediate halt points and campsites; and searched for stragglers. The unit's members were also detailed out for duties such as providing clerical and courier services to staff departments, guarding prisoners of war and stock in pasture, and acting as trail hands, driving stock to new locations, and as stable hands for the headquarters' stables.

LIFE OF THE SOLDIER IN THE FIELD

Confederate army regulations authorized one tent per thirteen mounted men. This was most likely the Sibley tent, patented in 1857 by Henry H. Sibley of Natchitoches, Louisiana, who would later become a brigadier general in the Confederate army. The cone-shaped, canvas Sibley tent measured approximately twelve feet tall and eighteen feet in diameter at the base. Supported by a central pole, the tent was ventilated by a circular opening at the top, which also vented a cone-shaped stove used for heating. Although the tent was designed to sleep approximately a dozen men, supply shortages during the war required occupancies of up to twenty. For a unit on the march, packing and transporting large pieces of canvas was difficult, and the tents were frequently jettisoned. In absence of a Sibley tent, soldiers often made use of a smaller piece of canvas that could be thrown over a low-hanging branch or any similar makeshift frame. These improvised shelters, housing one or two individuals, were a precursor to the shelter-half tents utilized by twentieth-century armies.[39]

Food service was accomplished by the men themselves. Rations were drawn by the company's commissary sergeant from higher-level commissary staff, or from depots, and issued to the men. When the unit was on the march, rations frequently were issued for three to five days at a time to account for the inability of the supply trains to keep up with the tactical units. The authorized standard daily ration (three meals for one person, unless specified otherwise) was as follows:

DAILY RATION: 1863 REGULATIONS	1864 REGULATIONS
.75 lb. pork or bacon, or 1.25 lb. fresh or salt beef	.5 lb. pork or bacon when in movement or at work; .33 lb. when stationary
18 oz. bread or flour, or 12 oz. hard bread, or 20 oz. corn meal	22 oz. flour or corn meal, or 12 oz. hard bread; 16 oz. hard bread when on a campaign, march, or onboard transports
2.5 oz. peas or beans, or .1 lb. rice	same
0.06 lb. (less than one ounce) coffee	same
0.12 lb. (just under 2 oz.) sugar	same
1 lb. potatoes	same
2 qt. salt per 100 men (approx. 1.25 tbsp. per man)	same
2 qt. molasses and 1–1.5 bushels dried apples per 100 rations (when available)	same
1.5 lb. tallow candles per 100 men	same
2.3 oz. soap	same

SOURCE: CONFEDERATE STATES WAR DEPARTMENT, 42, PARA. 1107; *OR*, SER. 1, VOL. 32, PT.2:608.

Soldiers would prepare and consume their food in groups, or messes, of four to eight men, who were usually connected by a common hometown, familial ties, or friendship. Regulations provided that on marches and in the field, the only "mess furniture" would be one tin plate and cup and one knife, fork, and spoon, all to be carried by the individual soldier. The members of the mess took turns cooking, cleaning the skillet, which belonged to the group, and going after rations. To put this in perspective, on a quiet day in camp, when Polk's Corps sat down to supper, there could be more than two thousand campfires, each with its mess group huddled around it. For the Army of Tennessee as a whole, this number could rise to as many as eight thousand campfires. This was the focal point of the social life of the army in the field.[40]

Each corps was allocated one or more hospitals, normally situated in major cities and operated by the centralized medical service of the Confederate States Army. For example, when Polk's Corps was stationed in Shelbyville, Tennessee, at the beginning of 1863, their allocated hospitals were located at Rome and Atlanta, Georgia. Each day those who required medical treatment, along with a corps surgeon, would take the six-to-eight-hour train ride to the hospital, where the medical staff would decide when the men were well enough to be released to their units. The medical service jealously guarded these facilities, as evidenced by the order issued by the adjutant general in March 1863 prohibiting medical directors of corps, armies, and departments from interfering with the hospitals.[41]

OPERATIONAL CONTEXT

For the majority of the war, the Orleans Light Horse served in a corps of the Army of Tennessee. In his books *Army of the Heartland* (1967) and *Autumn of Glory* (1971), Thomas L. Connelly compiled the story of this army and defined the conditions and limitations under which it operated. He also contrasted the Army of Tennessee with the Army of Northern Virginia (commanded by General Robert E. Lee), which has consistently garnered the lion's share of publicity and historical research. Connelly concludes that, comparatively, the Army of Tennessee "has been rather badly neglected," and the historical record unduly influenced by attempts to judge the Tennessee army using Virginia standards. He points out that the western army had to defend a much larger territory—225,600 square miles, more than ten times the area covered by the Virginia army—with fewer men. The entire Confederate line in northern Virginia stretched only about 125 miles, while the Army of Tennessee defended a line that extended some 400 miles, from the Mississippi River to the Appalachian Mountains, with no east-west river to block Union forces. Defending such a vast area required longer troop movements. Lee's army never traveled more than sixty miles north of the Virginia border, but in 1862 alone the Army of Tennessee traveled eight hundred miles.[42]

This operational context would not only frame the daily activities of the Orleans Light Horse, its corps, and the Army of Tennessee, but would also become an impossible hurdle that each commander and each unit in turn would struggle against, in effect preordaining an inevitable result. They could struggle manfully, even heroically, but they would not be able to prevail.

Louisiana pelican buckle; *courtesy of the Confederate Memorial Hall Museum Collection, 007.003.186*

NOTES

1 Williams and Hébert, 1, 2. On March 21, 1861, Louisiana's Constitutional Convention ratified the Constitution of the Confederate States of America. Winters, 19.

2 Nolan, 63–67.

3 *New Orleans Daily Picayune*, 23 and 25 Feb. 1861; *Gardner's New Orleans Directory*, 1861. Before the early 1900s, all states had militias, as established by the provisions of the US Militia Acts of 1792. These acts were updated periodically, and by 1861 they required that every free, able-bodied, white male citizen between the ages of eighteen and forty-five be enrolled in the militia of his state of residence (hence the term "enrolled militia"). Each state's militia was organized into local companies, which were then assigned to regiments, brigades, and divisions. The acts further established that for each battalion of infantry, there should be at least one company of artillery and one troop of horse. In all cases, members of the militia were expected to provide their own uniforms, weapons, and equipment, including horses for members of the cavalry. To minimize the disruption to the lives of militia members, the acts provided that no individual could be required to perform active service of more than three months in any one year. This last provision was the source of the ninety-day enlistments common in the mobilizations of 1861 and early 1862. It was changed by action of the Confederate States Congress in 1862 (see page 46). The militia acts were repealed by the Militia Act of 1903, which established the National Guard as the primary body of organized reserves for the armed forces of the United States.

4 Field, 3–5; Emerson, 5–6.

5 *New Orleans Daily Picayune*, 23 Feb. 1861.

6 In the early days of the war, the overall command structure of the Confederate States Army included a hierarchy of local districts (such as New Orleans, Mobile, and Vicksburg) and departments, both state-level and higher. For example, there was a Department of Louisiana, which was part of the higher-level Trans-Mississippi Department, and a Department of Mississippi, part of the higher-level Department

of Mississippi and East Louisiana. In concept, each department would have an army: the Army of Louisiana in the Department of Louisiana; the Army of Mississippi in the Department of Mississippi. These district and departmental designations all came and went, having brief flashes of importance and emphasis, then fading as priorities turned elsewhere as resources became more scarce and had to be focused to meet changing threats. Beginning in mid-1863, many of these structures and labels fell into disuse and were dropped, with only a few surviving into the last year or two of the war. On May 31, 1861, Major General Twiggs assumed command of Department No. 1, which was focused on the Gulf Coast and headquartered in New Orleans.

7 *New Orleans Daily Picayune*, 6 Mar. 1861. Braxton Bragg (b. 1817, Warrenton, NC; d. 1876, Galveston, TX), an 1837 graduate of the US Military Academy, served in the Second Seminole War (1835–42) and Mexican-American War (1846–48) and was posted in the Indian Territory before resigning from the service in 1856. Since his wife was originally from Louisiana, they settled there, and Bragg became a planter in addition to being active in the Louisiana Militia. After a short retirement, he was commissioned as a brigadier general in the Confederate army in 1861 and accepted promotion to major general later that year. Recognizing his personal ties to Louisiana, the military authorities selected him to command the Army of Louisiana. In this capacity, he provided executive supervision of the process of recruiting, mobilizing, equipping, and training the manpower levies imposed by the Confederate States Congress on the state of Louisiana.

8 NARA M320, reel 032; Bartlett, sec. 2:31.

9 *Richmond Daily Dispatch*, 7 Oct. 1861. The prisoners were bound for the parish prison on Orleans Street (near the rear of the present-day Municipal Auditorium), which had been emptied of its civil criminals. Arceneaux, 18. The Orleans Guards were an infantry regiment of the Louisiana Militia.

10 Bartlett, sec. 5:242–43; Rightor, 154–55; NARA M320, reel 032. On Oct. 9 General Twiggs had retired as commander of Department No. 1; Major General Lovell had assumed command on Oct. 18, sparking a burst of energy in the department. Winters, 64.

11 Rightor, 154–55; NARA M320, reel 032.

12 *New Orleans Daily Picayune*, 8 Jan. 1862.

13 In January 1862 there were two opera houses in New Orleans. The Théâtre d'Orléans on Orleans Street near Bourbon Street, which was frequently called the Old French Opera House, would burn down in 1866. The New Opera House, built in 1859 on Bourbon Street at Toulouse Street, became known as the French Opera House in the 1880s. Either opera house could have accommodated a ball. *Daily True Delta*, 3 Feb. 1861; *New Orleans Daily Picayune*, 7 Dec. 1866; Mardi Gras invitations, 1870–84, The Historic New Orleans Collection; Wharton, 210.

14 Invitation to Orleans Light Horse ball, 16 Jan. 1862, The Historic New Orleans Collection, 2003.0282.2.3.

15 Bartlett, sec. 5:240–42.

16 Pierre Gustave Toutant Beauregard (b. 1818, St. Bernard Parish, LA; d. 1893, New Orleans, LA), an 1838 graduate of the US Military Academy, served in the Mexican-American War (1846–48) and as a member of the staff of the Corps of Engineers in Louisiana before being commissioned as brigadier general in the Confederate army in 1861. He was quickly promoted to general and early in the war commanded the defenses of Charleston, South Carolina, resulting in the capture of Fort Sumter. He then became the first commander of the defenses in Northern Virginia and served at First Manassas. He was commander of the Confederate army's Department No. 2 and the Army of Mississippi from March 5, 1862, until March 29, 1862, when Albert Sidney Johnston assumed command. He was second-in-command of the Army of Mississippi at the Battle of Shiloh, and after Johnston's death, on the first day of the battle, he again assumed command of the army and the department. Department No. 2 (the Western Department) was created June 25, 1861. Its area of responsibility varied over time but, at its peak, it encompassed Arkansas, Tennessee, and parts of Alabama, Kansas, Kentucky, Louisiana, Mississippi, Missouri, and the Indian Territories to the west of Arkansas and Missouri.

17 *New Orleans Daily Picayune*, 1 Mar. 1862; Rightor, 155; Winters, 29–43.

---

18 *New Orleans Daily Picayune*, 4 and 9 Mar. 1862.

19 Williams, 346; Spence, "General Polk," 121–23.

20 By and large, the farmers were men of moderate landholdings and net worth. Large plantation owners were generally older than would be appropriate for a cavalry troop and would have opted for staff positions in higher-level headquarters. However, several of the cavalrymen were the younger sons of prominent landholders.

21 NARA M320, reel 032.

22 *New Orleans Daily Picayune*, 29 and 30 Mar. 1862.

23 Thomas L. Leeds to P. G. T. Beauregard, telegram, 4 Apr. 1862, P. G. T. Beauregard Papers, Rosenbach Collection, Philadelphia, PA (hereafter Beauregard Papers, Rosenbach Collection); Bartlett, sec. 2:31–34.

24 *New Orleans Daily Picayune*, 4 Apr. 1862; Thomas L. Leeds to Olivia Barbarin Leeds, 1 Apr. 1862, The Historic New Orleans Collection, gift of Dr. Elizabeth Eustis Wheeler in memory of Jane Eustis Suydam (hereafter THNOC, Wheeler donation), 2014.0279.3.

25 Thomas L. Leeds to P. G. T. Beauregard, telegram, 4 Apr. 1862, Beauregard Papers, Rosenbach Collection; Thomas L. Leeds to Olivia Barbarin Leeds, 6 Apr. 1862, THNOC, Wheeler donation, 2014.0279.4.

26 Bartlett, sec. 2:31–34.

27 Connelly, *Army of the Heartland*, 169–75.

28 Samuel W. Ferguson, lieutenant colonel and aide-de-camp, to Captain Leeds, order from General Beauregard, 8 Apr. 1862, THNOC, Wheeler donation, 2014.0279.5.

29 Bartlett, sec. 2:31–34; Thomas L. Leeds to Olivia Barbarin Leeds, 15 Apr. 1862, THNOC, Wheeler donation, 2014.0279.6.

30 Ibid.

31 Warner, 242–43; Carter and Carter, 51–53, 129–30, 206; *OR*, ser. 1, vol. 10, pt. 2:418–19.

32 *OR*, ser. 1, vol. 10, pt. 1:382; *OR*, ser. 1, vol. 10, pt. 2:370–71.

33 Johnson, "Confederate Staff Work," 1–4, 82–85; Henry Watterson, description of Leonidas Polk on the battlefield, quoted in Polk, 2:353.

34 Johnson, "Confederate Staff Work," 67–70.

35 *OR*, ser. 4, vol. 2:26; Notes on the Louisiana troops at the Battle of Chickamauga, box 5, folder 4, p. 10, Chalaron Papers, Tulane.

36 Johnson, "Confederate Staff Work," 71–72.

37 Ibid., 73–74.

38 Ibid., 75.

39 *OR*, ser. 1, vol. 16, pt. 2:746–47; Confederate States War Department, 106, para. 1031; Stoddard and Murphy, 199–200.

40 Confederate States War Department, 106, para. 1032; Wiley, 106. Despite the best of official intentions, the standard daily ration of food was very often not met by available supplies or transportation capabilities. In periods of constant rain, building a fire to transform flour into bread was impossible. In both the Confederate and Union armies, there were frequent wide swings between feast and famine, usually more famine than feast. Hunger was an ever-present condition in the life of a Civil War soldier.

41 *OR*, ser. 4, vol. 2:425; Crego, 142. Lieutenant General Polk's rejoinder to this general order, written one month later, presents an alternative corps-level system of management, preferred by both Polk and Hardee. *OR*, ser. 1, vol. 23, pt. 2:747–49.

42 Connelly, *Army of the Heartland*, ix–x.

❧ 2 ❧

APRIL–JUNE 1862

ESCORT, FIRST CORPS, ARMY OF
MISSISSIPPI, DEPARTMENT NO. 2

‹ • • • ›

THANKS TO THE EFFORTS OF THE ORLEANS LIGHT HORSE'S CAPTAIN,
Thomas L. Leeds, the middle of April 1862 found the unit newly assigned as escort
to Major General Leonidas Polk, commander of the First Corps of the Army
of Mississippi. Captain Leeds's procurement of this assignment would be one of
his last—and most enduring—accomplishments. His failing health had been a
matter of concern to family and associates for some time. During the voyage from
New Orleans, his lieutenants relieved him of many of his tasks so that he might
rest as much as possible. The symptoms were intermittent, but recurring, and on
April 21 he was examined by the staff surgeon, Samuel Choppin. He diagnosed
Leeds with bilious fever, and asserted that his condition could not be treated in
camp.[1] Leeds was ordered back to New Orleans for extended treatment, leading
to his resignation from command of the unit, as Napier Bartlett, a member
of the Washington Artillery of New Orleans, discussed in his *Military Record
of Louisiana* (1875):

> His rapidly failing strength warned his friends that it was imperative his services
> should be, for a time, lost. A consultation of surgeons resulted in his being ordered
> to New Orleans. The decision, however, came too late. On the journey South, it
> became evident to Lieutenant Greenleaf, his kinsman, who accompanied him,
> that the end was near. He stopped at Jackson; and there, on the 24th of April,

Thomas L. Leeds, second captain of the Orleans Light Horse, between June 1861 and March 1862;
*The Historic New Orleans Collection, gift of Dr. Elizabeth Eustis Wheeler in memory
of Jane Eustis Suydam, 2014.0279.1*

COMMANDERS OF THE FIRST CORPS, ARMY OF MISSISSIPPI

Commander	Maj. Gen. Leonidas Polk
First Division	Brig. Gen. Charles Clark
First Brigade	Col. Robert M. Russell
Second Brigade	Brig. Gen. Alexander P. Stewart
Second Division	Maj. Gen. Benjamin F. Cheatham
First Brigade	Col. Preston Smith
Second Brigade	Col. George E. Maney
Cavalry force	Col. Andrew J. Lindsay
Orleans Light Horse (escort)	Lt. William A. Gordon

SOURCE: *OR*, SER. 1, VOL. 10, PT.1:382, 405–12; *OR*, SER. 1, VOL. 10, PT.2:419.

1862, died Captain Thomas L. Leeds, as much a victim of the war as if he had been killed in battle. No purer, truer man laid down his life a sacrifice, for his country and his honor, in all the Southern army.[2]

When Captain Leeds was released from duty status, First Lieutenant William A. Gordon became acting commander of the Light Horse. After the death of Leeds, Gordon was confirmed as acting troop commander. At the same time, two privates in the Light Horse were promoted to noncommissioned ranks: J. Norman Jackson to sergeant and Josiah C. Patrick Jr. to corporal.[3]

The Light Horse's command, the Army of Mississippi, had withdrawn to Corinth in the aftermath of the Battle of Shiloh. Although Corinth was militarily significant as a rail junction, it was not a good location for the army. The vicinity was relatively indefensible against constant enemy probes, and poor drainage after recent rains had led to standing water and mud, making the area unhealthy for habitation. The already insufficient sources of drinking water were polluted, and dysentery and typhoid fever became rampant. Men of the Light Horse and other units fell ill in significant numbers, and the effective strength of the force was seriously depleted. By May 25, after unrelenting enemy pressure for some three weeks, the city came under siege, and General Beauregard, commander of the Army of Mississippi, was forced to evacuate Corinth and move the army farther south, toward Tupelo.[4]

During the months of May and June, the realities of field operations in a combat zone had a severe impact on the ranks of the Light Horse. Many of the older members were sent home, and the younger, more physically fit members were called upon to take on the burdens of leadership. Approximately twenty members of the unit—including Second Lieutenant George Foster; Corporal Jules N. Robelot; and Sergeants William A. Bell, J. Norman Jackson, and John F. Pollock—were discharged for age, illness, or physical limitations. Corporal William

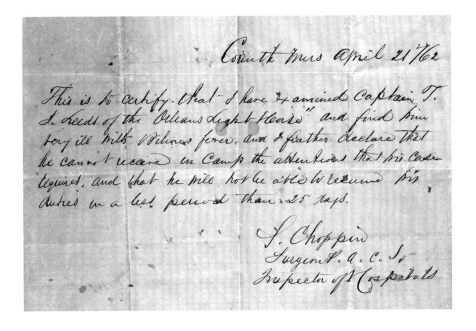

Certificate of examination of Thomas L. Leeds, by Surgeon Samuel Choppin, April 21, 1862;
*The Historic New Orleans Collection, gift of Dr. Elizabeth Eustis Wheeler in memory
of Jane Eustis Suydam, 2014.0279.2*

A. Freret II was granted a transfer to the Fifth Company of the Washington Artillery.[5] Corporals Philip M. Kenner, Aristide R. Hopkins, and Josiah C. Patrick Jr. were promoted to sergeant. Privates Robert S. Griffith, Amos B. Gunnison, John M. Kennedy, and Jackson W. Simmons were promoted to corporal. Junior Second Lieutenant J. Leeds Greenleaf was promoted to second lieutenant. Sergeants Henry M. Thornhill and Charles D. Lallande were elected junior second lieutenant. First Lieutenant William A. Gordon continued as troop commander.[6]

General Beauregard had suffered from poor health for some time and had petitioned the war department for a replacement so that he could recuperate. After numerous requests, the authorities finally responded on June 20, 1862, relieving Beauregard of his post and designating General Braxton Bragg as commander of the Army of Mississippi as well as Department No. 2, the area command to which that army belonged. Remaining in Tupelo through July, General Bragg continued to solidify the army's emplacements and to repair and refit after the recent action. Colonel Philip B. Spence, a member of Major General Polk's staff, recalled the positive influence General Bragg's appointment had on the morale of the men of the army: "Under this stern, strict disciplinarian the army was soon greatly improved, and the morale and spirits of the men were as cheerful as before our disastrous defeat on the second day's battle of Shiloh. Officers and men at this time had the utmost confidence in Gen. Bragg as commander of the Army of Mississippi."[7] They would need that confidence, as General Bragg had plans for the army that few could have anticipated.

ORLEANS LIGHT HORSE PERSONNEL ACCOUNTABILITY

APRIL–JUNE 1862

	APR. 1862	MAY–JUNE 1862
GAINS	2	6
LOSSES	2	20
Discharged	1	14
Transferred	0	2
Killed/died	1	0
Unspecified	0	4
ACCOUNTABLE	85	71
Present	82	38
Detailed to duty	1	4
Absent—leave	0	3
Absent—sick	0	24
Absent—w/o leave	1	1
Hospitalized	1	1

	APR. 1862	MAY–JUNE 1862
GAINS	Brooks, A. C.; Stewart, S. R.	Chew, ——; Elenterius, L. C.; Huntington, S.; Louis, ——; Payan, H.; Perkins, J. A.
LOSSES	Byrne, T. K.; Leeds, T. L.	Bell, W. A.; Bonfanti, H. T.; Brooks, A. C.; Bryan, W. H.; Davis, R. H.; Foster, G.; Freret, W. A.; Gardner, L. H.; Haney, M.; Hearn, E. O.; Jackson, J. N.; Lange, L.; May, T. P.; Monty, F. P.; Nichols, W. C.; Pollock, J. F.; Robelot, J. N.; Trepagnier, F. E.; Urquhart, R. P.; White, ——

NOTES

1   Bilious fever was a loose medical term for illnesses with vomiting, fever, and sometimes jaundice. According to Paul E. Steiner in *Disease in the Civil War*, "bilious fever was the most common diagnosis made that does not appear in the official disease tables." Steiner, 80.

2   Bartlett, sec. 2:31–34; Thomas L. Leeds to Olivia Barbarin Leeds, 1 Apr. 1862, THNOC, Wheeler donation, 2014.0279.3; Certificate of examination of Thomas L. Leeds, by Surgeon Samuel Choppin,

Evacuation of Corinth, Mississippi, wood engraving from a sketch by Henri Lovie, 1862;
Library of Congress Prints and Photographs Division

21 Apr. 1862, THNOC, Wheeler donation, 2014.0279.2. Junior Second Lieutenant J. Leeds Greenleaf
was Captain Thomas L. Leeds's cousin.

3   NARA M320, reel 032.

4   *OR*, ser. 1, vol. 10, pt. 1:764–65, 774–77; Cunningham, 385–86; Engle, 181.

5   The Washington Artillery of New Orleans was formed in 1838 as the Washington Artillery
Company. In 1845 the unit volunteered for service in the Mexican-American War. The unit was
mustered into service of the Confederate States Army on May 26, 1861, as an artillery battalion, and
four of its companies were sent to the Army of Northern Virginia, where they served principally with
James Longstreet's corps. For service in Virginia, the unit was awarded ten battle streamers. At the
time of its mustering in, some twenty-five members of the battalion remained in New Orleans and
formed a fifth company, which was mustered into the Confederate States Army on March 6, 1862.
Assigned initially to the Army of Mississippi (later the Army of Tennessee), this unit participated in
the Kentucky and Tennessee campaigns and in the defense of Atlanta and Mobile. For service in this
western theater of the Confederacy, the unit was awarded eight battle streamers. In wars subsequent to
1900, the Washington Artillery has been credited with service in World War I (one streamer), World
War II (fourteen streamers), and Operation Iraqi Freedom (one streamer). The unit survives today as the
141st Field Artillery Regiment of the Louisiana National Guard.

6   NARA M320, reel 032.

7   Spence, "Services in the Confederacy," 500–501.

✷ 3 ✷

JULY–AUGUST 1862

ESCORT, DEPARTMENT NO. 2

◄ • • • ►

JULY BEGAN WITH A BANG AS GENERAL BRAXTON BRAGG PROMULGATED a massive realignment of the forces assigned to him in Department No. 2. His intention was to imprint his personality on this new command, to ready it for the work he had planned for it, and to put in key positions individuals with whom he was most comfortable. Major General Leonidas Polk was relieved as a corps commander in the Army of Mississippi and designated as second-in-command of the forces of the department. Those forces consisted of the Army of Mississippi (32,126 effectives); the Army of the West (10,390 effectives); the garrison at Columbus, MS (2,607 effectives); and a cavalry force (270 effectives): a total of 45,393.[1] Major General William J. Hardee was appointed commander of the Army of Mississippi, with its corps redesignated as divisions.[2] The Light Horse continued as escort to Major General Polk and welcomed twelve new members on July 1, restoring some of the manpower lost the previous month.[3] This bolstering of its ranks would prove to be important in the coming months as General Bragg launched a large-scale initiative to take Kentucky into the Confederate States.

Shortly after the middle of July, General Bragg and Major General Edmund Kirby Smith, commander of the Department and Army of East Tennessee, had solidified plans for a massive joint operation in Kentucky. In the coming weeks the

---

General Braxton Bragg, from engraving of Confederate generals by Henry Wright Smith, 1863; *The Historic New Orleans Collection, 1986.96.3i–viii*

COMMANDERS OF DEPARTMENT NO. 2

Commander	Gen. Braxton Bragg
Second-in-command	Maj. Gen. Leonidas Polk
Army of Mississippi	Maj. Gen. William J. Hardee
Army of the West	Maj. Gen. Sterling Price
District of the Mississippi	Maj. Gen. Earl Van Dorn
District of the Gulf	Brig. Gen. John H. Forney
Columbus, MS, garrison	Brig. Gen. Daniel Ruggles
Cavalry force	Capt. William C. Bacot
Orleans Light Horse (escort)	Lt. William A. Gordon

SOURCE: *OR* SER. 1, VOL. 17, PT. 2:635, 636; *OR*, SER. 1, VOL. 10, PT. 2:419.

Army of Mississippi participated in the largest Confederate troop movement of the war, with more than thirty thousand men traveling by rail more than 770 miles from Tupelo, Mississippi, to Chattanooga, Tennessee, from which they would launch the Kentucky campaign. The other elements of Department No. 2 remained in the west, defending Mississippi and western Tennessee.[4]

Beginning on Wednesday, July 23, and on a daily basis for the next seven days, the infantry units of the Army of Mississippi mustered, accounted for personnel and equipment, then departed. They traveled by rail to Mobile, Alabama, by ferry across Mobile Bay, and by steamboat and rail to Montgomery, Alabama. From Montgomery, they continued by rail to West Point and Atlanta, Georgia, where they transferred to trains bound for Chattanooga. Meanwhile, the cavalry, artillery, and wagon trains journeyed overland via Columbus, Mississippi; Tuscaloosa, Alabama; and Rome, Georgia, a distance of some 350 miles.[5] The men of the Light Horse were divided between the rail and overland parties—some of its members traveled by train with the corps headquarters; others accompanied the livestock, spare horses, and wagon trains of supplies and equipment. By the end of the first week of August, the army, including the Light Horse, was reassembled at Chattanooga.

While preparing for redeployment, commanders had to take into account a change in army regulations on terms of service, resulting from the First Conscription Act of April 16, 1862. The new regulations, dated July 1, 1862, stipulated that those men under eighteen and over thirty-five were entitled to discharge ninety days after the expiration of their term of service; those between eighteen and thirty-five were required to reenlist for three years or for the duration of the war. From this point forward, all enlistments would be for this longer term. The early, popular conception of a short, decisive war had been completely dispelled.[6]

On July 25, just before leaving Tupelo, the members of the Light Horse between the ages of eighteen and thirty-five were reenlisted. During July and

August twenty-four older men were discharged by the unit, and seventeen younger replacements were received.[7] Sergeant Henry M. Thornhill was elected second lieutenant, and Private Auguste Viavant Jr. was promoted to sergeant. The troop was changing, becoming younger and more physically fit. But with the older ranks went a significant amount of experience that would require time to make up.

ORLEANS LIGHT HORSE PERSONNEL ACCOUNTABILITY
JULY–AUGUST 1862

GAINS	17	GAINS	Bein, H.; Blanton, R. M.; Campbell, J.; Cenas, E. H.; Guilfant, A. J.; House, J. A.; Hughes, E. A.; Jonas, J. J.; Kennedy, T. S.; Le Monnier, Y. R.; Macready, R.; Mandeville, T.; Moore, J. B.; Rogers, W. L.; Simmons, R. W.; Thuer, J.; Trist, N. P.
LOSSES	24		
Discharged	11		
Unspecified	13	LOSSES	Adam, ——; Adams, J.; Belknap, M. S.; Boisblanc, E.; Branham, W. H.; Campbell, M. G.; Carey, H. S.; Chew, ——; Converse, E. K.; Eberle, G.; Fazende, L. J.; Foley, T. W. P.; Freret, F. G.; Hite, C. M.; Hobart, E.; Huntington, B. W.; Louis, ——; Moreau, J. T.; Murphy, C.; Opdenweyer, W. C.; Parsons, J. W.; Shally, C. E.; Smith, E.; Williams, T. H.
ACCOUNTABLE	64		
Present	57		
Detailed to duty	4		
Absent—w/o leave	3		

NOTES

1 Individual strength figures for the District of the Mississippi and the District of the Gulf were not found.

2 *OR,* ser. 1, vol. 17, pt. 2:635–36. William J. Hardee (b. 1815, Camden County, GA; d. 1873, Wytheville, VA), an 1838 graduate of the US Military Academy, served in the Second Seminole War (1835–42) and Mexican-American War (1846–48) and was commandant of cadets at the US Military Academy before being commissioned as a colonel in the Confederate army in 1861. He was promoted to brigadier general in June 1861, to major general in October 1861, and to lieutenant general in October 1862.

3 NARA M320, reel 032.

4 *OR,* ser. 1, vol. 16, pt. 2:731, 733.

5 Connelly, *Autumn of Glory,* 203–4.

6 *OR,* ser. 4, vol. 2:1. During the course of the war, there would be a total of five acts of the Confederate States Congress regulating general military service: (1) the Act of March 6, 1861, which called for 100,000 volunteers and militia; (2) the Act of January 23, 1862, which called for 400,000 volunteers and militia; (3) the First Conscription Act of April 16, 1862, which required service of all white males between the ages of eighteen and thirty-five; (4) the Second Conscription Act of September 27, 1862, which extended general conscription to white males between the ages of seventeen and fifty; and (5) the Act of March 13, 1865, which called for 300,000 African American males. *OR,* ser. 4, vol. 1:1,095; Eicher and Eicher, 25, 26.

7 NARA M320, reel 032.

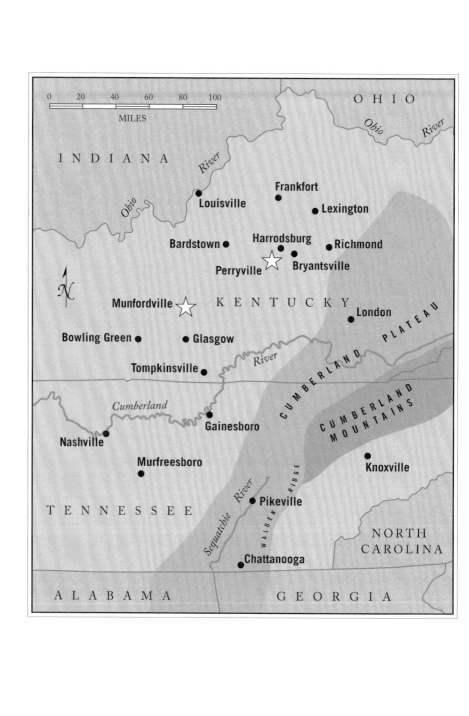

⚔ 4 ⚔

AUGUST–NOVEMBER 1862

ESCORT, RIGHT WING, ARMY
OF MISSISSIPPI

A<small>SSUMING COMMAND FROM</small> M<small>AJOR</small> G<small>ENERAL</small> W<small>ILLIAM</small> J. H<small>ARDEE</small>, General Braxton Bragg reorganized the Army of Mississippi in Chattanooga, consolidating the traditional corps structure into two wings. The Right Wing, commanded by Major General Leonidas Polk, with the Light Horse as his escort, consisted of two divisions, led by Major General Benjamin F. Cheatham and Brigadier General Jones M. Withers. The Left Wing, commanded by Major General Hardee, also consisted of two divisions, led by Brigadier Generals Samuel Jones and Sterling A. M. Wood. The total effective strength of the Army of Mississippi was reported as 27,320, divided evenly between the two wings.[1]

About the middle of August, Major General Edmund Kirby Smith and the Army of East Tennessee, moving north from Knoxville, had crossed the Cumberland Mountains and entered Kentucky. Reorganizing his command as the Army of Kentucky, Kirby Smith scored a major victory at Richmond and then moved on to take Lexington.[2] By the end of August, General Bragg and the Army of Mississippi were ready and began to move north from Chattanooga. Bragg accompanied the Left Wing as it moved up the Sequatchie River valley, between the Cumberland Plateau and Walden Ridge, into Pikeville, Tennessee. Polk's Right Wing ascended Walden Ridge and joined Bragg on September 1, near Pikeville.[3]

COMMANDERS OF THE RIGHT WING, ARMY OF MISSISSIPPI

Commander	Maj. Gen. Leonidas Polk
Cheatham's Division	Maj. Gen. Benjamin F. Cheatham
First Brigade	Brig. Gen. Daniel S. Donelson
Second Brigade	Brig. Gen. Alexander P. Stewart
Third Brigade	Brig. Gen. George E. Maney
Fourth Brigade	Brig. Gen. Preston Smith
Withers's Division	Brig. Gen. Jones M. Withers
First Brigade	Brig. Gen. Franklin Gardner
Second Brigade	Brig. Gen. James R. Chalmers
Third Brigade	Brig. Gen. John K. Jackson
Fourth Brigade	Col. Arthur M. Manigault
Orleans Light Horse (escort)	Lt. William A. Gordon

SOURCE: *OR*, SER. 1, VOL. 16, PT. 2:764; *OR*, SER. 1, VOL. 10, PT. 2:419.

Union Major General Don Carlos Buell reacted immediately to the Confederate advance, withdrawing from his base in the vicinity of Corinth, Mississippi, toward Nashville, Tennessee, where some of his units were situated. On September 5 Bragg, perceiving Buell to be withdrawing first to Murfreesboro and then to Nashville, sent Polk and the Right Wing forward, to the Cumberland River crossing at Gainesboro, Tennessee, in order to prevent Buell from turning and massing against Bragg. However, it quickly became apparent that Buell was falling back on Bowling Green. Once across the river at Gainesboro, the Right Wing was directed to move into Kentucky via Tompkinsville to Glasgow, joining up with the Left Wing there.[4]

On September 13 Brigadier General James R. Chalmers, commander of the Second Brigade of Withers's Division, initiated an attack on the Union force guarding the railroad bridge spanning the Green River at Munfordville, Kentucky, a stop on the Louisville and Nashville Railroad just north of Glasgow. Bragg had not intended to give battle there, but he took advantage of the situation that presented itself. While Polk's Right Wing was in a blocking position, the Left Wing laid siege to the Union force, which surrendered two days later.[5] Bragg now dominated the Union army's primary supply line to Louisville; by astute and aggressive action, he had pushed Buell's army back almost to the Ohio River, causing panic in Louisville and Cincinnati.[6]

Despite his advantageous position, Bragg was unsure of his ability to attack the Union formations in the vicinity of Bowling Green, some forty miles away. Remaining at Munfordville for several days, he was acutely aware of his dwindling supplies and decided to move northeast about half the distance to Louisville,

Battle of Perryville on October 8, 1862; *Library of Congress Prints and Photographs Division*

reaching Bardstown on September 22. In response, Buell moved to Louisville. Bragg temporarily handed command of the Army of Mississippi to Polk, then headed to Frankfort to oversee the installation of a Confederate government for the state of Kentucky.

By October 1 Buell had begun moving his force southeast from Louisville toward Bardstown, where Polk and the Army of Mississippi waited. Having conferred with Bragg, on October 3 Polk initiated withdrawal of his army east, toward Harrodsburg; Buell followed. By October 7 the Union force was approaching Perryville, approximately ten miles west of Harrodsburg, where Hardee and the Left Wing were located. Polk and the Right Wing moved from Harrodsburg to join Hardee, and, by the morning of October 8, Buell's army and the Army of Mississippi met just north of Perryville. Polk's Right Wing attacked, initially pushing one Union division back with heavy losses. Others held, however, and initiated a counterattack that restored their lines. Fierce fighting raged throughout the afternoon, terminating at dusk.

The day ended with the Confederate force in a stronger position overall, the heavier casualties on the Union side.[7] However, strong Union forces hovered on the periphery and threatened action the next day. Near midnight Bragg ordered a general withdrawal, first toward Harrodsburg, then toward Bryantsville, where a depot had been established for the stores evacuated from Lexington. The army was prepared for a counterattack at each location, but none came. In the Union army, Major General Buell was relieved by Major General William S. Rosecrans, who began reorganizing and planning a concentration at Nashville.[8]

On October 10 Polk was notified that he had been promoted to lieutenant general. Two days later General Bragg called a conference of generals at Bryantsville to review the army's status and options. After extensive discussion it was agreed that the Kentucky campaign should be terminated and the army withdrawn south, through the Cumberland Gap into Tennessee. The movement began the next day. Colonel Spence recalled:

> The march from Kentucky was a hard one, the enemy following, skirmishing with our rear guard as far as London [Kentucky].... Gen Polk would stop to make little encouraging talks when the boys were resting on the roadside, that would cheer him as he passed. On one of these occasions . . . a fine-looking, sunburned veteran . . . called out, "General, don't you think it would be a heap better if our faces were turned toward that firing we hear in the rear?" alluding to the skirmishing with our rear guard. . . . This created a laugh amongst these old soldiers. . . . Gen Polk made no reply. He doubtless hated the retreat from Kentucky more than any soldier in that grand army. . . . Why battle was not offered by Gen Bragg is not known.[9]

And so the Army of Mississippi withdrew southward, through London, Kentucky, and the Cumberland Gap. At London on October 17, General Bragg relinquished command to Polk and departed to Richmond, Virginia, for consultations; Polk led the army on to Knoxville, arriving there on October 21.[10]

In Knoxville the Orleans Light Horse saw a major change in leadership. Effective October 24, Lieutenant William A. Gordon, who had been acting troop commander for the last six months, was assigned to a staff position and transferred to the Gulf Coast.[11] Second Lieutenant J. Leeds Greenleaf was promoted to first lieutenant and acting commander, succeeding Gordon. On November 1 Greenleaf was promoted to captain and confirmed as permanent troop commander. Other promotions at this time included Second Lieutenant Charles D. Lallande to first lieutenant; Sergeant Josiah C. Patrick Jr. to second lieutenant; Corporal Jackson W. Simmons to sergeant; and Private James C. Walker to corporal. The unit had received nine new members during September and October, with only two losses. Its total strength was holding satisfactorily at seventy-one men now well seasoned from the activities and events of the Kentucky campaign.[12]

ORLEANS LIGHT HORSE PERSONNEL ACCOUNTABILITY
SEPTEMBER–OCTOBER 1862

GAINS	9	GAINS	Crain, P. W.; D'Aquin, T. A.; Delgado, A.; Egelly, C. R.; Frederic, S.; Le Sassier, G.; Lynd, S.; Martindale, F. B.; Sutherland, P. F.
LOSSES	2		
Discharged	1		
Unspecified	1		
ACCOUNTABLE	71	LOSSES	Robinson, E. T.; Simmons, R. W.
Present	47		
Detailed to duty	15		
Absent—leave	1		
Absent—sick	2		
Absent—w/o leave	6		

NOTES

1 *OR*, ser. 1, vol. 16, pt. 2:759, 784.

2 Blair, 96–97; Seitz, 165–68. At Richmond, of the 6,850 Confederate soldiers engaged, total casualties were approximately 451, or 6 percent (78 killed; 372 wounded; 1 missing). Of the 6,500 Union soldiers engaged, total casualties were 5,353, or 82 percent (206 killed; 844 wounded; 4,303 captured/missing).

3 Esposito, 60–63.

4 Seitz, 160–70.

5 Total casualties at Munfordville: Confederate, 714; Union, 4,148.

6 *OR*, ser. 1, vol. 16, pt. 2:784; Parks, 250–55; Seitz, 168–77.

7 Of the 16,000 Confederate troops engaged, total casualties were approximately 3,401, or 21 percent (532 killed; 2,641 wounded; 228 captured or missing). Of the 22,000 Union troops engaged, total casualties were approximately 4,276, or 19 percent (894 killed; 2,911 wounded; 471 captured or missing).

8 Blair, 96–97; Seitz, 168–201.

9 Spence, "Campaigning in Kentucky," 121–23.

10 Ibid., 23; *OR*, ser. 1, vol. 16, pt. 2:963–64.

11 In March 1864 Gordon was ruled medically unfit for field service because of congenital presbyopia. When the unit returned from Kentucky in October 1862, he would have been thirty-four years of age, entering that age span where the effects of presbyopia (progressively diminished ability to focus on near objects) become more acute. This condition would have made his continuation in the Light Horse increasingly problematic, justifying his transfer to a more controlled staff environment. Rutstein and Daum, 3, 157–58, 170.

12 NARA M320, reel 032.

✠ 5 ✠

NOVEMBER 1862–OCTOBER 1863

ESCORT, FIRST CORPS, ARMY
OF TENNESSEE

◆ • • ◆

IN RICHMOND GENERAL BRAXTON BRAGG AND THE WAR DEPARTMENT discussed a new offensive that Bragg was developing, focused on the central Tennessee heartland around Murfreesboro. Bragg argued for a combined force for this initiative, and the authorities in Richmond, recognizing the problems that resulted from two independent armies attempting to operate together in Kentucky, agreed with his assessment. Edmund Kirby Smith, who had been promoted to lieutenant general in October, remained in command of the Department of East Tennessee, but a general order was published permitting Bragg to draw on that department for "such troops . . . as may be disposable, and for such time as these operations may require." Kirby Smith was permitted to decide whether he would remain in Knoxville or go with the troops levied from him for the Murfreesboro campaign; he chose the latter option.[1]

In Knoxville Lieutenant General Leonidas Polk continued temporarily in command of the Army of Mississippi, which had been severely shaken by the withdrawal from Kentucky. Within the ranks, a significant number of the men were disappointed that Bragg had been unwilling to give battle there. At the same time, the army was suffering from the logistics system's inability to function effectively

COMMANDERS OF THE FIRST CORPS, ARMY OF TENNESSEE

Commander	Lt. Gen. Leonidas Polk
Cheatham's Division	Maj. Gen. Benjamin F. Cheatham
First Brigade	Brig. Gen. Daniel S. Donelson
Second Brigade	Brig. Gen. Alexander P. Stewart
Third Brigade	Brig. Gen. George E. Maney
Fourth Brigade	Brig. Gen. Preston Smith
Withers's Division	Brig. Gen. Jones M. Withers
First Brigade	Brig. Gen. Franklin Gardner
Second Brigade	Brig. Gen. James R. Chalmers
Third Brigade	Brig. Gen. John K. Jackson
Fourth Brigade	Col. Arthur M. Manigault
Wharton's Cavalry Brigade	Brig. Gen. John A. Wharton
Orleans Light Horse (escort)	Capt. J. Leeds Greenleaf

SOURCE: *OR*, SER. 1, VOL. 20, PT.2:393, 418–21, 431–32, 465.

at such a long distance from the sources of supply. Blankets were scarce, clothing was worn and tattered, and shoes were wearing out. Already, large numbers of men were marching barefoot, and the weather in Kentucky and northern Tennessee was rapidly turning cold. Straggling and unauthorized absences increased. By November 2 the Army of Mississippi consisted of an effective total of 27,360 men, but the army's aggregate strength was approximately 8 percent greater. Thus several thousand men were either sick, straggling, or on recuperative home leave.[2]

By November 7 General Bragg had returned from consultations in Richmond and resumed command of the Army of Mississippi. He immediately began pushing forces toward Murfreesboro, starting with a number of regiments drawn from the Department of East Tennessee; meanwhile, the men of Polk's and Hardee's Corps were recuperating and being reequipped and supplied. By November 14 the headquarters of the Army of Mississippi had moved 180 miles from Knoxville to Tullahoma, a town on the Nashville and Chattanooga Railroad southeast of Murfreesboro.[3] There, on November 20, General Bragg formalized his deployments, combining the elements drawn from Kirby Smith's command with the Army of Mississippi and creating the Army of Tennessee. The new organization, made up of some forty-seven thousand men, initially comprised three corps and a cavalry division. Designated commander of the First Corps, Lieutenant General Polk, with the Orleans Light Horse continuing as his escort company, was positioned at Murfreesboro. Lieutenant General William J. Hardee was assigned the Second Corps and positioned near Shelbyville. Lieutenant General Kirby Smith was assigned the Third Corps and positioned near Manchester.[4]

In a simultaneous development in Richmond, orders were published creating the Department of the West, commanded by General Joseph E. Johnston.[5] This command blanketed the region from the Blue Ridge Mountains to the Mississippi River, in essence supplanting Department No. 2. Within Johnston's new command, the Department of Mississippi and East Louisiana was created under the command of Lieutenant General John C. Pemberton to oversee the defense of Vicksburg.[6] A division comprising ten thousand men from Kirby Smith's Corps in the Army of Tennessee was assigned to Pemberton's department, leaving Kirby Smith with only one division. As a result, his corps was dissolved on December 18, and he returned to the Department of East Tennessee in Knoxville. The Army of Tennessee continued with Polk's and Hardee's Corps, but the time would come when it would feel the loss of the division and the maneuvering flexibility of Kirby Smith's Corps.[7]

Throughout December, the cavalry brigades kept Union patrols at a distance, as the Army of Tennessee settled into its new positions and rested from its recent operations. In the second week of December, Confederate President Jefferson Davis and General Joseph E. Johnston visited the army. The atmosphere in Murfreesboro during their visit was highly social, with a gala review of the army by the president and numerous parties and dances. Colonel Philip B. Spence remembered this period: "No one who was present could ever forget President Davis's first visit and his reviewing of the army at Murfreesboro. The President, a fine rider, splendidly mounted, and the general of the army and the lieutenant generals of the army corps with their staff officers riding rapidly around each corps, and then that grand body of old soldiers wheeling into column of companies and marching by our President and the reviewing officers, with their bright guns and shining cannons, was a sight never to be forgotten."[8]

On December 26, as severe winter rains began with a vengeance, Major General William S. Rosecrans began moving the Union force out of Nashville toward Murfreesboro. Over the next several days of miserable weather, his troops clashed repeatedly with the Army of Tennessee along the Stones River near Murfreesboro. After fighting Rosecrans's force to a standstill—albeit with heavy losses—on the night of January 3, 1863, Bragg elected to withdraw toward Tullahoma. Rosecrans occupied Murfreesboro but made no effort to pursue Bragg.[9] Polk's Corps had suffered greatly during the Battle of Murfreesboro, losing 4,682 of its 16,068 men (29.1 percent).

Bragg established the Army of Tennessee's winter quarters in the area around Tullahoma. The Orleans Light Horse was stationed with the headquarters of Polk's Corps in Shelbyville, a few miles to the northwest. They remained there for the next five months, until the middle of June, as the army replenished and trained its personnel and worked to improve its positions and fortifications. The routine of the Orleans Light Horse was relatively unchanged: providing local security for the corps headquarters; acting as couriers for the constant flow of messages, orders, and reports between the headquarters and its various subordinate units; and continuing local reconnaissance of unit locations, roads, bridges, and fords.[10]

During the first week of June, the leadership of the Light Horse underwent changes as Lieutenants Charles D. Lallande, Josiah C. Patrick Jr., and Henry M. Thornhill were transferred to other units. To replace them, Lieutenant Philip M. Kenner was promoted to first lieutenant; First Sergeant Samuel Huntington, Sergeant Aristide R. Hopkins, and Private E. Malcom Morse were elected second lieutenants; Sergeant Jackson W. Simmons was promoted to first sergeant; and Corporal John M. Kennedy and Private Austin W. Rountree were promoted to sergeant. All other individuals continued in their respective positions.[11]

A Union offensive led by Rosecrans, and days of seasonal rains, came in the fourth week of June. The assault began with an attack on Polk's Corps, a screen to conceal the primary effort against Hardee's Corps, some twenty-five miles to the east of Shelbyville, at Manchester. As the main attack developed at Manchester, Bragg's initial thought was to have Polk's Corps counterattack the Union flank. On the evening of June 26, Polk attempted to convince Bragg that the success of the attack against Hardee's Corps made withdrawal necessary, but Bragg did not agree, so the force settled down in the muck and mire to strengthen their defensive fortifications and await developments. By the afternoon of June 30, continued Union advances convinced Bragg of the correctness of Polk's assessment, and he ordered a general withdrawal to Allisonia (present-day Estill Springs), south of Manchester. By noon on July 1, the army was in position there. The rains continued.[12]

On July 2 Bragg's plan of action called for a line of battle on the plain between Cowan, a few miles southeast of Allisonia, and the mountains that screened Chattanooga. Along with the army, Polk's Corps withdrew toward Cowan, while the cavalry screening the rear reported being severely pressured by lead elements of Rosecrans's pursuing Union army. The Confederate troops continued south, crossing the Tennessee River near the mouth of Battle Creek (present-day South Pittsburg). On July 5, however, Bragg again changed his plan of action, and the entire army was put in motion across the mountains to Chattanooga; the last elements of Polk's Corps arrived there by the evening of July 7. Morale among the members of the Army of Tennessee was low as they reached Chattanooga. A year of fighting had brought them back to where they had started, without any victories to celebrate. Their confidence in Bragg faltered, as historian Joseph H. Parks described in his 1962 biography of Polk: "The Army of Tennessee was exhausted, but not from fighting. It was now back at the base from which it had started almost a year earlier, but under much different circumstances. . . . Retreat had become almost a habit; confidence was at a low ebb. Bragg was being vigorously censured

Battle of Stones River or Murfreesboro, January 1863; *Library of Congress Prints and Photographs Division*

by both officers and troops. Even so, his mistake had not been in retreating but in permitting his army to get into a situation where retreat was necessary."[13]

From July 3 to August 16, two Union commanders, Major Generals Rosecrans (at Tullahoma) and Ambrose E. Burnside (at Cincinnati), concentrated on resting their forces and shoring up their supply lines, thereby releasing pressure on the Army of Tennessee, which took advantage of this respite by resting its troops and fortifying Chattanooga. Both armies were suffering from the miserable conditions brought on by relentless rain. The roads, especially in the mountains, became impassable, and the rivers had reached flood stages. While at Chattanooga, Lieutenant General Hardee was relieved of his corps at his own request and transferred to command the forces of the Department of Mississippi and East Louisiana; Lieutenant General Daniel H. Hill was moved from the Army of Northern Virginia to join the Army of Tennessee as a corps commander.[14]

Rosecrans's force began moving toward Chattanooga on August 16. Bragg, anticipating that the enemy would cross the Tennessee River above Chattanooga, stationed his troops primarily northeast of the city.[15] By Friday, August 21, which had been designated by President Davis as "a day of fasting, humiliation and prayer," a Union brigade had advanced to the Tennessee River and had begun shelling the city.[16] However, on August 31, Bragg received a report that the enemy was crossing the river at Bridgeport and near Stevenson—both towns southwest of Chattanooga in Alabama—and pouring into the mountain passes leading to the city. It finally became clear to Bragg during the first week of September that Rosecrans's main effort would indeed be from the south.

On September 2 the Union troops of Major General Burnside took Knoxville, just over a hundred miles to the northeast of Chattanooga. By Monday, September 7, Rosecrans's troops had occupied Alpine (near present-day Menlo), Georgia, some fifty miles south of Chattanooga. With Burnside in Knoxville to the north and Rosecrans in strength to the south, Bragg decided to withdraw southward, to the vicinity of Chickamauga, Georgia, abandoning Chattanooga to Federal occupation. In taking this action, he avoided having to fight in the city and thereby gained more maneuvering room for himself without permitting a wide-open field to Rosecrans, whose back was still to the mountains. Chattanooga was a major rail hub, but the Chickamauga area, which Bragg controlled, channeled the rail lines southeast to Atlanta. For this reason, his choice of location was superior to that of Rosecrans, who was hoping that Bragg would withdraw even farther southeast, to Dalton or Rome, Georgia, a mistake the general did not make.[17]

Polk's Corps moved to the vicinity of Lee and Gordon's Mills in Chickamauga, with Hill's Corps farther south, in the vicinity of LaFayette. On Wednesday, September 9, Confederate Lieutenant General James Longstreet began moving his corps by rail from northern Virginia to reinforce the Army of Tennessee. Over the next several days, Rosecrans moved his force to the vicinity of West Chickamauga Creek, just north of Chickamauga. By September 18 Bragg's and Rosecrans's forces were positioned parallel to each other, in a line extending over eight miles along the creek.[18]

On September 19 and 20, the two armies collided in the Battle of Chickamauga—the bloodiest two days of the war in the western theater. Longstreet and his corps arrived at the end of the first day's fighting. That evening Bragg reorganized the Army of Tennessee into two wings, assigning the Right Wing to Polk (see table, right) and the Left Wing to Longstreet.

Near midnight Bragg issued orders for the next day. Polk was to attack at daybreak, Longstreet to follow. One of Polk's couriers, Trooper John H. Fisher of the Orleans Light Horse, was assigned the task of delivering these orders to Lieutenant General Hill. Traveling in the dark, amidst the confusion resulting from a day of movement and change, Fisher was unable to find Hill and distribute the orders in time. Trooper Yves R. Le Monnier Jr. of the Orleans Light Horse, on duty that night as a member of Polk's security detail, recalled the general's response to the courier's failed mission in an article published after the war:

> At break of day, or before General Polk was in the saddle, word was passed around from headquarters: "Has the courier returned?" We answered, "No." Scarcely was the answer given when the General spurred his horse, and off we went. The

COMMANDERS OF THE RIGHT WING, ARMY OF TENNESSEE

Commander	Lieut. Gen. Leonidas Polk
Cheatham's Division	Maj. Gen. Benjamin F. Cheatham
Jackson's Brigade	Brig. Gen. John K. Jackson
Smith's Brigade	Brig. Gen. Preston Smith
Maney's Brigade	Brig. Gen. George E. Maney
Wright's Brigade	Brig. Gen. Marcus J. Wright
Strahl's Brigade	Brig. Gen. Otho F. Strahl
Artillery	Maj. Melancthon Smith
Hill's Corps	Lieut. Gen. Daniel H. Hill
Cleburne's Division	Maj. Gen. Patrick R. Cleburne
Wood's Brigade	Brig. Gen. Sterling A. M. Wood
Polk's Brigade	Brig. Gen. Lucius E. Polk
Deshler's Brigade	Brig. Gen. James Deshler
Artillery	Maj. Thomas R. Hotchkiss
Breckinridge's Division	Maj. Gen. John C. Breckinridge
Helm's Brigade	Brig. Gen. Benjamin H. Helm
Adams's Brigade	Brig. Gen. Daniel W. Adams
Stovall's Brigade	Brig. Gen. Marcellus A. Stovall
Artillery	Maj. Rice E. Graves
Reserve Corps	Maj. Gen. William H. T. Walker
Walker's Division	Brig. Gen. States R. Gist
Gist's Brigade	Col. Peyton H. Colquitt
Ector's Brigade	Brig. Gen. Matthew D. Ector
Wilson's Brigade	Col. Claudius C. Wilson
Artillery	Capt. Evan P. Howell
Liddell's Division	Brig. Gen. St. John R. Liddell
Liddell's Brigade	Col. Daniel C. Govan
Walthall's Brigade	Brig. Gen. Edward C. Walthall
Artillery	Capt. Charles Swett
Orleans Light Horse (escort)	Capt. J. Leeds Greenleaf

SOURCE: *OR*, SER. 1, VOL. 30, PT.2:11–20.

situation was then as silent as it had been noisy all night. We, the privates, knew then that something was up.

We started for Alexander's bridge. As we reached the other side of the creek I saw the courier, Fisher, by a fire warming his hands, the bridle of his horse over his right shoulder. I cried to him, "Fisher, the General wants you," and through devilment added: "You are going to catch hell." He immediately jumped into the saddle and quickly rode to General Polk. I advanced to within respectful distance to where they were and distinctly heard Fisher say, " * * * and, having no answer, I stopped at the fire to warm my hands and did not think I was doing wrong." General Polk spurred his horse, a quick mover, and we followed at a rapid gait. We knew then by his face and his movements that something was wrong. . . . The mask had fallen; a terrible blunder had been made.[19]

The courier's failure to reach Hill led to a delay in the September 20 attack. Daybreak was at 5:47 a.m.; the attack did not begin until 9:45 a.m. Nonetheless, after a full day of fighting, the Confederates were in complete possession of the field as the Union army retreated in disorder.[20] Both sides had suffered heavy losses, each losing 28 percent of their armies—of the 66,326 Confederate troops, 18,454 had been killed, wounded, or taken prisoner; of the 58,222 Union troops, 16,179 had been killed, wounded, or taken prisoner.[21] Lieutenant Joseph A. Chalaron, a member of the Fifth Company of the Washington Artillery, recorded the Orleans Light Horse's activities during the Battle of Chickamauga: "Active as escort and couriers to Gen'l Polk, it accomplished these important duties during the battle, which amounted almost to staff duty, to the great satisfaction of the general. Although none were reported killed or wounded in skirmishing, its duties took it into the very heaviest fighting of the right wing. Captain Leeds Greenleaf acted as provost marshall [sic] of Polk's wing, Lieut. A. Hopkins acted on Gen'l Polk's staff and Lieut. [P. M. Kenner] was in command of the company."[22]

The Union force was in disarray as it retreated to Chattanooga on September 21. Brigadier General Nathan B. Forrest, whose cavalry corps hounded the fleeing troops, repeatedly urged Bragg to move on Chattanooga; however, Bragg, who seemed not to recognize the magnitude of his victory, demurred.[23] In an article published after the war, Lieutenant General Hill reflected on Bragg's indecision:

> Whatever blunders each of us in authority committed before the battles of the 19th and 20th, and during their progress, the great blunder of all was that of not pursuing the enemy on the 21st. The day was spent in burying the dead and gathering up captured stores. Forrest, with his usual promptness, was early in the saddle, and saw that the retreat was a rout. Disorganized masses of men were hurrying to the rear; batteries of artillery were inextricably mixed with trains of wagons; disorder and confusion pervaded the broken ranks struggling to get on. Forrest sent back word to Bragg that "every hour was worth a thousand men." But the commander-in-chief did not know of the victory until the morning of the 21st, and then he did not order a pursuit.[24]

By Tuesday, September 22, the entire Union force had regrouped within the Chattanooga defenses. Bragg positioned his men on Lookout Mountain, to the southwest of Chattanooga, cutting rail access and effectively placing the city under siege.[25]

Then, on September 29, Bragg suspended Polk for not obeying his attack orders at Chickamauga on September 20 and sent him and his personal staff to Atlanta to await further orders; the Light Horse remained with the army. On October 6 Polk requested a court of inquiry, which was denied on the grounds that Bragg had requested a court-martial. The matter dragged on through October with the gathering of statements and depositions from personnel of the command, including four cavalrymen of the Orleans Light Horse who had been on duty at the time: Lucien Charvet, John H. Fisher, John A. Perkins, and J. Minnick Williams. Ultimately, President Davis became involved and on October 29 notified Polk, "I have arrived at the conclusion that there is nothing attending them to justify a court-martial or a court of inquiry, and I therefore dismiss the application."[26]

On October 23 a directive was issued from Richmond: Lieutenant General Hardee, who had left the Army of Tennessee in July for the Department of Mississippi and East Louisiana, would be brought back to command the First Corps of the Army of Tennessee. Lieutenant General Polk, still waiting for the charges against him to be dropped, was ordered to Mississippi to serve in the Department of Mississippi and East Louisiana, now temporarily under the command of General Johnston.[27] When Polk reached Mississippi, the first thing he did was send for his escort company and several additional staff officers.[28]

During September and October, the Orleans Light Horse had received an infusion of twenty-seven men and was now at an all-time high in operational strength. After sixteen months of incessant skirmishing, a welcome change in tempo was in store for the Light Horse cavalrymen as they followed their general from the mountains of Tennessee to the plains of central Mississippi.

ORLEANS LIGHT HORSE PERSONNEL ACCOUNTABILITY
NOVEMBER 1862–OCTOBER 1863

	NOV.–DEC. 1862	JAN.–FEB. 1863	MAR.–APR. 1863	MAY–JUNE 1863	JULY–AUG. 1863	SEPT.–OCT. 1863
GAINS	4	3	3	8	2	27
LOSSES	1	1	7	7	3	2
Discharged	0	0	1	0	0	1
Transferred	0	0	1	3	2	0
Deserted	0	0	4	2	0	0
Killed/Died	0	0	0	1	0	0
Unspecified	1	1	1	1	1	1
ACCOUNTABLE	74	76	72	73	72	97
Present	52	54	52	56	46	71
Detailed to duty	8	8	12	11	16	15
Absent—leave	4	4	1	0	1	1
Absent—sick	2	4	4	6	3	1
Absent—w/o leave	8	6	3	0	1	0
Hospitalized	0	0	0	0	5	9

	NOV.–DEC. 1862	JAN.–FEB. 1863	MARCH–APR. 1863
GAINS	Charvet, L.; Haydel, E. C.; Macready, J.; Russell, M.	Gatch, J. A. R.; Keeble, R. C.; Lotspeich, J. T.	Allen, C. W.; Bickle, W. O.; Safford, H.
LOSSES	Crain, R. A.	Mandeville, T.	Bryan, C. A.; Bryan, T.; Crain, P. W.; Harrison, F. W.; Landreaux, P. F.; Mitchell, W. C.; St. Phar, A. H.

	MAY–JUNE 1863	JULY–AUG. 1863	SEPT.–OCT. 1863
GAINS	Borduzat, J. P.; Brown, J. B.; Byrd, J. G.; Ryall, H. C.; Tourtarel, J. B.; Tureman, T. Y. P.; Watters, S. B.; Williams, J. M.	Gribble, W. C.; Hartigan, J.	Armstrong, H. A.; Bellamy, J. T.; Bergeron, O. J.; Bethancourt, O. A.; Carey, R. S.; Cassady, B.; Dillon, J. W.; Fisher, J. H.; Floyd, T. M.; Glynn, M.; Hamilton, W. B.; Hankins, C. D.; Hébert, J. A.; Hurd, J. H.; Lawler, J.W.; Love, W. D.; Mallen, J. B.; Mansfield, R.; Mulholland, J.; Perkins, L. W.; Phillips, E. M.; Reynolds, T. S.; Rondeau, W. A. S.; Trellue, M. G.; Trellue, N. B.; Windsor, N. A.; Winn, J.
LOSSES	Bickle, W. O.; Gatch, J. A. R; Lallande, C. D.; Patrick, J. C.; Shaw, W. N.; Sprigg, H. S.; Thornhill, H. M.	Christian, P. J.; Fleitas, J. B.; Rogers, W. L.	Allen, C. W.; Watters, S. P.

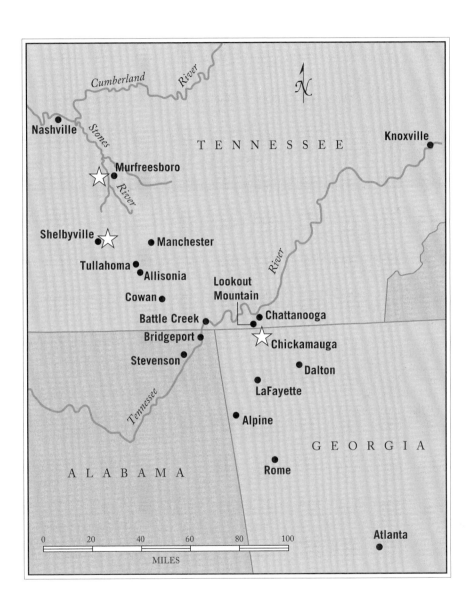

NOTES

1 *OR*, ser. 1, vol. 20, pt. 2:384–85; Connelly, *Autumn of Glory*, 14–15.

2 *OR*, ser. 1, vol. 16, pt. 2:784, 963–64; *OR*, ser. 1, vol. 20, pt. 2:385, 421–23; Spence, "General Polk and His Staff," 22–23.

3 *OR*, ser. 1, vol. 20, pt. 2:400, 402, 411, 426; Connelly, *Autumn of Glory*, 19–29.

4 *OR*, ser. 1, vol. 20, pt. 2:411–12, 418–21, 428–32; Seitz, 203–6; Parks, 250–55.

5 Joseph Eggleston Johnston (b. 1807, Farmville, VA; d. 1891, Washington, DC), an 1829 graduate of the US Military Academy, resigned from the service in 1837 to study engineering. In 1838 he reentered the service and was appointed a lieutenant. He received a brevet to captain for service in the Second Seminole War (1835–42) and Mexican-American War (1846–48). From 1848 to 1853 he was the chief topographical engineer of the Department of Texas. He then became a colonel and commanded the First US Cavalry at Fort Leavenworth, Kansas. In 1860 he was promoted to brigadier general and quartermaster general of the US Army. One year later, he was commissioned as brigadier general by the Confederate army. He organized the Army of the Shenandoah and reinforced Beauregard at the First Battle of Manassas. Later that year he was promoted to general and commanded the Confederate Army of the Potomac, later the Army of Northern Virginia, until he was wounded at the Battle of Seven Pines and succeeded by General Robert E. Lee. In 1862 Johnston was placed in command of the Department of the West.

6 Established on October 1, 1862, the Department of Mississippi and East Louisiana merged the District of the Mississippi and the District of Southern Mississippi and Eastern Louisiana. Its commanders were Lieutenant General John C. Pemberton (October 1, 1862–July 4, 1863); General Joseph E. Johnston (temporary; July 4–August 21, 1863); Lieutenant General William J. Hardee (August 21–December 2, 1863).

7 *OR*, ser. 1, vol. 17, pt. 2:782, 787, 800; *OR*, ser. 1, vol. 20, pt. 2:412, 418–20, 423–24, 461. After Kirby Smith's departure, Polk's Corps remained at Murfreesboro; Hardee's Corps (less one brigade) was positioned at Eagleville, approximately twenty miles away.

8 Parks, 282–83; Spence, "General Polk and His Staff," 22.

9 Parks, 282–95; Seitz, 237–70; Conservation Fund, 151–54. Confederate losses were estimated at ten thousand (29.4 percent); Union losses, thirteen thousand (29.5 percent).

10 *OR*, ser. 1, vol. 20, pt. 1:674–81; *OR*, ser. 1, vol. 20, pt. 2:465; Woodworth, *Six Armies in Tennessee*, 13–18.

11 NARA M320, reel 032.

12 *OR*, ser. 1, vol. 23, pt. 1:618–25; Parks, 311–15.

13 *OR*, ser. 1, vol. 23, pt. 1:624–27; *OR*, ser. 1, vol. 23, pt. 2:900–908; Parks, 315–17.

14 *OR*, ser. 1, vol. 23, pt. 2:522, 529, 531. Daniel Harvey Hill (b. 1821, York District, SC; d. 1889, Charlotte, SC), an 1842 graduate of the US Military Academy, was commissioned in the First US Artillery and served in the Mexican-American War (1846–48), where he received brevets to captain and major for bravery. He resigned from the service in 1849 to become professor of mathematics at Washington College in Lexington, Virginia (now Washington and Lee University). In 1854 he accepted the chair of the mathematics department at Davidson College in North Carolina, a position he held until 1859, when he resigned to become superintendent of the North Carolina Military Institute in Charlotte. He was commissioned a colonel by the Confederate army in 1861 and initially led the First North Carolina Infantry Regiment. Later that year he was promoted to brigadier general and then, in 1862, to major general. Hill's division distinguished itself at Second Manassas, South Mountain, and Sharpsburg. In 1863 he was commander of the Department of North Carolina before being called to defend Richmond during the Gettysburg campaign. He was promoted to lieutenant general in July 1863 and ordered to the Army of Tennessee. This promotion was short lived. Following the Confederate victory at Chickamauga, Hill called upon President Jefferson Davis to remove General Bragg from

his command on grounds of incompetence, a criticism that resulted in Hill's own dismissal and loss of his recent commission. Hill's service was limited thereafter, though he did command a division in General Johnston's force at Bentonville, North Carolina, in March 1865. He surrendered with Johnston at Durham Station, North Carolina.

15 *OR*, ser. 1, vol. 30, pt. 4:518, 519, 529, 540–41.

16 In his proclamation declaring Friday, August 21, 1863, to be "a day of fasting, humiliation and prayer," President Davis called upon all "people who believeth that the Lord reigneth and that his overruling Providence ordereth all things—to unite in prayer and humble submission under his chastening hand, and to beseech his favor on our suffering country." Military duties were suspended for the day, and divine services were offered in churches across the Confederacy. His proclamation was part of a religious movement among the Confederate troops that became known as the Great Revival. During the course of the war, Davis declared a total of ten such days of fasting and prayer. Bennett, 273, 316–17, 371.

17 Hill, 642–47; Seitz, 328–32.

18 Parks, 322–33; Hill, 650–54; Gabel, 10; Seitz, 325–37.

19 Le Monnier, 17–19.

20 Hill, 652; Seitz, 343–58.

21 Wert, 318–19; Connelly, *Autumn of Glory*, 232–34.

22 Notes on the Louisiana troops at the Battle of Chickamauga, box 5, folder 4, p. 10, Chalaron Papers, Tulane. As the company's first lieutenant, Philip M. Kenner was the second-in-command. When the captain was called upon to perform a special duty (acting as provost marshal, in this case), it would be normal for the first lieutenant to assume many of the functions of command.

23 *OR*, ser. 1, vol. 30, pt. 2:22–23; Nathan Bedford Forrest (b. 1821, Bedford County, TN; d. 1877, Memphis, TN) was a self-educated, successful businessman before enlisting as a private in the Tennessee Mounted Rifles. In 1861 he was commissioned as a lieutenant colonel in the Confederate army and authorized to recruit and train a battalion of mounted rangers. After serving with distinction at the Battle of Fort Donelson, he was promoted to brigadier general and commanded a brigade at the Battle of Shiloh. He again served with distinction at the Battle of Chickamauga and was promoted to major general and assigned to independent command, targeting Union supply depots and transportation routes in Mississippi and western Tennessee. With the Army of Tennessee, Forrest participated in the Franklin-Nashville Campaign. He commanded the rear guard in the army's withdrawal, for which he was promoted to lieutenant general. In 1865 he led a five-thousand-man cavalry corps in Alabama and Georgia. When notified of Lieutenant General Taylor's surrender of the Department of Alabama, Mississippi, and East Louisiana, he issued a farewell address and disbanded his corps at Gainesville, Alabama, on May 9.

24 Hill, 662.

25 Wert, 318–19; Connelly, *Autumn of Glory*, 232–34.

26 *OR*, ser. 1, vol. 30, pt. 2:64–70; Seitz, 378–81.

27 *OR*, ser. 1, vol. 31, pt. 3:582–83.

28 Beginning on November 23, the Army of Tennessee fought the Battle of Missionary Ridge. In his papers, Lieutenant Chalaron states that the Orleans Light Horse was not there; by that date, they had already left Tennessee, en route to central Mississippi. That overland trek, a distance of some 320 miles, would require a march of ten to twelve days. Notes on the Louisiana troops at the Battle of Chickamauga, box 5, folder 4, p. 10, Chalaron Papers, Tulane.

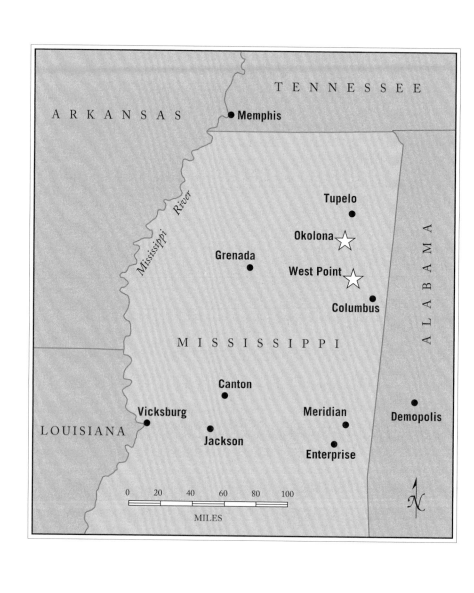

⚔ 6 ⚔

NOVEMBER 1863–APRIL 1864

ESCORT, DEPARTMENT OF ALABAMA, MISSISSIPPI, AND EAST LOUISIANA

◀ • • ▶

IN RESPONSE TO HIS ORDERS FROM RICHMOND, ON NOVEMBER 7, 1863, Lieutenant General Leonidas Polk set out from Atlanta, accompanied by his wife and his aides-de-camp. Their destination was Enterprise, Mississippi, about eighteen miles south of Meridian, where his headquarters was to be located. Polk went to work on Friday, November 13, in an office in a small country town, a far cry from the activity of leading an army corps. He had his faithful aides with him, but little else. His main task would be rounding up and organizing paroled and exchanged Confederate soldiers, principally those who had surrendered at Vicksburg, Mississippi, and Port Hudson, Louisiana.[1]

In Georgia, on November 29, General Braxton Bragg asked to be relieved of command of the Army of Tennessee. President Jefferson Davis accepted Bragg's request and offered the position to Lieutenant General William J. Hardee; he refused the post but agreed to act as commander on a temporary basis. On December 16 General Joseph E. Johnston was ordered to turn over to Lieutenant General Polk command of the Department of Mississippi and East Louisiana and to take command of the Army of Tennessee. The change of command in Mississippi took place on Wednesday, December 23. Having gone there with only the prospects of an administrative position, Polk now found himself once again in command of an extensive area and an operational corps-sized force. His escort company, the Orleans Light Horse, which had arrived in Enterprise around December 1, would have its work cut out for it.[2]

COMMANDERS OF DEPARTMENT OF ALABAMA, MISSISSIPPI, AND EAST LOUISIANA

Commander	Lt. Gen. Leonidas Polk
Loring's Division	Maj. Gen. William W. Loring
Buford's Brigade	Brig. Gen. Abraham Buford
Featherston's Brigade	Brig. Gen. Winfield S. Featherston
Adams's Brigade	Brig. Gen. John Adams
French's Division	Maj. Gen. Samuel G. French
Ector's Brigade	Brig. Gen. Matthew D. Ector
McNair's Brigade	Brig. Gen. Evander McNair
Missouri Brigade	Brig. Gen. Francis M. Cockrell
Forney's Command	Maj. Gen. John H. Forney
Baldwin's Brigade	Brig. Gen. William E. Baldwin
Mackall's Brigade	Brig. Gen. William W. Mackall
Heavy artillery brigade	Lt. Col. Daniel Beltzhoover
Cavalry in Mississippi	Maj. Gen. Stephen D. Lee
Jackson's Cavalry Division	Brig. Gen. William H. Jackson
First Brigade	Brig. Gen. George B. Cosby
Second Brigade	Col. Hinche P. Mabry
Adams's Brigade	Brig. Gen. William W. Adams
Ross's Brigade	Col. Lawrence S. Ross
Chalmers's Cavalry Division	Brig. Gen. James R. Chalmers
Slemons's Brigade	Col. William F. Slemons
McCulloch's Brigade	Col. Robert McCulloch
Ferguson's Brigade	Brig. Gen. Samuel W. Ferguson
Orleans Light Horse (escort)	Capt. J. Leeds Greenleaf

SOURCE: *OR*, SER. 1, VOL. 31, PT.3:725–28, 746–47, 865–66; *OR*, SER. 1, VOL. 32, PT. 2:583.

On January 28 the war department defined Polk's command as the Department of Alabama, Mississippi, and East Louisiana, adding Alabama to the area but removing Mobile and the District of the Gulf. The effective strength of active military units at Polk's disposal was 19,671. This force was about to be tested by a severe incursion from Vicksburg.[3]

On February 4, 1864, Union Major General William T. Sherman left Vicksburg with a force of approximately 27,000 men and headed east toward Meridian via Jackson. Sherman was acting in concert with Brigadier General William Sooy Smith, whose cavalry column of 7,500 was to depart Memphis, Tennessee, no later than February 2 for Meridian via Grenada and Columbus, Mississippi. Sherman and Smith were to rendezvous in Meridian no later than February 10. Sherman's intention was to wreak havoc on Confederate rail and logistics systems, and as his troops progressed across Mississippi, they did indeed destroy elements of the railway infrastructure.[4]

Polk reacted immediately. His force was not sufficient to stop or repel Sherman, but he could deny Sherman his objective. Meridian was a major logistics hub in addition to a rail junction. Since most of the railroad rolling stock was at Meridian, Polk utilized large segments of his force to load the trains with supplies and materiel from the depots as quickly as possible, sending them out of reach of Union raiders. Working around the clock, they completed the task during the week of February 7 through 13. Thus, when Sherman arrived in Meridian on February 14, he found empty warehouses and bare rails.

Smith and his cavalry never reached Meridian. Their departure was delayed by ten days, then they progressed at a leisurely pace, until they were stopped by Confederate forces. Polk had sent Major General Nathan B. Forrest and his cavalry force of twenty-five hundred men, reinforced by the cavalry corps of Major General Stephen D. Lee, to intercept the enemy.[5] On February 22 Forrest collapsed Smith's stand at West Point, Mississippi, northwest of Columbus, and forced the Union column into retreat. Having withdrawn some thirty miles northward, Smith then turned and attempted a second stand at Okolona, but Forrest again drove them from the field in disorder; the remainder of Smith's brigade then retreated to Memphis.[6]

Aware that Polk was being reinforced by Hardee's Corps from the Army of Tennessee, Sherman, having not heard from Smith by February 19, dismissed any further aggressive options, such as moving on to Selma or Mobile, Alabama. Instead, he turned back toward Vicksburg, waiting in Canton for a week in hopes of a communication from Smith. When he realized that none was to come, the remnants of the Union force continued to Vicksburg. For the next two months, Polk was able to turn his attention to housekeeping functions: conscription, depots, transportation, and maintenance of order.[7]

By the end of April, Sherman had moved from Vicksburg to Chattanooga, where he began amassing troops and materiel. Lieutenant General Ulysses S. Grant had given him a new mission, and his sights were now set on Georgia. On May 4 Polk was directed to move, with all available force, to Rome, Georgia, northwest of Atlanta, to unite with General Johnston and his Army of Tennessee. Major General Stephen D. Lee replaced Polk as commander of the Department of Alabama, Mississippi, and East Louisiana.[8]

During five months in Mississippi, the Orleans Light Horse, which continued to maintain a high level of operational strength, had been well fed, refurbished its equipment, and acquired a good stock of mounts and replacements. Additionally, many of the men from the region enjoyed home leave. All in all, the men of the Light Horse were well prepared to move back into the line.[9]

ORLEANS LIGHT HORSE PERSONNEL ACCOUNTABILITY
NOVEMBER 1863–APRIL 1864

	NOV.–DEC. 1863	JAN.–FEB. 1864	MAR.–APR. 1864
GAINS	0	3	11
LOSSES	3	11	2
Discharged	1	0	0
Transferred	1	2	1
Captured	0	1	0
Killed/Died	1	0	0
Unspecified	0	8	1
ACCOUNTABLE	94	86	95
Present	48	62	74
Detailed to duty	18	19	17
Absent—leave	15	1	0
Absent—sick	6	2	2
Absent—w/o leave	2	0	0
Hospitalized	5	0	1
Wounded/Medically disqualified	0	2	1

	NOV.–DEC. 1863	JAN.–FEB. 1864	MAR.–APR. 1864
GAINS	—	Cowarden, S. L.; Jordan, J. D.; Shepherd, H. H.	Butler, J. M.; Fox, W. H.; Hulburt, B. M.; Penn, M. A.; Rabby, J. M.; Ryall, J. S.; Spratt, R. B.; Tennison, W. H.; Waller, W. M.; Weathersby, A. D.; Wrester, J.
LOSSES	Claiborne, A. J.; Mansfield, R.; Phillips, E. M.	Blanton, R. M.; Carey, R. S.; Elenterius, L. C.; Hankins, C. D.; House, J. A.; Keeble, R. C.; Moriarty, W. A.; Peters, B. F.; Russell, M.; Sutherland, P. F.; Tourtarel, J. B.	Gordon, W. A.; Safford, H.

NOTES

1   *OR*, ser. 1, vol. 31, pt. 3:751, 773–74; *OR*, ser. 1, vol. 32, pt. 2:546; Parks, 353–56. In wars of the nineteenth century, when two opposing armies had taken prisoners of war, it was customary to exchange the captives as soon as possible after their capture to avoid having to provide them with food, housing, and medical treatment. After a battle, under a flag of truce, agreements on numbers would be struck, and the respective prisoners would be trotted out and handed over to their own army's representatives. Each man exchanged gave his word of honor that he would not participate in military activities until an agreed-upon date. Once that date arrived, the man was free to go back into the ranks. After Vicksburg and Port Hudson, three thousand to four thousand Confederate soldiers had been exchanged, and many returned to their homes. Polk's task was to find them, determine when their paroles expired, and get them back into the army by forming them into companies and regiments, equipping them, and marching them off to a new division.

2   *OR*, ser. 1, vol. 31, pt. 2:682; *OR*, ser.1, vol. 31, pt. 3:771, 775, 835–36, 857–58; *OR*, ser. 1, vol. 32, pt. 2:583–86.

3   *OR*, ser. 1, vol. 31, pt. 2:682; *OR*, ser. 1, vol. 31, pt. 3:775, 835–36; *OR*, ser. 1, vol. 32, pt. 1:332–34; *OR*, ser. 1, vol. 32, pt. 2:583–86.

4   *OR*, ser. 1, vol. 32, pt. 1:172–74. In *Rails to Oblivion,* Christopher Gabel notes, "It is more difficult to do lasting damage to a railroad deliberately than one might assume. Consider the problem confronting a Union raider who rides up to a Confederate rail line on horseback, carrying nothing but a carbine and a few hand tools. . . . Any damage he inflicts can probably be repaired with little more effort than the raider expended in causing it. Union cavalry raiders operating around Atlanta in 1864 discovered that rail lines that took a day to 'destroy' would be back in operation two or three days later" (22).

5   *OR*, ser. 1, vol. 32, pt. 1:181–82, 189, 336–38; Blair, 143.

6   *OR*, ser. 1, vol. 32, pt. 1:251–60, 345, 350–56; Blair, 143–44.

7   *OR*, ser. 1, vol. 32, pt. 1:173, 343–45; *OR*, ser. 1, vol. 52, pt. 2:621; Parks, 360–63.

8   *OR*, ser. 1, vol. 32, pt. 3:822, 831–32; *OR*, ser. 1, vol. 38:661; *OR*, ser. 1, vol. 52, pt. 2:627; Connelly, *Autumn of Glory*, 294. Stephen Dill Lee (b. 1833, Charleston, SC; d. 1908, Vicksburg, MS), an 1854 graduate of the US Military Academy, was commissioned in the Fourth Infantry Regiment and served during the Third Seminole War (1857) and in Kansas and the Dakota Territory from 1858 to 1861. In 1861 he was commissioned as an artillery captain in the Confederate army and served as an aide-de-camp to Brigadier General P. G. T. Beauregard at the capture of Fort Sumter, Charleston. Promoted to major later in 1861, Lee commanded an artillery battery in the Army of Northern Virginia. Early in 1862 he was promoted to lieutenant colonel and served as chief of artillery for a division of the Army of Northern Virginia. In July of that year he was promoted to colonel and became commander of an artillery battalion in Longstreet's Corps for Second Manassas and Antietam. In November he was promoted again, to brigadier general, and took command of an infantry brigade in the Department of Mississippi and East Louisiana, a position he held until taking command of the artillery defending access to the Mississippi River at Vicksburg in May 1863. He was credited with being the hero of the Battle of Champion Hill, where he was wounded. Lee remained at Vicksburg through the surrender, was taken prisoner, and was later paroled. In August he was promoted to major general and assigned command of the cavalry of the Department of Mississippi and East Louisiana. He replaced Polk in command of that department in May 1864. In June he became the youngest member of the Confederate army to hold the rank of lieutenant general, and in July he took command of a corps in the Army of Tennessee. He served in that capacity through the Franklin-Nashville Campaign and commanded the rearguard action in the withdrawal to Mississippi. After that, Lee led the remnants of his corps with the Army of Tennessee to the Carolinas for the final campaign and surrendered with Johnston at Durham Station, North Carolina, in April 1865.

9   NARA M320, reel 032.

⚔ 7 ⚔

MAY–JULY 1864

ESCORT, ARMY OF MISSISSIPPI

◄ • • • ►

WHEN LIEUTENANT GENERAL LEONIDAS POLK RECEIVED ORDERS ON May 4, 1864, to "move with Loring's division, and any other available force at your command, to Rome, Ga., and there unite with General Johnston," he sprang into action immediately. The forces available to him included the divisions of Major Generals Samuel G. French and William W. Loring; a brigade of Brigadier General James W. Cantey; and the cavalry force of Brigadier General William H. Jackson. Scattered across Alabama and Mississippi, these units would have to be disentangled from their current tasks and moved to the designated gathering place. Simultaneously, General Joseph E. Johnston, under severe pressure from Major General William T. Sherman's force in the vicinity of Dalton, Georgia, some fifty miles north of Rome, was insisting that brigades be deployed as they were ready, rather than waiting for the divisions to assemble.

Polk, with the Orleans Light Horse at his side, established his headquarters in Demopolis, Alabama, to orchestrate the assembly of his new command as the Army of Mississippi and respond to Johnston's call. It was about 175 miles by rail from Demopolis to Blue Mountain (present-day Anniston), Alabama, the terminus of the railroad, and an additional 70 miles from there to Rome, which would have to be made on foot. If trains could be made available, infantry and staff could go by rail as far as Blue Mountain. Cavalry, artillery, and wagon trains would have to go by road. It would take time, even under the best of conditions. By May 6

General Joseph E. Johnston, by the New York Photographic Co., ca. 1865;
The Historic New Orleans Collection, gift of John Armstrong, 1987.43.5

COMMANDERS OF THE ARMY OF MISSISSIPPI

Commander	Lt. Gen. Leonidas Polk
Loring's Division	Maj. Gen. William W. Loring
Featherston's Brigade	Brig. Gen. Winfield S. Featherston
Adams's Brigade	Brig. Gen. John Adams
Scott's Brigade	Col. Thomas M. Scott
Division artillery	Maj. John D. Myrick
French's Division	Maj. Gen. Samuel G. French
Ector's Brigade	Brig. Gen. Matthew D. Ector
Cockrell's Brigade	Brig. Gen. Francis M. Cockrell
Sears's Brigade	Brig. Gen. Claudius W. Sears
Division artillery	Maj. George S. Storrs
Cantey's Division	Brig. Gen. James W. Cantey
Reynolds's Brigade	Brig. Gen. Daniel H. Reynolds
Murphey's Brigade	Col. Virgil S. Murphey
Division artillery	Maj. William C. Preston
Cavalry division	Brig. Gen. William H. Jackson
Armstrong's Brigade	Brig. Gen. Frank C. Armstrong
Ross's Brigade	Brig. Gen. Lawrence S. Ross
Ferguson's Brigade	Brig. Gen. Samuel W. Ferguson
Division artillery	Not specified
Orleans Light Horse (escort)	Capt. J. Leeds Greenleaf

SOURCE: *OR*, SER. 1, VOL. 38, PT. 3:645–46.

Polk estimated to authorities in Richmond that he expected to take some fourteen thousand men—ten thousand infantry and four thousand cavalry—to Georgia.[1]

For the next three days, a flurry of orders was generated, and couriers from the Orleans Light Horse circulated between the headquarters and the units preparing for movement around the clock. Captain J. Leeds Greenleaf, who had acted as Polk's provost marshal in Mississippi, hurriedly handed off to Major General Stephen D. Lee's staff the activities of that position; meanwhile, First Lieutenant Philip M. Kenner and First Sergeant Jackson W. Simmons raced to get the Light Horse packed and organized for movement. An augmented security detail would travel with the general by rail, as would Captain Greenleaf and designated members of the company. The remainder would travel by road as couriers and security for the wagon trains, and also to move the company's spare horses and baggage to the new assembly area.[2]

Lieutenant General Polk arrived in Montevallo on Monday, May 9, and found things in serious disarray. Planning had been fairly explicit, but by mid-1864 the Confederate transportation and logistics systems were not as capable of supporting this magnitude of troop movement as they had been during the 1862 move to Chattanooga. Major General French had arrived two days earlier with one of his brigades and found a second brigade sitting there, awaiting transportation. There were no trains, and no meals at the commissary. The staff worked valiantly, but the resources were insufficient. The Army of Mississippi was not going to get to the scene of battle as quickly as the generals would have liked.[3]

Polk notified General Johnston that he expected to be in Rome by Tuesday, May 10. Johnston responded with instructions for Polk to concentrate at Resaca, some thirty miles north of Rome, and to take command of that location as well as Rome. Leaving French's division at Rome, Polk ordered the remainder of his force to move on to Resaca.[4]

Late in the evening on Wednesday, May 11, Polk arrived in Resaca with Major General Loring and positioned his Army of Mississippi at the left flank of the Army of Tennessee.[5] Brigadier General Cantey, traveling from Mobile, had been able to get to Resaca by May 7, in time to be an effective reinforcement there. But the main body of the Light Horse, which had traveled by road, did not arrive until May 17, and the remainder of Polk's units did not close with the Army of Tennessee until May 18. By this time, the Army of Tennessee was operating with three corps: Polk's corps (which he continued to call the Army of Mississippi), Lieutenant General John B. Hood's corps, and Lieutenant General William J. Hardee's corps.[6]

Skirmishing between the Army of Tennessee and General William T. Sherman's force from May 12 through 15 had ended with Johnston's decision to retire southward, first from Dalton, and then from Resaca, on May 16. Polk covered the retreat and destroyed the Oostanaula River bridge at Resaca when the passage had been effected. By the afternoon of May 18, the Confederate force was in position at Cassville, approximately thirty miles south of Resaca, with Hardee on the left, Polk in the center, and Hood on the right. Johnston had planned to attack about midmorning on May 19, but Hood, reacting to a reported sighting of a heavy Union force to his right, began to pull back, spoiling the plans. By evening, Polk had determined that he also needed to withdraw to a more favorable location. Johnston agreed, and plans were made to withdraw to Allatoona Pass, some fifteen miles to the southeast.

The Union force outflanked Johnston's position to the west, driving on to Dallas, fourteen miles to the southwest of Allatoona. The Confederates were again forced to withdraw, this time to New Hope Church, twenty miles west of Marietta. Union forces attempted a number of probes in the last week of May, but they were met with heavy losses. Seasonal rains made conditions miserable for the armies in the field; roads were quagmires, and the men fought in place for days on end, through the second week of June.[7]

On Tuesday, June 14, 1864, Polk, in company with General Johnston, Lieutenant General Hardee, and Brigadier General Jackson, rode out to Pine Mountain, north of Marietta, to review the terrain and plan deployments. They reached their destination about 11:00 a.m. The rains of the previous two days had stopped. Leaving their horses near the base of the mountain, the men moved on foot to a knoll with a clear view of the Union lines. A battery of the Washington Artillery of New Orleans was on the summit of the mountain, and a Union artillery battery had recently been emplaced on a lower elevation at a range of about nine hundred yards; the Confederate generals and their staffs were in plain view of the Union artillery.

A shot from the Union battery landed nearby, causing the generals to disperse. As they scattered, moving quickly to safety, Lieutenant General Polk moved to the center of the clearing, still studying the deployments.[8] A second round struck Polk and killed him instantly. His staff members—Lieutenant Colonel Thomas Jack, Lieutenants William D. Gale and Aristide R. Hopkins, and cavalrymen of his escort—ran to him, established a defensive perimeter, and, under increasing fire, carried his body to shelter. From there, under heavy escort by the Orleans Light Horse, Polk was taken in an ambulance to Marietta, with Jerry, Polk's horse, walking behind the ambulance.[9] That afternoon, General Johnston issued a memorial to Lieutenant General Polk in General Field Orders No. 2: "Comrades, you are called to mourn your first captain, your oldest companion in arms. Lieutenant-General Polk fell today at the outpost of this army, the army he raised and commanded, in all of whose trials he shared, to all of whose victories he contributed. In this distinguished leader we have lost the most courteous of gentlemen, the most gallant of soldiers. The Christian patriot soldier has neither lived nor died in vain. His example is before you; his mantle rests with you."[10]

Major General Loring assumed command of the Army of Mississippi on an interim basis; Major General Alexander P. Stewart, a division commander in Hood's Corps, was selected to be Polk's permanent replacement. Promoted to lieutenant general on June 23, Stewart assumed command of the Army of Mississippi on July 7.[11]

On Monday June 27, Johnston summarized the army's situation for the authorities in Richmond: "Since May 7 in almost daily skirmishes and the attacks upon different points of our lines (which have been reported to you by telegraph), we have lost about 9,000 men in killed and wounded. Long and cold, wet weather, which ended five days ago, produced a great deal of sickness. Our superior officers think that we have inflicted a loss on the enemy treble our own, as our men have almost always fought under cover or favorable circumstances."[12] Then, in another message later that same day, Johnston reported, "The enemy advanced upon our whole line to-day. . . . Their loss is supposed to be great; ours is known to be small."[13] Johnston was describing the Battle of Kennesaw Mountain, which began on the

Death of General Polk, Pine Mountain, Kennesaw, Georgia, by Alfred R. Waud, June 14, 1864;
Morgan Collection of Civil War Drawings, Library of Congress Prints and Photographs Division

Lieutenant General John B. Hood, ca. 1865;
The Historic New Orleans Collection, gift of John Armstrong, 1987.43.15

morning of June 27, when Sherman, concerned that the constant war of maneuver was becoming too predictable, decided to change the pace with a frontal assault of Confederate positions.[14] Beginning with a heavy artillery preparation, the infantry of three corps attacked Johnston's heavily fortified positions across the front. Fierce battles raged for more than two hours; Union troops were forced to climb the mountain slopes under withering fire, through underbrush and broken terrain, to reach their objectives. The Confederate line held, and the Union force was compelled to withdraw, having been massively punished. Union losses were on the order of three thousand; Confederate losses were a third of that. Sherman reverted once again to the more time-consuming and less spectacular war of maneuver.[15]

By July 1 the rains had stopped, the summer heat set in, and the roads began to dry, facilitating force movement. Johnston, concerned with the regularity of flanking actions against him, elected to withdraw to the line of the Chattahoochee River, the last natural barrier before Atlanta. This line was more than militarily significant; it was politically significant as well. The authorities in Richmond were growing increasingly restive with Johnston's continual withdrawals, urging him to go on the offensive. Johnston was convinced that he faced an enemy double his strength and therefore was taking every option to preserve his force. When pressed by Sherman, on July 9, Johnston fell back again, crossing the Chattahoochee. The reaction from Richmond was swift. On Sunday, July 17, Johnston received this message from Adjutant General Samuel Cooper:

> Lieut. Gen. J[ohn] B. Hood has been commissioned to the temporary rank of general under the late law of Congress. I am directed by the Secretary of War to inform you that as you have failed to arrest the advance of the enemy to the vicinity of Atlanta, far in the interior of Georgia, and express no confidence that you can defeat or repel him, you are hereby relieved from the command of the Army and Department of Tennessee, which you will immediately turn over to General Hood.[16]

The replacement of General Johnston was a shock to the Army of Tennessee. Johnston occupied a special place in the hearts of his soldiers. The morale and confidence of the army had improved significantly since the departure of General Braxton Bragg, and the soldiers gave Johnston credit for this. General Hood did not lack respect, but his leadership came on top of so many changes. The army had lost Polk only a month before; that shock had not yet fully subsided. Stewart had been in place as Polk's successor for only ten days.

With Hood's promotion, Major General Benjamin F. Cheatham assumed temporary command of Hood's Corps. The Army of Tennessee's three corps were now led by Stewart, Cheatham, and Hardee.[17] Then, the army's chief of staff resigned and was replaced by Brigadier General Francis Shoup—another new face in a key position.[18] This was an inordinate degree of flux in the leadership structure, which certainly would have resulted in a tenuous condition even under the best of circumstances. But the continuing pressure from Sherman meant that these were not the best of conditions. Each of the corps commanders petitioned Johnston, Hood, and the authorities in Richmond to delay Johnston's departure until the present offensives were decided; all met with refusal. Hood would have to hit the ground running, and mistakes would bear a severe penalty.

ORLEANS LIGHT HORSE PERSONNEL ACCOUNTABILITY
MAY–JUNE 1864

GAINS	3	GAINS	Dubose, F. M.; Dubose, N. W.; Hosmer, C. H.
LOSSES	7		
Transferred	4	LOSSES	Bellamy, J. T.; Floyd, T. M.; Fox, W. H.; Gribble, W. C.; Hughes, E. A.; Spratt, R. B.; Trist, N. P.
Captured	1		
Killed/Died	1		
Unspecified	1		
ACCOUNTABLE	91		
Present	55		
Detailed to duty	19		
Absent—leave	1		
Absent—sick	10		
Absent—w/o leave	1		
Hospitalized	3		
Wounded/Medically disqualified	2		

NOTES

1 *OR*, ser. 1, vol. 38, pt. 4:661–65, 668, 670–71; Parks, 373–74.

2 *OR*, ser. 1, vol. 38, pt. 2:659–61; *OR*, ser. 1, vol. 39, pt. 2:585; *OR*, ser. 1, vol. 52, pt. 2:666; NARA M320, reel 032; Connelly, *Autumn of Glory*, 332–34.

3 *OR*, ser. 1, vol. 32, pt. 3:598, 772–74; Connelly, *Autumn of Glory*, 302; French, 192–95; Gabel, 24. A revealing narrative of this time is contained in F. Jay Taylor, ed., *Reluctant Rebel*, 159*ff*. The diary of Robert Draughon Patrick, a quartermaster sergeant in Cantey's Brigade, *Reluctant Rebel* provides an instructive and useful commentary on the Atlanta Campaign and succeeding transitional events from Resaca to Tuscumbia (April–November 1864).

4 *OR*, ser. 1, vol. 38, pt. 4:695, 701, 704, 720.

5 William Wing Loring (b. 1818, Wilmington, NC; d. 1886, New York, NY) enlisted in the Florida Militia at the age of fourteen and served in the Second Seminole War (1835–42). He was promoted to lieutenant and in 1846 joined the Regiment of Mounted Rifles. He was then promoted to major and served in the Mexican-American War (1846–48). Loring received brevet promotions to lieutenant colonel and to colonel. From 1849 to 1851, he commanded the Oregon Territory. In 1861 he was commissioned as a brigadier general in the Confederate army with command of the Army of the Northwest. He was promoted to major general in 1862 and commanded the Department of Southwestern Virginia. In 1863 he became a division commander in the Department of Alabama, Mississippi, and East Louisiana. He continued as a division commander within Polk's Army of Mississippi, when the army became a corps in the Army of Tennessee during the 1864 Atlanta Campaign. When Polk was killed, Loring briefly succeeded him as corps commander. He then returned to being a division commander until he

was wounded at Ezra Church during the Atlanta Campaign. He returned for the Franklin-Nashville Campaign (1864) and the Carolinas Campaign (1865). He surrendered with Johnston at Durham Station, North Carolina.

6 *OR*, ser. 1, vol. 38, pt. 4:694, 710, 711, 715, 720; Connelly, *Autumn of Glory*, 341; Esposito, 144–45. John Bell Hood (b. 1831, Bath County, KY; d. 1879, New Orleans, LA), an 1853 graduate of the US Military Academy, served in California and Texas before being commissioned as a colonel in the Fourth Texas Infantry in 1861. He commanded a brigade during the Seven Days' Battles in northern Virginia, after which he was promoted to major general with divisional command at Second Manassas, Antietam, Fredericksburg, and Gettysburg. He was transferred with Longstreet's Corps to Tennessee and served with distinction at the Battle of Chickamauga. In 1864 he was promoted to the temporary rank of general and relieved General Joseph E. Johnston in command of the Army of Tennessee at Atlanta. Following that campaign, he led the Army of Tennessee through the Franklin-Nashville Campaign, withdrawing afterward to Tupelo, where he resigned his command.

7 *OR*, ser. 1, vol. 38, pt. 4:706, 708, 758; Parks, 375–80; Castel, 140–80; Elliott, 183–88; Esposito, 146–49.

8 *Macon Daily Telegraph*, 17 June 1864.

9 Burnam, n.p.; Williams, 346.

10 *OR*, ser. 1, vol. 38, pt. 4:776.

11 *OR*, ser. 1, vol. 38, pt. 4:776, 787; Parks, 382–86; Elliott, 191–97. Alexander Peter Stewart (b. 1821, Rogersville, TN; d. 1908, Biloxi, MS), an 1842 graduate of the US Military Academy, resigned from the service in 1845 to become a college professor. He accepted a commission in the Tennessee Militia in 1861 as a major of artillery, and shortly thereafter entered the Confederate army in the same capacity. Later in 1861 he was appointed brigadier general and commanded a brigade in the Columbus District of Department No. 2. He continued as a brigade commander in the Army of Mississippi's First Corps during the Battle of Perryville. He was promoted to major general and commanded a division in the Army of Tennessee during the Tullahoma Campaign and at the Battle of Chickamauga, where he was wounded.

12 *OR*, ser. 1, vol. 38, pt. 4:795–96.

13 *OR*, ser. 1, vol. 38, pt. 4:796.

14 War of maneuver is taking advantage of favorable terrain and using frequent or rapid movement of forces to gain an advantageous position so as to neutralize or capture an enemy, rather than directly assaulting and destroying him, which is called war of attrition.

15 *OR*, ser. 1, vol. 38, pt. 4:795–96; Connelly, *Autumn of Glory*, 359–60; Esposito, 144–49.

16 *OR*, ser. 1, vol. 38, pt. 3:617–18; *OR*, ser. 1, vol. 38, pt. 5:885, 887, 891; Connelly, *Autumn of Glory*, 391–426; Elliott, 200–201.

17 *OR*, ser. 1, vol. 38, pt. 5:891. There was also a fourth corps: Major General Joseph Wheeler's cavalry corps. Invaluable for the screening of flanks, shock action at particular places and times, and the probing of problematic areas, Wheeler's Corps was subject to separate deployment for extended periods, such as its forays into Tennessee, and was not always fully integrated with the infantry corps. The integrated "combined arms team" was a concept not yet fully present in the minds of many of the senior commanders. Benjamin Franklin Cheatham (b. 1820, Nashville, TN; d. 1886, Nashville, TN) was commissioned as a captain in the First Tennessee Infantry in 1846. He served in the Mexican-American War (1846–48), after which he was released from active duty and served as a brigadier general in the Tennessee Militia. In 1861 he was commissioned as a brigadier general in the Confederate army and became a brigade commander in the Western District, Department No. 2. He was promoted to major general in 1862 and commanded the Second Division of the First Corps of the Army of Mississippi. He was wounded at the Battle of Shiloh but went on to serve at the Battles of Perryville, Murfreesboro, and Chickamauga. He became a corps commander for the Battle of Missionary Ridge and continued in that capacity through the Atlanta and Franklin-Nashville Campaigns. After returning from Tennessee, he joined General Johnston in the Carolinas Campaign and surrendered with him at Durham Station, North Carolina.

18 *OR*, ser. 1, vol. 52, pt. 2:712–13; *OR*, ser. 1, vol. 38, pt. 5:887–91, 907, 910; Connelly, *Autumn of Glory*, 421–23. For more on the appointment of Brigadier General Francis Shoup as chief of staff of the Army of Tennessee for the period of July 24 through September 14, 1864, see *OR*, ser. 1, vol. 38, pt. 5:907 and *OR*, ser. 1, vol. 39, pt. 1:804. For Shoup's journal, see *OR*, ser. 1, vol. 39, pt. 1:803–8.

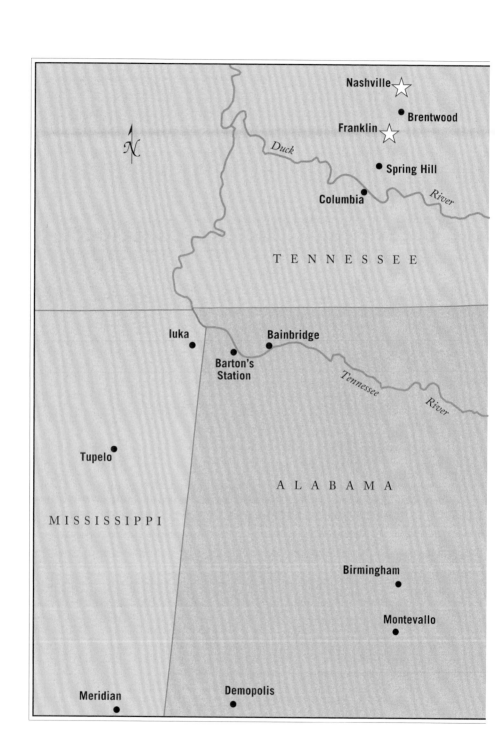

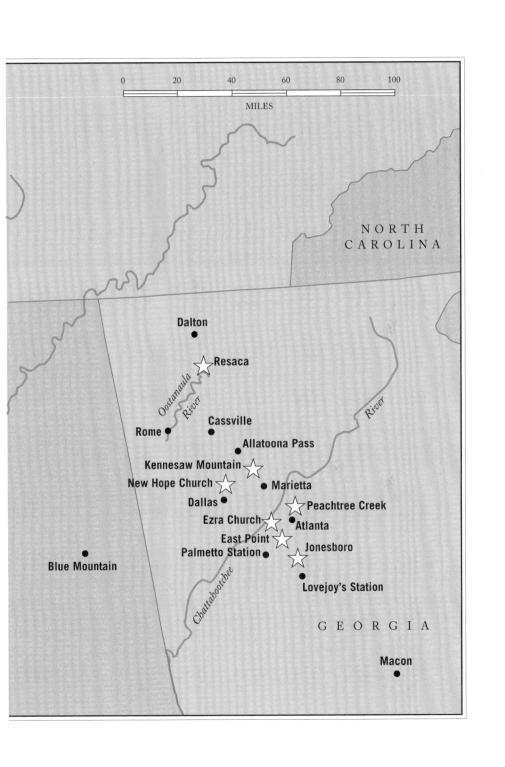

Lt. Genl. A. P. Stewart

⚒ 8 ⚒

JULY 1864–JANUARY 1865

ESCORT, STEWART'S CORPS, ARMY OF TENNESSEE

——— ◄ • • • ► ———

On Monday, July 18, 1864, the Orleans Light Horse and the Army of Mississippi began to accustom themselves to their new commanders. General John B. Hood had been wounded twice and had lost one leg and the use of one arm. As a division and corps commander, he was known to be gallant and fearless, if somewhat impetuous, in combat. He was an offensive, rather than defensive, general who preferred to attack rather than to fortify. Lieutenant General Alexander P. Stewart had a highly respected combat reputation as a brigade and division commander; he had been a college professor, mathematician, and philosopher and was somewhat more introspective than Hood. For these two very different individuals, there would be no grace period; both would be severely tested in short order.[1]

After the Army of Tennessee had withdrawn across the Chattahoochee River, Major General William T. Sherman's Union armies spread out on a broad front, approaching Atlanta from the north and northeast. Johnston had chosen the Confederate positions south of Peachtree Creek, an east-to-west-flowing stream approximately three miles north of Atlanta, as the location for the Army of Tennessee. It was from there that Hood initiated the first of four efforts to save Atlanta.[2] On July 20 Hood launched a preemptive attack in an effort to catch elements of the Union force before they reached their intended positions. After

Lieutenant General Alexander P. Stewart, by Alfred R. Waud, between 1864 and 1865; *Morgan Collection of Civil War Drawings, Library of Congress Prints and Photographs Division*

COMMANDERS OF STEWART'S CORPS, ARMY OF TENNESSEE

Commander	Lieut. Gen. Alexander P. Stewart
Loring's Division	Maj. Gen. William W. Loring
Featherston's Brigade	Brig. Gen. Winfield S. Featherston
Adams's Brigade	Brig. Gen. John Adams
Scott's Brigade	Brig. Gen. Thomas M. Scott
Division artillery	Maj. John D. Myrick
French's Division	Maj. Gen. Samuel G. French
Ector's Brigade	Brig. Gen. Matthew D. Ector
Cockrell's Brigade	Brig. Gen. Francis M. Cockrell
Sears's Brigade	Brig. Gen. Claudius W. Sears
Division artillery	Maj. George S. Storrs
Walthall's Division	Maj. Gen. Edward C. Walthall
Reynolds's Brigade	Brig. Gen. Daniel H. Reynolds
Quarles's Brigade	Brig. Gen. William A. Quarles
Shelley's Brigade	Brig. Gen. Charles M. Shelley
Division artillery	Maj. William C. Preston
Orleans Light Horse (escort)	Capt. J. Leeds Greenleaf

SOURCE: *OR*, SER. 1, VOL. 38, PT. 3:659–61.

approximately two hours of furious fighting late in the afternoon, the Confederates were unable to break the Union line and were beaten back at a cost of about five thousand casualties; Hood pulled his force back into the prepared defenses of the city of Atlanta.[3]

Hood's second effort came quickly. On the evening of Thursday, July 21, he ordered troop movements to prepare for an attack the next morning. An attempted turning movement by Hardee's Corps against the Union flank was initially successful, but then stalled, after which the two armies engaged in a massive struggle supported by large numbers of artillery. The only notable outcome was the killing of Union Major General James B. McPherson. With his death, the men of the Army of Mississippi felt that the killing of Lieutenant General Leonidas Polk had been avenged. The Confederate casualties for the day approached 8,500; the Union casualties, 3,600. After the exertions of the past several days, the armies had reached the point of exhaustion; a period of relative quiet, lasting almost a week, ensued.[4]

Hood used this time to firm up his ongoing reorganization of the Army of Tennessee. On July 26 Stephen D. Lee, who had been promoted to lieutenant general in June, was received as the permanent replacement for command of Hood's Corps, permitting Benjamin F. Cheatham, the temporary commander, to return to his own division in Hardee's Corps. Hood also completed the assimilation of the Army of Mississippi, redesignating it as Stewart's Corps. The army's corps commanders were now Lieutenant Generals Hardee, Lee, and Stewart, plus Major General Joseph Wheeler, commander of the cavalry corps.[5]

For the Orleans Light Horse, July marked the beginning of a period of net losses of personnel. Constant rains, continuous shifting of positions, and ever-present skirmishing were taking a toll on the men, and replacements were not being received as frequently as they had been earlier in the year. The leadership of the troop remained relatively unchanged: J. Leeds Greenleaf, captain; Philip M. Kenner, first lieutenant; Samuel Huntington, Aristide R. Hopkins, and E. Malcolm Morse, second lieutenants; Jackson W. Simmons, first sergeant. Sergeant Austin W. Rountree left the unit in July and was replaced by the promotion of Private Charles R. Egelly to commissary sergeant. The unit's mission and functions continued unchanged under the new corps commander.[6]

Meanwhile, Sherman continued to shift and reposition his force in an attempt to encircle and isolate Atlanta, now focusing on the area to the west and southwest of the city. Major General Oliver O. Howard, who had succeeded McPherson, was sent to cut the railroad supply line that approached Atlanta from the southwest. This would be the scene of Hood's third offensive initiative, on July 28. Lee, reinforced by Stewart, led the movement to intercept the Union force, colliding with Howard's troops near Ezra Church, a small log chapel. Throughout the day, successive Confederate attacks were repelled; the Union line held, but Howard was unable to cut the railroad. When the day ended, the Confederates had sustained on the order of five thousand casualties, including the wounding of Lieutenant General Stewart and Major General Loring; the Union casualties were reported as seven hundred. Hood designated Major General Cheatham as interim commander of Stewart's Corps during Stewart's convalescence, from July 28 until August 15.[7]

Union raids against the railroads from July 29 through August 1 were met by Wheeler's Cavalry Corps, augmented by Brigadier General Jackson's Cavalry Division, and ended in a devastating setback to the Union cavalry. Countering a massive Union cavalry offensive, Wheeler captured 950 members of Brigadier General Edward M. McCook's cavalry division plus Major General George Stoneman and 700 members of his cavalry corps. The total Union cavalry losses of this one operation—including killed, wounded, missing, and captured—exceeded 4,200 troopers, nearly half of Sherman's cavalry.[8] Despite his losses, Sherman continued to attempt to complete the encirclement of Atlanta. His efforts to take a railroad junction at East Point, southwest of the city, on August 4 and 5 were repulsed. Growing increasingly impatient with his inability to complete the siege of Atlanta, Sherman began a systematic long-range heavy-artillery bombardment of the city on August 9, which lasted for a few days then abated noticeably.[9] For the next two weeks, other activity slowed as well. By August 22 railroad raids ceased altogether; within a week it was apparent that Sherman was changing his tactics, and the Union forces were falling back from their positions north of Atlanta. On August 26 Stewart and Lee moved their corps forward and occupied the deserted Union positions, reaping a bonanza in abandoned food and equipment.

For two days the Confederate commanders were perplexed, and all cavalry resources were employed in an attempt to fathom Sherman's activity. By August 28 the situation became clearer: Sherman's entire army had moved from the north and northeast of Atlanta to southwest of the city, threatening to cut off the Macon and Western Railroad at Jonesboro, the last remaining supply line. In the last of Hood's four offensive efforts to hold on to Atlanta, he sent Hardee, supported by Lee, to Jonesboro, where they took up positions on August 31. Stewart's Corps and the Orleans Light Horse remained in the city with the army headquarters. The next day, after a full day of heavy fighting, three Union corps were able to break the Confederate line and take control of the railroad. Confederate losses for the day were approximately two thousand; Union losses were in excess of twelve hundred. As a result of losing this last rail connection, Hood elected to evacuate Atlanta and fall back in the direction of Macon, to the southeast. Sherman's force entered Atlanta on September 2.[10]

As Hood gathered his corps at Lovejoy's Station, on the Macon and Western Railroad southeast of Atlanta, Sherman issued an edict that all civilians were to be evicted from Atlanta. Hood was shocked and, in a letter to Sherman, wrote, "the unprecedented measure you propose transcends, in studied and ingenious cruelty, all acts ever before brought to my attention in the dark history of war."[11] With Sherman in an obdurate frame of mind, however, there was no alternative for Hood but to agree to a ten-day truce, from September 12 to 21, to implement the eviction. For days thereafter, refugees from Atlanta plodded along the roads or huddled at railway stations, mostly without shelter, supplies, or assistance of any kind. During this enforced lull in activity, Hood relocated the army some twenty-five miles westward to the vicinity of Palmetto Station on the Atlanta and West Point Railroad. It was here that President Davis arrived on September 25 for a three-day conference with Hood and his corps commanders on the continuation of the campaign.[12]

In his formal report of operations south of the Chattahoochee River from July 18 to September 29, 1864, Lieutenant General Stewart complimented "those who distinguished themselves by acts of special gallantry," mentioning by name, among others, Lieutenant Aristide R. Hopkins and Private J. Minnick Williams of the Orleans Light Horse. Stewart went on, "to Captain Greenleaf and his company (the Orleans Light Horse), I acknowledge my obligations for valuable services."[13] One hundred twenty days had passed since Polk had been ordered to move from Mississippi with his command to reinforce Johnston. From June

City of Atlanta, by George N. Barnard, 1864; *Library of Congress Prints and Photographs Division*

through September 1864, the personnel strength of the Light Horse had fallen from ninety-two to sixty-two, with losses due to high rates of illness, hospitalization, and physical disqualification.[14]

Atlanta's defense had come at a terrible price for the Army of Tennessee. Its ranks had been severely reduced by battle casualties and by illness outbreaks that could not be contained. The replacement stream had nearly dried up, and straggling and desertion were rife. By mid-September Hood's total effective force was fewer than forty thousand. The Confederate high command in Richmond had searched high and low for a general without Bragg's and Johnston's tendency to maneuver and withdraw. They had found a candidate in Hood, but his aggressiveness had seriously depleted the army. In the aftermath of Atlanta, senior authorities attempted to answer the question "What do we do now?"[15]

Unable to defeat Sherman's army in a massed confrontation, Hood's new plan was to attack the Union army's more lightly defended base in Tennessee, in hopes of cutting their supply lines and thereby forcing Sherman to abandon his plan to march from Atlanta to Savannah. To that end, and with governmental approval from his conference with President Davis, on September 29 Hood and the Army of Tennessee recrossed the Chattahoochee River heading northwest toward Nashville, the defense of which had been assigned by Sherman to Major General George H. Thomas.[16]

As Hood reached the Tennessee River near Florence, Alabama, his army's fighting strength was approximately thirty-five thousand men.[17] Its first objective in Tennessee was to respond to reports of Major General John M. Schofield's Union force of approximately fifteen thousand men massing at Columbia, about seventy-five miles north. By the afternoon of November 27, the Army of Tennessee was in position around the city. Union troops abandoned Columbia overnight, withdrawing to the north side of the Duck River. The weather had turned cold, with intermittent snow—a problem for the Army of Tennessee, which was not equipped for winter. Hood pursued Schofield twenty-five miles north to Franklin, Tennessee, where his troops made a frontal assault on the entrenched Union positions late in the day on November 30. Repeated assaults and bitter face-to-face confrontations took place in a hailstorm of musketry. The battle continued until midnight, with some skirmishing after that. Under the cover of night, the Union force quietly withdrew in the direction of Nashville.

With the light of dawn came a sickening reality: Confederate losses were frighteningly heavy. Stewart's Corps had sustained on the order of 40 percent combat losses. Of the 8,708 men participating in the campaign, 3,387 were killed, wounded, missing, or captured; 27 of these were irreplaceable unit commanders. For the Army of Tennessee as a whole, total losses were more than 6,200, and within the command structure, 1 division commander, 10 brigade commanders, and 54 regimental and company commanders had been lost. The leadership was in a shambles; as a functional entity, the army had essentially been destroyed.[18]

After a grim day spent burying the dead, collecting battle debris, and assessing the residual effective strength of the army, the Army of Tennessee moved twenty miles to the vicinity of Nashville, on Friday, December 2. By December 7 the army had taken its positions two to three miles from the defenses of Nashville, and there the men waited. Hood had decided to take a defensive posture, letting Thomas attack him rather than taking the initiative as he had at Franklin. On December 8 the weather turned cold: ten degrees Fahrenheit with freezing rain, sleet, and snow lasting for the next five days. The frozen ground impeded the preparation of positions; the men, unprotected from the extreme elements, suffered miserably.

Lieutenant General Ulysses S. Grant urged Thomas to attack on December 6 and again on December 11, but Thomas wasn't ready.[19] The attack came on the morning of Thursday, December 15, with the main offensive developing against Stewart's Corps. By 1 p.m. the attack reached its critical point, and despite Hood's reinforcement of Stewart, the line began to break. By 2 p.m. the entire line had to be withdrawn. Falling back two miles, the Army of Tennessee regrouped overnight, expecting a continuation of the attack on Friday morning. The assaults came throughout that day, over and again, and always under the incessant bombardment of massed artillery. By 4 p.m., in the midst of a cold drizzle, the Union force surged in a massed onslaught against Cheatham's Corps, which gave way. Some brigades disappeared altogether; some began a hasty retreat only to find that the withdrawal route was blocked, at which time they panicked.[20]

Abandoning everything, they fled, disorganized, to the Franklin Pike and then southward toward the Tennessee River, more than one hundred miles away. Lee's Corps, relatively lightly pressed during the attack, undertook an organized withdrawal, providing a measure of cover to the disorganized remainder. Hood had anticipated, in the event of a withdrawal, making a stand at Columbia. But there was no force left to make a stand. Under freezing conditions, several thousand men, the majority without shoes of any kind and all clad in thin cotton clothing, now in tatters, abandoned everything—weapons, artillery, baggage—and streamed southward. Only gradually would they be regrouped.[21]

Stewart's after-action report of the Franklin-Nashville Campaign describes the return to the Tennessee River as it was experienced by the men of the Orleans Light Horse: "On reaching Brentwood, . . . about dark [Friday, December 16], I received orders to move on to Franklin, and next morning to move toward Spring Hill and Columbia. Arriving at the latter place on the morning of the 18th, this corps took position on the north bank of Duck River, covering the passage of the entire army, and crossing about daylight of the 20th; so, the following week at Tennessee River, Bainbridge [near present-day Florence, Alabama], this corps covered the operations, and was the last to cross, which it did on the morning of December 28."[22]

As Stewart's escort company, the Orleans Light Horse remained attentive to him and supportive of his needs. The unit suffered from the climatic conditions and logistics deficiencies along with everyone else in the army, and the mortality rate of the unit's horses was appallingly high due to lack of forage, loss of shoes, lameness, and broken legs resulting from the ice-encrusted mud. However, they were spared the combat losses suffered by many units, despite the fact that the cavalrymen were constantly in the thick of the action and that Stewart's Corps sustained the brunt of the casualties, especially at Franklin. The Light Horse lost only three men during November and December, two of whom, Troopers Octave J. Bergeron and Henry C. Ryall, were captured at Nashville and Shelbyville, respectively. None of the leadership of the unit was lost.[23]

From the Tennessee River, the remnants of the Army of Tennessee had continued southwest into Mississippi, and finally, after four long weeks of slogging along frozen, muddy roads, they reached Tupelo during the second week of January 1865.[24]

Writing after the war, Lieutenant Bromfield Ridley, an aide-de-camp to Stewart, recalled the last night of 1864:

Our skeleton army plodded its weary way from Nashville, Tenn., to Iuka, Miss. [northeast of Tupelo]. Through the bleak and chilling blasts of December 31 our ill-clad, barefooted, hungry soldiers marched in slush and mud, and at nightfall drew their foot-sore and weary bodies into a tentless camp.

Stewart's corps had bivouacked. He and those of his staff were building fires to warm, when an order came from Gen. Hood to send a staff officer with three couriers back to Barton's Station [in Alabama, twenty miles east of their encampment] . . . and from thence establish communications with Gen. W. [William] H. Jackson, to ascertain whether the enemy had crossed at Bainbridge, and the extent of his pursuit. . . . For once our General hesitated to particularize. Said he: "Is there a member of my staff who will volunteer to execute this order?" . . . The silence was painful until a faint and slow answer, "General, I will go," was involuntarily made by me.

Capt. Greenleaf, of the escort, besought three volunteer couriers to accompany me. . . . We started back over the road that was cut up into mud and mire, but now was frozen, making travel on it dangerous. Our poor horses, jaded from the sore trials of the Nashville campaign, would slide over the icy road, and sometimes break in and sink up to their bodies. . . . There was no moon to light us on the journey. . . . Along the route we would . . . run across a dead horse or something that always kept us on the lookout. . . . Well, about daybreak we crossed the Big Bear Creek a short distance from the station. Now came my time, on reaching the destined point, to select one of my couriers . . . to see Gen. Jackson. I asked who would volunteer. . . . One courier started, but returned in less than an hour reporting that he had met Gen. Jackson at the head of his cavalry command coming that way. . . . I wired Gen. Stewart from the station, and got a reply to put my horses and men in the only remaining box car at the station, and return to Iuka. Thus was spent the last night of 1864.[25]

In the Franklin-Nashville Campaign, the Army of Tennessee lost in excess of 14,500 men, more than 40 percent of its effective force. Combining these numbers with the high percentage of senior leadership losses, it was apparent that the army was wrecked as a fighting force.[26] As always, however, it was the soldiers themselves who delivered the ultimate verdict. As they struggled home from Nashville, there was little to sing about. But, in the sometimes perverse manner of soldiers enmeshed in hardship, someone made up a new set of words to the popular melody of "The Yellow Rose of Texas":

Oh, my feet are torn and bloody, and my heart is full of woe,

I'm going back to Georgia to find my Uncle Joe;

You may talk about your Beauregard, and sing of Bobbie Lee,

But the gallant Hood of Texas, he played hell in Tennessee.[27]

View of the outer trenches on the last day of the Battle of Nashville, by Jacob F. Coonley, December 16, 1864; *Civil War Photograph Collection, Library of Congress Prints and Photographs Division*

ORLEANS LIGHT HORSE PERSONNEL ACCOUNTABILITY
JULY–DECEMBER 1864

	JULY–AUG. 1864	SEPT.–OCT. 1864	NOV.–DEC. 1864
GAINS	0	1	0
LOSSES	29	1	3
Discharged	0	1	0
Transferred	2	0	0
Deserted	0	0	1
Captured	0	0	1
Unspecified	27	0	1
ACCOUNTABLE	62	62	59
Present	45	48	45
Detailed to duty	13	12	11
Absent—leave	0	2	1
Hospitalized	2	0	1
Wounded/Medically disqualified	2	0	1

	JULY–AUG. 1864	SEPT.–OCT. 1864	NOV.–DEC. 1864
GAINS	—	Peters, B. F.	—
LOSSES	Beauregard, C.T.; Buord, L.A.; Campbell, J.; Clough, J. A.; D'Aquin, T. A.; Dubose, F. M.; Egelly, C. R.; Gallwey, C.; Griffith, R. S.; Hardin, J. O.; Hartigan, J.; Huntington, S.; Le Sassier, G.; Lynd, S.; Macready, J.; Mallen, J. B.; Mulholland, J.; Penn, M. A.; Rondeau, W. A. S.; Rountree, A. W.; Ryall, J. S.; Seiler, F. W.; Shepherd, H. H.; Stewart, S. R.; Tennison, W. H.; Viavant, A.; Waller, W. M.; Weathersby, A. D.; Wrester, J.	Hamilton, W. B.	Bergeron, O. J.; Byrd, J. G.; Ryall, H. C.

NOTES

1 Connelly, *Autumn of Glory*, 429–39; Elliott, 200–201.

2 Horn, 350.

3 Connelly, *Autumn of Glory*, 447–51; Elliott, 201–9; French, 219–20; Groom, 49–50.

4 *OR*, ser. 1, vol. 38, pt. 3:952–53; *OR*, ser. 1, vol. 38, pt. 5:899–903; Connelly, *Autumn of Glory*, 445–50; Elliott, 209–10; French, 218–19; Groom, 49–50.

5 *OR*, ser. 1, vol. 38, pt. 5:910, 912; *OR*, ser. 1, vol. 38, pt. 3:661–67. Joseph Wheeler (b. 1836, Augusta, GA; d. 1906, Brooklyn, NY), an 1859 graduate of the US Military Academy, was first commissioned in the First US Dragoons, then attended the US Cavalry School, and was assigned to the Regiment of Mounted Rifles in the New Mexico Territory. In 1861 he was commissioned by the Confederate army and took command of the Nineteenth Alabama Infantry Regiment. After being promoted to

colonel that September, he transferred to cavalry and commanded the Second Cavalry Brigade in the Army of Mississippi. He proved his value in successive rearguard actions at the Battle of Perryville. In October 1862 he was promoted to brigadier general and became commander of the cavalry of the Second Corps of the Army of Tennessee. In January 1863 he was promoted to major general and performed several independent raids against logistics and transportation centers of the Union army in Tennessee throughout that year. He continued with the Army of Tennessee through the Atlanta, Franklin-Nashville, and Carolinas Campaigns. When the Confederate government withdrew from Richmond in May 1865, Wheeler provided a cavalry escort for the attempted escape of President Davis and was captured on May 9 at Conyers Station, Georgia. He was paroled in June 1865.

6 *OR*, ser. 1, vol. 38, pt. 5:912; NARA M320, reel 032.

7 *OR*, ser. 1, vol. 38, pt. 3:688–89, 870–73; *OR*, ser. 1, vol. 38, pt. 5:917, 930; Connelly, *Autumn of Glory*, 453–55; Elliott, 210–14; Groom, 51.

8 *OR*, ser. 1, vol. 38, pt. 3:953–57; *OR*, ser. 1. Vol. 38, pt. 5:921, 924; Horn, 362–63; Connelly, *Autumn of Glory*, 452–53.

9 *OR*, ser. 1, vol. 38, pt. 3:688–89; *OR*, ser. 1, vol. 38, pt. 5:917, 930; Connelly, *Autumn of Glory*, 453–55; Elliott, 210–14; Groom, 51.

10 *OR*, ser. 1, vol. 38, pt. 3:668–75, 680–83; Connelly, *Autumn of Glory*, 456–67; Elliott, 214–17; Bonds, 278–305.

11 Horn, 369; Bonds, 313–17, 324–32.

12 A significant topic on the agenda for the visit of the president was Lieutenant General Hardee's tenure with the army. Hardee and General Hood had both previously requested that he be relieved of his command, but prior to the Battle of Jonesboro, the president had appealed to them to maintain the status quo for the good of the country. In the aftermath of the battle, the president relented and, on September 28, relieved Hardee of his corps in the Army of Tennessee and reassigned him to command the Department of South Carolina, Georgia, and Florida, which he assumed on October 5. Major General Cheatham replaced Hardee within the Army of Tennessee; Cheatham, Lee, and Stewart would take their respective corps into Tennessee. *OR*, ser. 1, vol. 39, pt. 1:803–5; Horn, 369–74; Sherman, 2:117–30; Connelly, *Autumn of Glory*, 470–78; Elliott, 217–18; Groom, 54–58; Bonds, 313–17, 324–32.

13 *OR*, ser. 1, vol. 38, pt. 3:872–73.

14 NARA M320, reel 032.

15 *OR*, ser. 1, vol. 38, pt. 3:872–73; Connelly, *Autumn of Glory*, 467–69; Groom, 59–64; Esposito, 148–49.

16 *OR*, ser. 1, vol. 39, pt. 1:803–5; *OR*, ser. 1, vol. 39, pt. 3:162–202; Connelly, *Autumn of Glory*, 476–80; Groom, 59–63.

17 *OR*, ser. 1, vol. 39, pt. 1:803–5; Connelly, *Autumn of Glory*, 480–90; Elliott, 218–22; Esposito, 150–51.

18 *OR*, ser. 1, vol. 45, pt. 1:664, 678, 684–86; *OR*, ser. 1, vol. 45, pt. 2:707–8; Connelly, *Autumn of Glory*, 502–6; Elliott, 235–45; Groom, 156–220; Esposito, 152–57.

19 Connelly, *Autumn of Glory*, 507–9; Elliott, 245–47.

20 *OR*, ser. 1, vol. 45, pt. 1:709–11; Elliott, 248–56; Groom, 221–65.

21 *OR*, ser. 1, vol. 45, pt. 1:710–11; Connelly, *Autumn of Glory*, 510–12.

22 *OR*, ser. 1, vol. 45, pt. 1:711.

23 *OR*, ser. 1, vol. 45, pt. 1:711; NARA M320, reel 032.

24 *OR*, ser. 1, vol. 45, pt. 1:664–75; *OR*, ser. 1, vol. 45, pt. 2:707–12; Connelly, *Autumn of Glory*, 507–12; Elliott, 248–56; Groom, 221–65.

25 Ridley, "The Last Night of Sixty-Four," 539.

26 Conservation Fund, 392–96; Groom, 268–75.

27 A traditional folksong of unknown origins, "The Yellow Rose of Texas" has been known with various lyrics since the late 1830s. This verse originated during the return march from Nashville in December 1864. Watkins, 458–60; Groom, 271.

⊰ 9 ⊱

FEBRUARY–APRIL 1865

ESCORT, STEWART'S CORPS, ARMY OF TENNESSEE

‹ • • • ›

AFTER THE FALL OF ATLANTA, IN SEPTEMBER 1864, UNION MAJOR General William T. Sherman initially pursued Hood in his move northward but soon determined that Thomas and Schofield could fend for themselves in Tennessee. He returned to Atlanta and began preparations for his next campaign, the March to the Sea, which he commenced in mid-November with the approval of Lieutenant General Ulysses S. Grant. Sherman burned the undefended city of Atlanta as he departed, then laid waste to the countryside as he moved eastward, reaching Savannah before Christmas. He waited out the holidays there, and on January 19, 1865, he set off northward into South Carolina.[1]

Opposing Sherman in Georgia and the Carolinas was Lieutenant General William J. Hardee, who had left the Army of Tennessee in September to command the Department of South Carolina, Georgia, and Florida. After Sherman had reached Savannah, Hardee, responding to Sherman's overwhelming strength, had withdrawn into South Carolina and called for reinforcements. The war department in Richmond looked to the Army of Tennessee as a resource. General John B. Hood warned that the Tennessee veterans, who had been back in Tupelo for only one week, needed rest. They were not equipped or in condition to participate in another campaign. When General P. G. T. Beauregard, now commander of the

COMMANDERS OF STEWART'S CORPS, ARMY OF TENNESSEE

Commander	Lieut. Gen. Alexander P. Stewart
Loring's Division	Maj. Gen. William W. Loring
Featherston's Brigade	Brig. Gen. Winfield S. Featherston
Lowry's Brigade	Brig. Gen. Robert Lowry
Shelley's Brigade	Brig. Gen. Charles M. Shelley
Anderson's Division	Maj. Gen. James P. Anderson
Elliott's Brigade	Brig. Gen. Stephen Elliott Jr.
Rhett's Brigade	Col. William B. Butler
Walthall's Division	Maj. Gen. Edward C. Walthall
Harrison's Brigade	Col. George P. Harrison, Jr.
Connor's Brigade	Brig. Gen. John D. Kennedy
Artillery	Maj. Andrew B. Rhett
Orleans Light Horse (escort)	Capt. J. Leeds Greenleaf

SOURCE: *OR*, SER. 1, VOL. 47, PT. 1:1063–64.

Department of the West, and Lieutenant General Richard Taylor, commander of the Department of Alabama, Mississippi, and East Louisiana, realized with horror to what levels the army had descended, they supported Hood's call for a delay. But that delay would be measured in days rather than weeks or months.[2]

On January 13 Hood submitted his resignation as commander of the Army of Tennessee and was succeeded temporarily by Lieutenant General Taylor. Beginning on January 19, in response to orders from Richmond, the corps of Stephen D. Lee and Benjamin F. Cheatham set off by rail for Augusta, Georgia, from whence they would march to meet Hardee in South Carolina. Stewart's Corps initially was selected to remain in Mississippi as part of Taylor's departmental defense force, but by January 30 the developing situation in South Carolina demanded its release by Taylor to head east as well.[3]

On February 8 Lieutenant E. Malcolm Morse of the Orleans Light Horse arrived at Meridian with eighteen couriers from the unit. They constituted the lead element of Stewart's Corps in the movement to Augusta and would establish a line of couriers, one pair of men at each of the nine stations along the way, as the means by which Stewart would maintain contact with his troops en route and with his new commander in South Carolina.[4]

The cross-country train trip to Augusta, a distance of 750 miles, required two weeks under very unpredictable conditions. Derailings, increasingly common, resulted in many hours spent with soldiers sitting by the tracks as repairs were made. A break in the rail lines of twenty-five miles or more between Milledgeville and Sparta, Georgia, was traversed on foot or on horseback, with inundating rains as frequent as the rail failures had been. The absence of connecting trains contributed to protracted delays, with the units often moving on in forced marches.[5]

The soldiers had been sent from Mississippi in a completely deficient condition. Beauregard's staff in Mobile had warned him on January 25 that "Lee's corps, now passing through, is destitute of clothing.... Cheatham is, I learn, in like condition."[6] Stewart's Corps was in no better shape than the two preceding corps. The centralized supply system was scrambling to get clothing, shoes, weapons, ammunition, and artillery issued to the troops on the move—a massive undertaking. The situation was compounded by the fact that the corps were without their normal allowance of transportation resources.[7] Back in early January, as the men made their way from Tennessee to Tupelo, what little remained of the wheeled vehicles of the army— wagons, ambulances, caissons, and artillery pieces—was unserviceable and had been sent directly to depots in Columbus, Mississippi, for repair; to date, nothing had been returned. The units were dependent on rail transportation and could not deploy far from railway resources, a severe limitation in their usefulness.[8]

Despite the obstacles, the three corps made their way to Georgia. Lee's Corps arrived in Augusta on February 3, Cheatham's on February 7, and Stewart's on February 11. The gaining commanders in South Carolina—expecting normal-sized corps of approximately eight thousand to ten thousand men fully staffed, trained, and equipped—were unpleasantly surprised by the quantity and condition of the troops they received. There were approximately half of what had been expected, and the men, unclothed and unequipped, were weary, sick, and dispirited. The commanders initially thought that the units were suffering from a 50 percent desertion rate, but Stewart pointed out that he had granted furloughs to some twenty-five hundred members of his corps on their arrival in Tupelo; these men were expected to begin filtering in over time, as indeed they did, but not in time to assist in the operations in South Carolina.[9]

From Augusta, the corps continued on toward Newberry, South Carolina, in a piecemeal fashion. With Hood gone and Taylor remaining behind in Mississippi,

Spurs of General P. G. T. Beauregard;
courtesy of the Confederate Memorial Hall Museum Collection, 007.004.006

there was a noticeable lack of central leadership. Stewart's Corps was the last to arrive in Newberry, on February 23, six days after Sherman took Columbia, South Carolina, and the Confederates evacuated Charleston.[10] A constraining circle of enemy forces was drawing tighter.

On February 22 General Joseph E. Johnston assumed command of the Army of Tennessee once again, to the delight of the soldiers, who referred to him affectionately as Uncle Joe. It was a greatly reduced army from the time of Johnston's earlier command; the three corps now ranged in size from nine hundred to three thousand effectives, totaling just over five thousand. Johnston also assumed command of all troops in Hardee's Department of South Carolina, Georgia, and Florida (approximately seventy-five hundred men) and the Department of North Carolina (approximately sixty-five hundred men), which was under the command of General Braxton Bragg. For too long, scattered units and fragmentary operations had been a major problem for these forces, so Johnston combined the entities into the Army of the South; within this force structure, Lieutenant General Stewart would command the Army of Tennessee, with the ever-present Orleans Light Horse as his escort company.[11]

From Columbia, Sherman continued into North Carolina and took Fayetteville on March 11. On March 19 Johnston moved his troops to Bentonville, North Carolina, forty-five miles northeast of Fayetteville, aware that he had an opportunity to catch the left wing of Sherman's army in isolation. The armies collided in Bentonville that same day, and the Army of the South surged fiercely, collapsing a portion of the Union defenses. As darkness fell, the Confederates retired to the positions from which they had begun the day, carrying off several pieces of captured artillery. Incessant rain fell through the night. On March 20 Johnston adjusted his front for improved defense, held his ground, and waited to see if Sherman would attack; by early afternoon, he faced Sherman's entire army of sixty thousand. The morning of March 21 dawned with the two armies still in place, skirmishing across the front under heavy rain. After dark, having evacuated his wounded and buried his dead, Johnston withdrew his army north, to Smithfield. Casualty estimates for the Battle of Bentonville were on the order of fifteen hundred Union and twenty-six hundred Confederate.[12]

Sherman did not follow Johnston but moved east in the direction of Goldsboro for his planned assembly with Major General John M. Schofield's army. The Union force in the Carolinas would now total approximately 100,000 men, whereas Johnston could claim just over 16,800. Both armies observed several weeks of rest and refitting.[13]

Despite the valiant efforts of so many, the war was winding down. The first week of April, there was a review of the Army of Tennessee, now a skeleton of the thirty-five-thousand-member army that only one year earlier had marched past an admiring president, weapons glinting in the sunlight and colorful battle flags

Opening fight at Bentonville, by Alfred R. Waud, March 19, 1865;
Morgan Collection of Civil War Drawings, Library of Congress Prints and Photographs Division

fluttering in the breeze. Now the men filed grimly past General Johnston, their uniforms makeshift, ill fitting, tattered and torn, their shoes worn or long gone. Many passed without weapons. The realities of death, desertion, dismemberment, sickness, and famine were imprinted on their ranks, which were so depleted that many had only twenty to forty men per regimental color. This slow march resembled little more than a funeral procession.[14]

On April 9 Johnston reorganized his command, incorporating all troops into the Army of Tennessee, with its three corps commanded by Hardee, Stewart, and Lee. He then withdrew the army from Smithfield, first thirty miles to Raleigh, then another seventy-five miles westward to Greensboro, encamping the corps individually in that vicinity. The stage was set; it was time for the final scene to begin.[15]

ORLEANS LIGHT HORSE PERSONNEL ACCOUNTABILITY
JANUARY–MARCH 1865

	JAN.–FEB. 1865	MAR. 1865
GAINS	0	0
LOSSES	1	4
Discharged	1	0
Captured	0	2
Killed/Died	0	1
Unspecified	0	1
ACCOUNTABLE	58	54
Present	44	41
Detailed to duty	8	9
Absent—leave	4	1
Hospitalized	1	3
Wounded/Medically disqualified	1	0

	JAN.–FEB. 1865	MAR. 1865
GAINS	—	—
LOSSES	Borduzat, J. P.	Armstrong, C. D.; Cassady, B.; McKnight, J. H.; Peters, B. F.

NOTES

1 Sherman, 2:137–229.

2 *OR*, ser. 1, vol. 45, pt. 2:772, 780–81, 785–86, 789. Richard Taylor (b. 1826, Jefferson County, KY; d. 1879, New York, NY) graduated from Yale College in 1845 and went on to serve in the Mexican-American War (1846–47) as a voluntary aide-de-camp to his father, Major General Zachary Taylor. In July 1861 he was elected colonel of the Ninth Louisiana Infantry Regiment and served at the First Battle of Manassas. After being promoted to brigadier general, in October 1861, he commanded a Louisiana brigade in the Shenandoah Valley Campaign and the Seven Days' Battles of the Peninsula Campaign. In July 1862 he was promoted to major general and initially served in the District of West Louisiana in the Trans-Mississippi Department. His successes at Brashear City, Mansfield, and Pleasant Hill, Louisiana, effectively terminated the Union army's Red River Campaign of 1864. He was promoted to lieutenant general in April 1864 and became commander of the Department of Alabama, Mississippi, and East Louisiana, which included the defenses of Mobile. As department commander, he temporarily succeeded General Hood as commander of the Army of Tennessee, on the latter's resignation in January 1865. He surrendered his department to Major General Edward R. S. Canby at Citronelle, Alabama, on May 8, 1865.

3 *OR*, ser. 1, vol. 45, pt. 2:768–92; *OR*, ser. 1, vol. 47, pt. 2:1059; *OR*, ser. 1, vol. 49, pt. 1:949, 951; Connelly, *Autumn of Glory*, 513–14; Elliott, 259–60.

4 *OR*, ser. 1, vol. 47, pt. 2:1084, 1133.

5 *OR*, ser. 1, vol. 47, pt. 1:1080–81.

6 *OR*, ser. 1, vol. 47, pt. 2:1043.

7 *OR*, ser. 1, vol. 47, pt. 2:1061, 1085. Depending on their strength levels, brigades were authorized twenty-five or more four-horse wagons and two-horse ambulances as the means by which they moved the sick and wounded as well as their baggage and equipment. In addition to this allowance of vehicles, they would have an ordnance train of five four-horse wagons per two thousand men. With all these horses came an additional allowance of four-horse wagons for food for the animals. When the army retreated from Tennessee, it had little equipment left. Horses had become lame or had died and the corresponding wagons and artillery had been destroyed or abandoned. The relocation to the Carolinas, so shortly after the army's return from Tennessee, had not allowed time to replace this equipment, and so the mobility of these units was seriously limited.

8 *OR*, ser. 1, vol. 44:1005–6; *OR*, ser. 1, vol. 45, pt. 2:753–54, 756, 757–58, 768; *OR*, ser. 1, vol. 47, pt. 2:374, 1043, 1061, 1120, 1174, 1185, 1224, 1269, 1285–86.

9 *OR*, ser. 1, vol. 45, pt. 2:788; *OR*, ser. 1. vol 47, pt. 2:1083, 1088, 1174, 1194; Elliott, 560–61.

10 *OR*, ser. 1, vol. 47, pt. 2:374, 1043, 1061, 1120, 1174, 1185, 1224, 1269, 1285–86; Elliott, 560–61.

11 *OR*, ser. 1, vol. 47, pt. 2:1386; *OR*, ser. 1, vol. 47, pt. 3:686, 698; Connelly, *Autumn of Glory*, 517–21. The Army of the South comprised the Army of Tennessee, under Lieutenant General Stewart (Lee's, Stewart's, and Cheatham's Corps); the Department of North Carolina, under General Braxton Bragg (Hoke's Division); the Department of South Carolina, Georgia, and Florida, under Lieutenant General William J. Hardee (Taliaferro's and McLaws's Divisions); Lieutenant General Wade Hampton's Cavalry Command (Butler's Division); and Wheeler's Cavalry Corps (Humes's, Allen's, and Dibrell's Divisions).

12 *OR*, ser. 1, vol. 47, pt. 1:1054–60; Connelly, *Autumn of Glory*, 525–30; Elliott, 263–69.

13 Connelly, *Autumn of Glory*, 531–32; Elliott, 267–70. As of April 17 the strength figures for the Army of Tennessee were as follows: General Staff, 16; Hardee's Corps, 7,029; Stewart's Corps, 5,558; Lee's Corps, 3,077; artillery, 841; engineers, 351—a total of 16,872. *OR*, ser. 1, vol. 47, pt. 3:808.

14 Ridley, *Battles and Sketches*, 456.

15 *OR*, ser. 1, vol. 47, pt. 3:773.

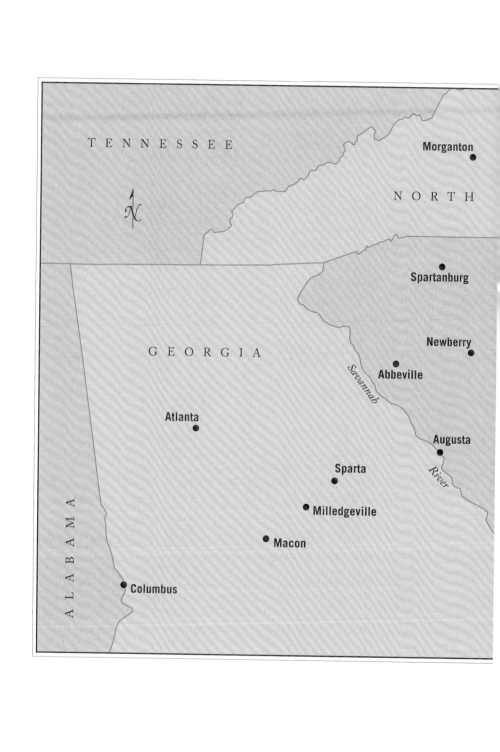

TENNESSEE

Morganton

NORTH

Spartanburg

GEORGIA

Newberry

Abbeville

Savannah

Atlanta

Augusta

Sparta

River

Milledgeville

ALABAMA

Macon

Columbus

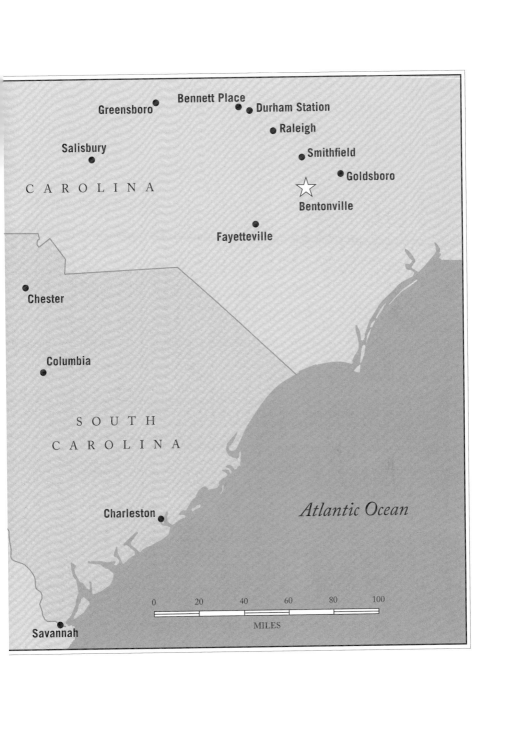

Greensboro

Bennett Place

Durham Station

Raleigh

Salisbury

Smithfield

CAROLINA

Goldsboro

Bentonville

Fayetteville

Chester

Columbia

SOUTH

CAROLINA

Charleston

Atlantic Ocean

Savannah

0   20   40   60   80   100

MILES

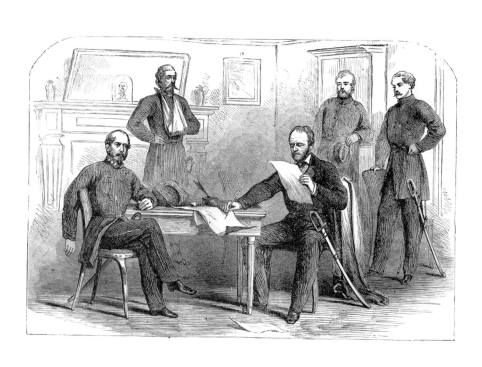

✶ 10 ✶

THE CLOSING SCENE

On April 11, 1865, General Joseph E. Johnston attended a meeting with governmental leaders in Greensboro, North Carolina, to discuss courses of action in the aftermath of the Battle of Bentonville. The next day, Johnston and the authorities in Greensboro received a report that the Army of Northern Virginia had surrendered at Appomattox. After extensive discussions, and with the tacit approval of President Jefferson Davis and the cabinet officers, on April 14 Johnston sent a letter to Major General William T. Sherman suggesting a meeting under a flag of truce to discuss peace terms. The two commanders chose a location between their headquarters, the farmhouse of James and Nancy Bennitt near Durham Station, North Carolina. Finally, on April 26, Johnston accepted the terms offered by Sherman and surrendered the Army of Tennessee and all other forces under his command.[1] Just a few days later, Lieutenant General Richard Taylor, commander of the Department of Alabama, Mississippi, and East Louisiana, surrendered his command on May 4 at Citronelle, Alabama, northwest of Mobile. And on May 5 Major General Dabney H. Maury, commander of the District of the Gulf, surrendered his command, also at Citronelle. The war came to an end in stages.[2]

These three acts of surrender resulted in a total of fifty-eight cavalrymen of the Orleans Light Horse laying down their arms. At the end of the war, thirty-one members of the unit were with the Army of Tennessee in North Carolina, while the other twenty-seven members were serving in Alabama, Georgia, Mississippi, and Tennessee.[3]

Surrender of General Johnston to Major General Sherman, April 26, 1865, from John Gilmary Shea, *A Child's History of the United States*, 1872; *The Print Collector/Heritage Images*

The members deployed in North Carolina were Captain J. Leeds Greenleaf; First Lieutenant Philip M. Kenner; Second Lieutenant Aristide R. Hopkins; Third Lieutenant Reuben C. Stewart; Sergeants Auguste Viavant Jr. and Julian J. Jonas; Corporal Amos B. Gunnison; and Privates Henry A. Armstrong, Hagart Bein, Octave A. Bethancourt, John B. Brown, James M. Butler, Thomas D. Cammack, Lucien Charvet, Harvey N. Crumhorn, J. W. Dillon, John H. Fisher, Michael Glynn, Jules A. Hébert, Charles A. Hildreth, Charles H. Hosmer, J. H. Hurd, Yves R. Le Monnier Jr., René Macready, Christophal C. Mitchell, Thomas S. Reynolds, John Thuer Jr., Marcus G. Trellue, Thomas Y. P. Tureman, J. Minnick Williams, and Nathaniel A. Windsor. Twelve members were deployed in Alabama: First Sergeant Jackson W. Simmons and Privates Edgar H. Cenas, Samuel L. Cowarden, Alexander Delgado, N. W. Dubose, B. M. Hulburt, J. Dillon Jordan III, Thomas S. Kennedy, James T. Lotspeich, William D. Love, James B. Moore, and Jacob M. Rabby. Ten members were deployed in Georgia: Sergeant John M. Kennedy; Corporal James C. Walker; and Privates Christian D. Armstrong, B. Cassady, Edouard C. Haydel, Fenelon B. Martindale, John A. Perkins, Louis W. Perkins, Bernard Riley, and Napoleon B. Trellue. Second Lieutenant E. Malcolm Morse was in Meridian, Mississippi, and Private Jonathan W. Dowsing was in Memphis, Tennessee. Additionally, three cavalrymen were hospitalized: Privates A. J. Guilfant and John W. Lawler in Macon, Georgia, and J. Winn in Montgomery, Alabama.

Many of these members of the Orleans Light Horse had served together for a long time. J. Leeds Greenleaf, Aristide R. Hopkins, and Jackson W. Simmons had enlisted together for militia service shortly after the unit's founding in February 1861. Eleven additional members had been present in New Orleans when the unit was mustered into active service on March 22, 1862. And of the fifty-eight, all but seven had served under Lieutenant General Leonidas Polk, their first corps commander and mentor, whose imprint, planted early, remained with them to the end. They were a band of brothers; they had lived and fought that way and they would return home that way. Napier Bartlett reflected on the hardships experienced by the Light Horse and their lasting contributions to the war in his *Military Record of Louisiana*: "The loss of the troop, in proportion to the losses experienced by similar commands throughout the service, was heavy; and the last man of the Confederate Army killed [east] of the Mississippi, was John H. McKnight, an original member of the Orleans Light Horse."[4]

The war was over, but at the Army of Tennessee's headquarters in Greensboro, there were still things to do before the soldiers could start their long trip home. In accordance with the negotiated terms, musters had to be taken to account for persons present and absent; certificates of parole (about thirty-six thousand of them) had to be made out, sworn, and signed; weapons and equipment had to be inventoried and deposited at Greensboro; and the normal myriad of tasks incidental to maintenance of order and discipline among a large number of men had to be accomplished. At the same time, food for men and animals still had to be procured, transported, distributed, and prepared; medical treatment had to be provided to injured and ill soldiers; and essential provisions of shelter and sanitation had to be maintained. All of these tasks took time and required a significant logistics establishment. Therefore, after the formalities of surrender, the members of the Army of Tennessee could not simply walk off and go home.

Naturally, this was contrary to the individual inclinations of most of the members of the army, and desertion rates were high. It required the strongest urgings and leadership of the general officers to maintain even a semblance of order. For several days, the remnants of the Army of Tennessee, no longer an instrument of war, remained in the vicinity of Greensboro. Beginning on May 1, paroles were issued for several days from Greensboro. Then, on May 2, General Johnston issued a farewell statement to the army in General Orders No. 22, as follows:

> Comrades: In terminating our official relations, I earnestly exhort you to observe faithfully the terms of pacification agreed to and to discharge the obligations of good and peaceful citizens, as well as you have performed the duties of thorough soldiers in the field. By such a course, you will best secure the comfort of your families and kindred, and restore tranquility to our country. You will return to your homes with the admiration of our people, won by the courage and noble devotion you have displayed in this long war. I shall always remember with pride the loyal support and generous confidence you have given me. I now part with you with deep regret—and bid you farewell with feelings of cordial friendship, and with earnest wishes that you may have hereafter all the prosperity and happiness to be found in the world.[5]

As part of the process of disbanding, General Sherman authorized the issuance of ten-day rations to Confederate soldiers for their journey home, as well as horses and mules for them to use in the rehabilitation of their farms.[6]

In his biography of Lieutenant General Alexander P. Stewart, Sam Davis Elliott summarized the final days at Greensboro:

> The final surrender was concluded April 26, 1865. Stewart spent the following days attending to the final affairs of his corps, including reporting on the arms, ammunition, and equipment held by his command, trying to straighten out transportation for his men, and waiting to see his men paroled. On a more personal level, the general spent time exchanging farewells with various officers in the army. On May 2, the army marched in its organized corps to Salisbury, where on May 5, it separated into three columns, one marching via Morgantown [sic], North Carolina, another via Spartanburg and Abbeville, South Carolina, and the remainder via Chester and Newberry, South Carolina. Thus, "the noble Army of Tennessee was disbanded."[7]

Tens of thousands of men now faced the prospect of making their way home, most on foot, across hundreds of miles of devastated, war-torn countryside. Travel was hazardous, with bushwhackers, desperate men roaming the countryside with no other means of support, preying on travelers, especially in mountainous areas. Safety was found in numbers, and the men of the Orleans Light Horse remained loyal to each other and to their general. They were fortunate that they had been cavalrymen and therefore had their horses.

At the dissolution, Stewart, his escort, two of his sons, and several of his staff chose to travel through Spartanburg and Abbeville, crossing the Savannah River into Georgia. They traveled together for some time; then, in the vicinity of Sparta, Georgia, the party separated. Stewart, his sons, and others from Tennessee turned northwest toward Chattanooga; the men of the Orleans Light Horse continued in the direction of Macon, crossing into Alabama near Columbus. New Orleans was still more than five hundred miles, and many days, away.

Though the corps, companies, and regiments had been dismissed from military service, there still remained a cohesiveness among the veterans that would endure for years.[8] The relationship between Light Horse Second Lieutenant Aristide R. Hopkins and Lieutenant General Stewart exemplifies the lasting bonds formed during the war. Hopkins, described as a "blonde, blue-eyed, favorite of his comrades," had been chosen by Major General Leonidas Polk to serve as his aide-de-camp early in the war.[9] After Polk's tragic death, at which Hopkins was said to have supported the dying general in his arms, Stewart retained Hopkins as his aide for the remainder of the war. They continued to be close after the war, and Hopkins was with Stewart at his death many years later: "It was the fortune of the aide to soothe the last moments of the corps commander, for when General Stewart died at Biloxi, in 1908, Hopkins was at his bedside, and from the General's hand received his sword, given in parting acknowledgement of friendship."[10]

The men of the Orleans Light Horse, more than 40 percent of whom were not native to Louisiana, came from diverse backgrounds and held a wide range of political preferences. Their common dedication to defending home and family brought them together and motivated them to go to war. To their homeland, whether native or adopted, they gave the full measure of their devotion. They acquitted themselves with honor on dozens of battlefields and won the unqualified respect of the generals whom they served. After the war, returning home, they adjusted to their changed circumstances and went on with their lives, many becoming pillars of the communities their fathers had served. No man can do more than this; their memories live in their deeds.

NOTES

1 *New York Times*, 12 May 1865. In the 1840s in rural Orange County, North Carolina, Hillsborough Road was the connecting artery between the cities of Raleigh and Hillsborough, a distance of about forty miles. In 1846 James Bennitt acquired several hundred acres of fertile land along this road and

built a simple square farmhouse with a stone chimney and a big loft. Here, James, Nancy, and their three children settled down to a life of farming. In 1849 a depot station for the newly established North Carolina Railroad was built approximately three miles east of the Bennitt homestead, on land donated by Dr. Bartlett S. Durham. The depot, one of many stops on the railroad, became known as Durham Station. Durham Station and Bennett Place, as the farmhouse became known (although the family name was recorded as "Bennitt"), lay approximately midway between Greensboro, the headquarters of Confederate General Joseph E. Johnston, and Raleigh, the headquarters of Union Major General William T. Sherman. In his memoirs, Sherman itemized the numbers of men encompassed in these negotiations as "Total number paroled at Greensboro, NC: 36,817. Total number surrendered in Georgia and Florida: 52,453. Aggregate surrendered by Gen'l J. E. Johnston: 89,270." Sherman, 2:370.

2 The termination of hostilities between the Confederate States and the United States took place in several stages during the spring of 1865. On April 9 Confederate General Robert E. Lee met with Union Lieutenant General Ulysses S. Grant at McLean House in Appomattox, Virginia, resulting in the surrender of the Confederate Army of Northern Virginia. On April 26 Confederate General Joseph E. Johnston met with Union Major General William T. Sherman at Bennett Place near Durham Station, North Carolina, resulting in the surrender of the Confederate Army of Tennessee, Department of Tennessee and Georgia, Department of South Carolina, Georgia, and Florida, and Department of North Carolina and Southern Virginia. On April 30 Confederate Lieutenant General Richard Taylor met with Union Major General Edward R. S. Canby north of Mobile, Alabama, resulting in the surrender of the Confederate Department of Alabama, Mississippi, and East Louisiana on May 4 at Citronelle, Alabama. On May 5 Confederate Major General Dabney H. Maury met with Union Major General Canby at Citronelle, Alabama, resulting in the surrender of the Confederate District of the Gulf. On May 10 Confederate Major General Samuel Jones met with Union Brigadier General Edward M. McCook at Tallahassee, Florida, resulting in the surrender of the Confederate Department of Florida and South Georgia. On May 9 Confederate Brigadier General M. Jeff Thompson met with representatives of Union Major General Grenville M. Dodge in Clay County, Arkansas, resulting in the surrender of the Confederate Northern Sub-District of Arkansas on May 11. On May 12 Confederate Brigadier General William T. Wofford met with Union Brigadier General Henry M. Judah at Kingston, Georgia, resulting in the surrender of the Confederate forces in north Georgia. On May 26 representatives of Confederate General Edmund Kirby Smith met with representatives of Union Major General Canby at Shreveport, Louisiana, resulting in the surrender of the Confederate Trans-Mississippi Department.

One by one, the major commands of the Confederate States Army laid down their arms during the months of April and May. In essence the fighting on the major domestic battlefields had ended, but there were elements of the Confederate armed forces yet to be heard from. On June 23 Confederate Brigadier General Stand Watie, commander of the Cherokee Mounted Rifles, surrendered the Confederate Indian forces at Fort Towson, Indian Territory (in present-day Oklahoma). General Watie was the last Confederate general to surrender. On November 6 Captain James I. Waddell, Confederate States Navy, surrendered the cruiser CSS *Shenandoah* at Liverpool, England, to Captain J. A. D. Paynter, captain of HMS *Donegal* of the British Royal Navy. This was the last combat vessel of the Confederate States Navy to surrender. Finally, on August 20, 1866, a proclamation was issued by President Andrew Johnson declaring the formal end of the war.

3 *Muster Rolls and Lists of Confederate Troops Paroled in North Carolina*, M1781, reel 006; NARA M320, reel 032.

4 Bartlett, sec. 2:34.

5 *OR*, ser. 1, vol. 47, pt. 1:1061.

6 Flood, *Grant and Sherman*, 347.

7 Elliott, 272.

8 Ridley, *Battles and Sketches*, 472–79, 482.

9 Williams, "Aristide Hopkins," 346.

10 Ibid.

PART 2 RECORDS OF SERVICE AND EXTENDED BIOGRAPHICAL DATA

PART 2 WAS CREATED BY SEARCHING FOR ALL INDIVIDUALS WHO AT any time enlisted for service with the Orleans Light Horse in three microfilm sets from the War Department Collection of Confederate Records (Record Group 109) published by NARA:

- *Compiled Service Records of Confederate Soldiers Who Served in Organizations from the State of Louisiana.* NARA M320.

- *Index to Compiled Service Records of Confederate Soldiers Who Served in Organizations from the State of Louisiana.* NARA M378.

- *Muster Rolls and Lists of Confederate Troops Paroled in North Carolina.* NARA M1781.

Some of the enlistments were for Louisiana Militia service only; some were for Confederate active duty only; and some were for both. From this effort a baseline company roster of 215 names was derived. Ten additional men listed on the Light Horse's constitution and bylaws (see appendix A), printed between June and October 1861, were not found in the compiled service records for the unit and resigned from the unit prior to November 1861. Therefore, the following individuals are not included in the company roster: James Blanc, Adolphe Boudousquie, M. J. Brenan, Adolphe Faure, James Miltenberger, George J. Olivier, Thomas M. Simmons, Norman Story, W. Wallace, and L. A. Welton.

The next step was to compile the military service résumés for the 215 members of the Light Horse from the following microfilm sets in Record Group 109:

- *Compiled Service Records of Confederate Soldiers Who Served in Organizations from the State of Louisiana.* NARA M320.

- *Index to Compiled Service Records of Confederate Soldiers Who Served in Organizations from the State of Tennessee.* NARA M231.

- *Selected Records of the War Department Relating to Confederate Prisoners of War, 1861–1865.* NARA M598.

The details extracted from these service résumés were compiled into individual data files for each of the identified servicemen, and were summarized in the personnel accountability tables at the end of each chapter.

The third step was to compile biographical and genealogical data on Light Horse members using the following NARA microfilm sets:

- *Passenger Lists of Vessels Arriving at New York, 1820–1897.* NARA M237.

- *Compiled Service Records of Confederate General and Staff Officers, and Nonregimental Enlisted Men.* NARA M331.

- *Internal Revenue Assessment Lists for New York and New Jersey, 1862–1866.* NARA M603.

- *Registers of Letters Received by the Office of the Adjutant General, 1812–1889.* NARA M711.

- *Internal Revenue Assessment Lists for Alabama, 1865–1866.* NARA M754.

- *Internal Revenue Assessment Lists for Louisiana, 1863–1866.* NARA M769.

- *Index to Compiled Service Records of Confederate Soldiers Who Served in Organizations Raised Directly by the Confederate Government and of General and Staff Officers and Nonregimental Enlisted Men.* NARA M818.

The final step was to search the public record for further biographical and genealogical information on the Light Horse cavalrymen. This was accomplished through the use of a wide variety of published, unpublished, and online sources (see bibliography). Ancestry.com was the central source, providing federal and state census data; city directories; local newspaper articles and obituary archives; birth, marriage, and death archives; and immigration and passport data. The grave-site records available through Findagrave.com were also indispensable. Where a public-record-data match could be made, the individual's page was augmented with birth and death dates, and parentage, marriage, occupation, and residence data. In twenty-six cases, available evidence was insufficient for determining a positive identification; the personal data forms for these individuals only include their military résumés. In a number of cases, an individual's name was listed in the various records with different spellings (e.g., Gilfant, A. and Guilfant, A.; Hayne and Haney; Robinson, J. T. and Robinson, E. T.). Where there was an absence of evidence suggesting two different people and multiple sources for one spelling, the author selected the dominant spelling, and indicated the alternate spellings in the additional information section of the personal narrative.

In the course of this research, the author created multigenerational family trees for each individual on Ancestry.com. In many cases, descendants and other interested parties have assisted materially in the compilation of the data shown. To each and all who have participated in this manner, the author extends his most fervent thanks.

Each record in part 2 has been formatted in the following manner:

NAME

BIRTH
DEATH

Birth (date/place) and death (date/place)

RECORD OF SERVICE
MILITIA SERVICE
CSA ENLISTMENT
ORLEANS LIGHT HORSE TRANSFER DATA
    INBOUND
    OUTBOUND
SERVICE RÉSUMÉ
SEPARATION

The record of service includes militia service (enlistment date/status), CSA enlistment (date/place/term), transfers in and out of the Orleans Light Horse (date/rank), a service résumé for militia as well as CSA service within the Orleans Light Horse, and data on the individual's separation from military service (date/place/basis).

PERSONAL NARRATIVE
OCCUPATION
GENEALOGY
RESIDENCES
ADDITIONAL INFORMATION
SOURCES

The personal narrative contains a variety of pre- and postwar personal and family information. In the genealogy section, the parents' city/country of residence for the 1860–70 time frame is provided, when available.

ADAM, ——

RECORD OF SERVICE

CSA ENLISTMENT   22 Mar. 1862/New Orleans, LA/90 days
ORLEANS LIGHT HORSE TRANSFER DATA
    INBOUND   22 Mar. 1862/Private
    OUTBOUND   June 1862/Private
SERVICE RÉSUMÉ
    22 Mar. 1862   New Orleans, LA/Mustered into service of CSA with the Orleans Light Horse
    22 Mar.–25 May 1862   Present
    6 June 1862   Camp Williamson, Tupelo, MS/Approved for discharge
SEPARATION   June 1862/Tupelo, MS/Discharge, unspecified

SOURCES

Booth, 1:25
NARA M320, reel 032

ADAMS, James

BIRTH   ca. 1827

RECORD OF SERVICE

CSA ENLISTMENT   22 Mar. 1862/New Orleans, LA/90 days
ORLEANS LIGHT HORSE TRANSFER DATA
    INBOUND   22 Mar. 1862/Private
    OUTBOUND   16 July 1862/Private
SERVICE RÉSUMÉ
    22 Mar. 1862   New Orleans, LA/Mustered into service of CSA with the Orleans Light Horse
    22 Mar.–25 May 1862   Present
    6 June 1862   Present
SEPARATION   16 July 1862/Tupelo, MS/Discharge, over age

SOURCES

Booth, 1:28
NARA M320, reel 032

ALLEN, Charles W.

RECORD OF SERVICE

CSA ENLISTMENT   7 Apr. 1863/Shelbyville, TN/Duration of the war
ORLEANS LIGHT HORSE TRANSFER DATA
    INBOUND   7 Apr. 1863/Private
    OUTBOUND   Oct. 1863/Private
SERVICE RÉSUMÉ
    7 Apr. 1863   Shelbyville, TN/Received into the Orleans Light Horse
    Mar.–Apr. 1863   Detached on duty with Signal Corps

May–June 1863	Present, detailed as trumpeter
9 July 1863	Present, detailed as bugler
9 Aug. 1863	Absent without leave
July–Aug. 1863	Absent without leave

PERSONAL NARRATIVE

OCCUPATION   Industrial pressman

RESIDENCES   1861, New Orleans, LA
1890, New Orleans, LA
1895, New Orleans, LA
1900, New Orleans, LA

SOURCES

Booth, 1:45
Gardner's New Orleans Directory, 1861
NARA M320, reel 032
Soards' New Orleans City Directory, 1890, 1895, 1900

ARMSTRONG, Christian Daniel

BIRTH   30 Jan. 1843/New Orleans, LA

DEATH   21 May 1908/New Orleans, LA

RECORD OF SERVICE

CSA ENLISTMENT   22 Mar. 1862/New Orleans, LA/90 days
25 July 1862/Tupelo, MS/Duration of the war

ORLEANS LIGHT HORSE TRANSFER DATA

     INBOUND   22 Mar. 1862/Private

     OUTBOUND   1 May 1865/Private

SERVICE RÉSUMÉ

22 Mar. 1862	New Orleans, LA/Mustered into service of CSA with the Orleans Light Horse
22 Mar.–25 May 1862	Present
6 June 1862	Camp Williamson, Tupelo, MS/Present
Sept.–Oct. 1862	Present, detached on duty
Nov.–Dec. 1862	Present
Jan.–June 1863	Present
July–Aug. 1863	Present
Sept.–Oct. 1863	Marietta, GA/Absent, detailed at government bakery
Nov.–Dec. 1863	Marietta, GA/Absent, furlough
May–June 1864	Macon, GA/Detailed with Maj. Buckley, assistant chief of staff, by order of Gen. Joseph E. Johnston
20–21 Apr. 1865	Macon GA/Captured

SEPARATION   1 May 1865/Macon, GA/Parole, released from military service

PERSONAL NARRATIVE

OCCUPATION   Engineer

GENEALOGY	Son of Augustus and Anna Maria (Meier) Armstrong, St. Bernard Parish, LA
	Brother of Henry A. Armstrong
	Married, 13 Feb. 1877, St. Bernard Parish, LA, Charlotte Ann "Martha" Draper (b. 30 Oct. 1828, Ireland; d. 7 Feb. 1907, St. Bernard Parish, LA)
RESIDENCES	1850, St. Bernard Parish, LA
	1860, St. Bernard Parish, LA
	1870, St. Bernard Parish, LA
	1880, St. Bernard Parish, LA
	1900, St. Bernard Parish, LA

SOURCES

Louisiana Marriages, 1718–1925
NARA M320, reel 032
New Orleans, LA, Birth Records Index, 1790–1899
New Orleans, LA, Death Records Index, 1804–1949
Obituaries: *New Orleans Item*, 22 May 1908; Mrs. Armstrong, *New Orleans Times-Picayune*, 8 Feb. 1907
US Census 1850, 1860, 1870, 1880, 1900
www.findagrave.com, 90110923

ARMSTRONG, Henry Albert

| BIRTH | 20 Aug. 1844/New Orleans, LA |
| DEATH | 28 Dec. 1919/New Orleans, LA |

RECORD OF SERVICE

| CSA ENLISTMENT | 24 Sept. 1862/Chattanooga, TN/90 days |
| | 24 Oct. 1863/Chickamauga, GA/Duration of the war |

ORLEANS LIGHT HORSE TRANSFER DATA

| INBOUND | 24 Oct. 1863/Private |
| OUTBOUND | 1 May 1865/Private |

SERVICE RÉSUMÉ

24 Oct. 1863	Chickamauga, GA/Received into the Orleans Light Horse from Capt. Jules Delery's St. Bernard Horse Rifles
Sept.–Dec. 1863	Present
May–June 1864	Present
26 Apr. 1865	Durham Station, NC/Surrendered
SEPARATION	1 May 1865/Greensboro, NC/Parole, released from military service

PERSONAL NARRATIVE

OCCUPATION	Engineer
GENEALOGY	Son of Augustus and Anna Maria (Meier) Armstrong, St. Bernard Parish, LA
	Brother of Christian D. Armstrong
	Married, 30 Nov. 1880, New Orleans, LA, Elizabeth B. "Lillie" Wigginton (b. Oct. 1862, Jeffersonville, IN; d. 1 Nov. 1925, New Orleans, LA)

1860, St. Bernard Parish, LA
1870, St. Bernard Parish, LA
1880, St. Bernard Parish, LA
1910, New Orleans, LA

SOURCES

Confederate Pension Applications Collection, Louisiana State Archives
Louisiana Marriages, 1718–1925
NARA M320, reel 032; M1781, reel 006
New Orleans, LA, Birth Records Index, 1790–1899
New Orleans, LA, Death Records Index, 1804–1949
Obituary: Mrs. H. A. Armstrong, *New Orleans Times-Picayune*, 2 Nov. 1925
US Census 1850, 1860, 1870, 1880, 1910
www.findagrave.com, 70466416

BEAUREGARD, Charles Toutant

BIRTH	ca. 1836/Louisiana
DEATH	18 Nov. 1882/New Orleans, LA

RECORD OF SERVICE

CSA ENLISTMENT	22 Mar. 1862/New Orleans, LA/90 days
	25 July 1862/Tupelo, MS/Duration of the war

ORLEANS LIGHT HORSE TRANSFER DATA

INBOUND	22 Mar. 1862/Private
OUTBOUND	5 May 1864/Private

SERVICE RÉSUMÉ

22 Mar. 1862	New Orleans, LA/Mustered into service of CSA with the Orleans Light Horse
22 Mar. –25 May 1862	Present
6 June 1862	Camp Williamson, Tupelo, MS/Absent, sick
May–June 1862	Absent, detailed with Maj. ——, by order of Maj. Gen. Leonidas Polk
Sept.–Oct. 1862	Present
Nov.–Dec. 1862	Absent with leave
Jan.–Feb. 1863	Absent without leave
Mar.–Apr. 1863	Reported as deserter
May–June 1863	Absent, special duty (recruiting, Mobile, AL)
July–Aug. 1863	Present
Sept.–Oct. 1863	Rome, GA/Absent, sick in hospital
Nov.–Dec. 1863	Mobile, AL/Absent, sick in hospital
Mar. 1864	Disabled, unfit for field service (syphilitic rheumatism)
June–Aug. 1864	Mobile, AL/Detailed as clerk, office of provost marshal
SEPARATION	5 May 1865/Mobile, AL/Parole, released from military service

PERSONAL NARRATIVE

OCCUPATION	Cotton inspector

GENEALOGY	Son of Joseph Emile Toutant and Aimée (Cavelier) Beauregard, New Orleans, LA
	Third cousin of Gen. P. G. T. Beauregard
RESIDENCES	1840, New Orleans, LA
	1850, New Orleans, LA
	1880, New Orleans, LA

SOURCES

Booth, 1:150

NARA M320, reel 032

New Orleans, LA, Death Records Index, 1804–1949

New York Passenger Lists, 1820–1957

US Census 1850, 1880

BEIN, Hagart

BIRTH	26 May 1843/New Orleans, LA
DEATH	1 Mar. 1902/Houston, TX

RECORD OF SERVICE

CSA ENLISTMENT	1 July 1862/Tupelo, MS/Duration of the war

ORLEANS LIGHT HORSE TRANSFER DATA

INBOUND	1 July 1862/Private
OUTBOUND	1 May 1865/Private

SERVICE RÉSUMÉ

1 July 1862	Tupelo, MS/Received into the Orleans Light Horse
Sept.–Dec. 1862	Present
Jan.–June 1863	Present
July–Dec. 1863	Present
Jan.–June 1864	Present
26 Apr. 1865	Durham Station, NC/Surrendered
SEPARATION	1 May 1865/Greensboro, NC/Parole, released from military service

PERSONAL NARRATIVE

GENEALOGY	Son of Dr. Richard and Mary Liddle (Milligan) Bein, New Orleans, LA
RESIDENCES	1850, New Orleans, LA
	1860, New Orleans, LA
	1880, New Orleans, LA
	1900, Houston, TX

SOURCES

Booth, 1:157

Confederate Pension Applications Collection, Louisiana State Archives

NARA M320, reel 032; M1781, reel 006

Obituaries: *Houston Chronicle*, 3 Nov. 1902; *New Orleans Times-Democrat*, 3 and 9 Nov. 1902; *New Orleans Daily Picayune*, 3 and 9 Nov. 1902

US Census 1850, 1860, 1880, 1900

www.findagrave.com, 64407741

BELKNAP, Morris Shepard

BIRTH	12 Aug. 1845/New Orleans, LA
DEATH	19 July 1890/Louisville, KY

RECORD OF SERVICE

CSA ENLISTMENT	22 Mar. 1862/New Orleans, LA/90 days

ORLEANS LIGHT HORSE TRANSFER DATA

INBOUND	22 Mar. 1862/Private
OUTBOUND	11 July 1862/Private

SERVICE RÉSUMÉ

22 Mar. 1862	New Orleans, LA/Mustered into service of CSA with the Orleans Light Horse
6 June 1862	Present
SEPARATION	11 July 1862/Tupelo, MS/Discharge, under age

PERSONAL NARRATIVE

OCCUPATION	Builder
GENEALOGY	Son of James T. and Martha J. (Shepard) Belknap, New Orleans, LA
	Married, about 1870, Louisville, KY, Mary Ormsby Dumesnil (b. 25 Nov. 1850, Louisville, KY; d. 29 May 1894, Louisville, KY)
RESIDENCES	1850, New Orleans, LA
	1870, Louisville, KY
	1880, Louisville, KY
	1890, Louisville, KY

SOURCES

Booth, 1:158
NARA M320, reel 032
Obituary: *New Orleans Daily Picayune,* 22 July 1890
US Census 1850, 1860, 1870, 1880
www.findagrave.com, 74635069

BELL, William A.

BIRTH	1803/Belfast, Ireland
DEATH	4 July 1879/New Orleans, LA

RECORD OF SERVICE

MILITIA SERVICE	23 Nov. 1861/Active
CSA ENLISTMENT	22 Mar. 1862/New Orleans, LA/90 days

ORLEANS LIGHT HORSE TRANSFER DATA

INBOUND	1861/Private
OUTBOUND	6 June 1862/Sergeant

SERVICE RÉSUMÉ

23 Nov. 1861	New Orleans, LA/Militia service with the Orleans Light Horse; present

22 Mar. 1862	New Orleans, LA/Mustered into service of CSA in the position of acting commissary sergeant
22 Mar.–25 May 1862	Present
SEPARATION	6 June 1862/Tupelo, MS/Discharge, over age

PERSONAL NARRATIVE

GENEALOGY	Son of William Alexander and Mary Ann (Patrick) Bell, Belfast, Ireland
	Arrived in New Orleans, LA, 1849
RESIDENCES	1850, Tensas Parish, LA
	1861, New Orleans, LA
	1866, New Orleans, LA
	1879, New Orleans, LA

SOURCES

Booth, 1:160
NARA M320, reel 032
Gardner's New Orleans Directory, 1861
New Orleans, LA, Death Records Index, 1804–1949
New Orleans Passenger List Quarterly Abstracts, 1820–1875
Obituary: *New Orleans Daily Picayune*, 5 July 1879
US Census 1850
US Federal Census Mortality Schedules Index, 1850–1885
US IRS Tax Assessment Lists, 1862–1918

BELLAMY, John Thomas

BIRTH	13 Sept. 1840/Montgomery County, TN
DEATH	4 Apr. 1901/Montgomery County, TN

RECORD OF SERVICE

CSA ENLISTMENT	1 July 1861/Memphis, TN/90 days
	1 Sept. 1863/Chattanooga, TN/Duration of the war

ORLEANS LIGHT HORSE TRANSFER DATA

INBOUND	1 Sept. 1863/Private
OUTBOUND	15 June 1864/Private

SERVICE RÉSUMÉ

1 Sept. 1863	Chattanooga, TN/Received into the Orleans Light Horse from the Twelfth Tennessee Regiment (dismounted)
Sept.–Oct. 1863	Present
Nov.–Dec. 1863	Present
May–June 1864	Atlanta, GA/Wounded, in hospital

PERSONAL NARRATIVE

OCCUPATION	Farmer
GENEALOGY	Married (1), 24 Feb. 1861, Montgomery, TN, Elizabeth D. Wimberly (b. ca. 1844, Robertson, TN; d. 7 Aug. 1873, Montgomery, TN)
	Married (2), 1874, Montgomery, TN, Nannie L. Keesee (b. 6 Feb. 1844, Montgomery, TN; d. 12 Dec. 1933, Montgomery, TN)

SOURCES
Booth, 1:161
NARA M320, reel 032; M231, reel 003
Tennessee State Marriages, 1780–2002
US Census 1860, 1870, 1880, 1900

BERGERON, Octave Jules

| BIRTH | 17 Dec. 1842/Assumption Parish, LA |
| DEATH | 8 Oct. 1921/Assumption Parish, LA |

RECORD OF SERVICE

| CSA ENLISTMENT | 1 July 1861/Memphis, TN/One year |
| | 1 Sept. 1863/Chattanooga, TN/Duration of the war |

ORLEANS LIGHT HORSE TRANSFER DATA

| INBOUND | 1 Sept. 1863/Private |
| OUTBOUND | 15 Dec. 1864/Private |

SERVICE RÉSUMÉ

1 Sept. 1863	Chattanooga, TN/Received into the Orleans Light Horse from the Twelfth Tennessee Regiment (dismounted)
Sept.–Oct. 1863	Chickamauga, GA/Present
Nov. 1863–June 1864	Present
15 Dec. 1864	Nashville, TN/Captured
18 Dec. 1864	Transferred to US military prison, Louisville, KY
22 Dec. 1864	Imprisoned at Camp Douglas, IL, until 18 June 1865
SEPARATION	18 June 1865/Camp Douglas, IL/Parole, released from military service

PERSONAL NARRATIVE

OCCUPATION	Farmer
GENEALOGY	Son of Jules and Feliciane (Truxillo) Bergeron, Berwick, St. Mary Parish, LA
	Married, 16 June 1880, Assumption Parish, LA, Arvilla Delphine Gautreaux (b. 2 Dec. 1851, Assumption Parish, LA; d. 23 Jan. 1923, Napoleonville, LA)
RESIDENCES	1850, Terrebonne Parish, LA
	1860, St. Mary Parish, LA
	1870, Terrebonne Parish, LA
	1910, Napoleonville, LA
	1920, Napoleonville, LA

SOURCES
Booth, 1:173
Civil War Prisoner of War Records, 1861–1865

Confederate Pension Applications Collection, Louisiana State Archives
Louisiana Statewide Death Index, 1900–1949
NARA M320, reel 032
Obituary: *New Orleans Times-Picayune*, 13 Oct. 1921
US Census 1850, 1860, 1870, 1910, 1920
www.findagrave.com, 94569223

BETHANCOURT, Octave Antoine

BIRTH	1838/Ascension Parish, LA
DEATH	27 Apr. 1884/New Orleans, LA

RECORD OF SERVICE

CSA ENLISTMENT	1 July 1861/Memphis, TN/One year
	1 Sept. 1863/Chattanooga, TN/Duration of the war

ORLEANS LIGHT HORSE TRANSFER DATA

INBOUND	1 Sept. 1863/Private
OUTBOUND	1 May 1865/Private

SERVICE RÉSUMÉ

1 Sept. 1863	Chattanooga, TN/Received into the Orleans Light Horse from the Twelfth Tennessee Regiment (dismounted)
Sept. 1863–Dec. 1863	Present
May–June 1864	Present
26 Apr. 1865	Durham Station, NC/Surrendered
SEPARATION	1 May 1865/Greensboro, NC/Parole, released from military service

PERSONAL NARRATIVE

OCCUPATION	Carpenter
GENEALOGY	Son of Patrice Antoine and Marie Rosalie (Duhe) Bethancourt, St. John the Baptist Parish, LA
	Married, 28 Jan. 1880, Orleans Parish, LA, Azema Thiberville (b. 25 Apr. 1856, Louisiana; d. 9 May 1884, New Orleans, LA)
RESIDENCES	1860, St. Mary Parish, LA
	1880, St. Charles Parish, LA

SOURCES

Booth, 1:186
Louisiana Marriages, 1718–1925
NARA M320, reel 032; M1781, reel 006
New Orleans, LA, Death Records Index, 1804–1949
New Orleans, LA, Marriage Records Index, 1831–1920
US Census 1850, 1860, 1880

BICKLE, William O.

BIRTH   May 1840/Orange County, NC

RECORD OF SERVICE

CSA ENLISTMENT   22 Apr. 1863/Shelbyville, TN/Duration of the war

ORLEANS LIGHT HORSE TRANSFER DATA

  INBOUND   22 Apr. 1863/Private

  OUTBOUND   4 Jun. 1863/Private

SERVICE RÉSUMÉ

  22 Apr. 1863   Shelbyville, TN/Received into the Orleans Light Horse;
           substitute for Courtland A. Bryan, discharged

  Mar.–June 1863 Present

SEPARATION   4 June 1863/Shelbyville, TN/Deserter, dropped from rolls

SOURCES

Booth, 1:189

NARA M320, reel 032

BLANC, Jules Arnaud, Jr.

BIRTH   12 Oct. 1846/New Orleans, LA

DEATH   1 Oct. 1867/New Orleans, LA

RECORD OF SERVICE

MILITIA SERVICE   23 Nov. 1861/Active

ORLEANS LIGHT HORSE TRANSFER DATA

  INBOUND   1861/Private

  OUTBOUND   22 Mar. 1862/Private

SERVICE RÉSUMÉ

  23 Nov. 1861   New Orleans, LA/Militia service with the
           Orleans Light Horse; present

SEPARATION   22 Mar. 1862/New Orleans, LA/Declined enlistment

PERSONAL NARRATIVE

GENEALOGY   Son of Jules Arnaud and Harriet Angelique (Peters) Blanc,
           New Orleans, LA
           Nephew of Benjamin F. Peters

RESIDENCES   1850, St. John the Baptist Parish, LA
           1860, New Orleans, LA

SOURCES

Booth, 2:4

NARA M320, reel 012

New Orleans, LA, Death Records Index, 1804–1949

Obituaries: *New Orleans Crescent*, 2 Oct. 1867; *New Orleans Daily Picayune*, 2 and 6
  Oct. 1867

US Census 1850, 1860

www.findagrave.com, 11811162

BLANTON, R. M.

BIRTH   1845/New Orleans, LA
DEATH   Louisiana

RECORD OF SERVICE

CSA ENLISTMENT   29 June 1861/New Orleans, LA/One year
                          25 July 1862/Tupelo, MS/Duration of the war

ORLEANS LIGHT HORSE TRANSFER DATA

   INBOUND   22 July 1862/Private
   OUTBOUND   Feb. 1864/Private

SERVICE RÉSUMÉ

   22 July 1862   Tupelo, MS/Received into the Orleans Light Horse from Co. I,
                          Twenty-First Louisiana Volunteer Infantry (disbanded)

   Sept.–Oct. 1862   Absent with leave
   Nov.–Dec. 1862   Absent without leave
   Jan.–Oct. 1863   Present
   9 Aug. 1863   Detailed in charge of stock in pasture
   Nov.–Dec. 1863   Absent without leave

SOURCES

Booth, 2:9
NARA M320, reel 032

BOISBLANC, Edgard

BIRTH   1824/Louisiana
DEATH   2 Jan. 1884/New Orleans, LA

RECORD OF SERVICE

MILITIA SERVICE   23 Nov. 1861/Active
CSA ENLISTMENT   22 Mar. 1862/New Orleans, LA/90 days

ORLEANS LIGHT HORSE TRANSFER DATA

   INBOUND   1861/Private
   OUTBOUND   Aug. 1862/Private

SERVICE RÉSUMÉ

   23 Nov. 1861   New Orleans, LA/Militia service with the
                          Orleans Light Horse; present
   22 Mar. 1862   Mustered into service of CSA
   22 Mar.–25 May 1862 Present
   6 June 1862   Camp Williamson, Tupelo, MS/Present

PERSONAL NARRATIVE

OCCUPATION   Accountant
GENEALOGY   Married, ca. 1875, New Orleans, LA, Marie Eliza Darcantel
                          (b. ca. 1842, Louisiana; d. 14 Jan. 1897, New Orleans, LA)
RESIDENCES   1870, New Orleans, LA
                          1880, New Orleans, LA
ADDITIONAL INFORMATION Alternate spelling: Edgar Boisblanc

SOURCES
Gardner's New Orleans Directory, 1866
NARA M320, reel 032
New Orleans, LA, Death Records Index, 1804–1949
Soards' New Orleans City Directory, 1876
US Census 1870, 1880

BONFANTI, H. T.

BIRTH	1845/Louisiana

RECORD OF SERVICE

CSA ENLISTMENT	22 Mar. 1862/New Orleans, LA/90 days
	25 July 1862/Tupelo, MS/Duration of the war

ORLEANS LIGHT HORSE TRANSFER DATA

INBOUND	22 Mar. 1862/Private
OUTBOUND	14 June 1862/Private

SERVICE RÉSUMÉ

Mar. 1862	New Orleans, LA/Mustered into service of CSA with the Orleans Light Horse
22 Mar.–25 May 1862	Present
6 June 1862	Camp Williamson, Tupelo, MS/Absent without leave
SEPARATION	14 June 1862/Tupelo, MS/Discharge, unspecified

SOURCES
NARA M320, reel 032

BORDUZAT, James P.

BIRTH	1840/Bordeaux, France
DEATH	12 Apr. 1865/New Orleans, LA

RECORD OF SERVICE

CSA ENLISTMENT	25 May 1863/Shelbyville, TN/Duration of the war

ORLEANS LIGHT HORSE TRANSFER DATA

INBOUND	25 May 1863/Private
OUTBOUND	6 Jan. 1865/Private

SERVICE RÉSUMÉ

25 May 1863	Shelbyville, TN/Received into the Orleans Light Horse; enlistment bounty, $50
May–June 1863	Present
July–Aug. 1863	Absent, sick in hospital
9 Aug. 1863	Sent to hospital at Rome, GA
Sept.–Oct. 1863	Rome, GA/Absent, sick in hospital
Nov.–Dec. 1864	Absent, sick
4 Mar. 1864	Paid for service 1 July 1863 to 29 Feb. 1864
Feb. 1864	Mobile, AL/Employed on extra duty as a hospital nurse
Mar.–Apr. 1864	Mobile, AL/Employed in hospital as a nurse overseer

May–June 1864	Mobile, AL/Detailed in hospital by order of
	Lt. Gen. Leonidas Polk
12 Dec. 1864	Mobile, AL/Approved for discharge
SEPARATION	6 Jan. 1865/Mobile, AL/Discharge, physical disability

PERSONAL NARRATIVE

| RESIDENCES | 1850, New Orleans, LA |
| | 1861, New Orleans, LA |

SOURCES

Gardner's New Orleans Directory, 1861
NARA M320, reel 032
Obituary: *New Orleans Bee*, 24 Apr. 1865
US Census 1850

BRANHAM, William Henry

| BIRTH | 1830/Harris County, GA |

RECORD OF SERVICE

| CSA ENLISTMENT | 22 Mar. 1862/New Orleans, LA/90 days |
| | 25 July 1862/Tupelo, MS/Duration of the war |

ORLEANS LIGHT HORSE TRANSFER DATA

| INBOUND | 22 Mar. 1862/Private |
| OUTBOUND | 5 July 1862/Private |

SERVICE RÉSUMÉ

22 Mar. 1862	New Orleans, LA/Mustered into service of CSA with the
	Orleans Light Horse
22 Mar.–25 May 1862	Present
6 June 1862	Camp Williamson, Tupelo, MS/Absent, sick
SEPARATION	5 July 1862/Tupelo, MS/Discharge, physical disability

PERSONAL NARRATIVE

OCCUPATION	Portrait painter, school teacher
GENEALOGY	Son of Joel and Emily (Cooper) Branham, Macon, GA
RESIDENCES	1830, Harris County, GA
	1840, Putnam County, GA
	1850, Putnam County, GA
	1870, Floyd County, GA
	1880, Chattanooga, GA

SOURCES

Booth, 2:106
NARA M320, reel 032
US Census 1830, 1840, 1850, 1870, 1880

BROADWELL, Charles B.

BIRTH	Sept. 1824/Clermont County, OH
DEATH	12 Apr. 1886/New Orleans, LA

RECORD OF SERVICE

MILITIA SERVICE	23 Nov. 1861/Active

ORLEANS LIGHT HORSE TRANSFER DATA

INBOUND	1861/Private
OUTBOUND	22 Mar. 1862/Private

SERVICE RÉSUMÉ

23 Nov. 1861	New Orleans, LA/Militia service with the Orleans Light Horse; present
SEPARATION	22 Mar. 1862/New Orleans, LA/Declined enlistment

PERSONAL NARRATIVE

OCCUPATION	Livestock broker and merchant
GENEALOGY	Son of Josiah and Susan (Bowsher) Broadwell
	Brother of James P. Broadwell
	Married, ca. 1864, New Orleans, LA, Marie Eulalie Peyroux (b. 2 Aug. 1842, New Orleans, LA; d. 12 July 1880, New Orleans, LA)
RESIDENCES	1860, New Orleans, LA
	1870, New Orleans, LA
	1880, New Orleans, LA

SOURCES

Booth, 2:123
Gardner's New Orleans Directory, 1861
NARA M320, reel 032
New Orleans, LA, Death Records, 1804–1949
New Orleans Passenger Lists, 1813–1945
US Census 1860, 1870, 1880

BROADWELL, James P.

BIRTH	about 1820/New Orleans, LA

RECORD OF SERVICE

MILITIA SERVICE	23 Nov. 1861/Absent, on leave

ORLEANS LIGHT HORSE TRANSFER DATA

INBOUND	1861/Private
OUTBOUND	22 Mar. 1862/Private

SERVICE RÉSUMÉ

23 Nov. 1861	New Orleans, LA/Militia service with the Orleans Light Horse; absent with leave, on service in Mississippi
SEPARATION	22 Mar. 1862/New Orleans, LA/Declined enlistment

PERSONAL NARRATIVE

OCCUPATION	Clerk

GENEALOGY	Son of Josiah and Susan (Bowsher) Broadwell
	Brother of Charles B. Broadwell
RESIDENCES	1860, New Orleans, LA
	1891, New Orleans, LA

SOURCES
Booth, 2:123
Gardner's New Orleans Directory, 1861
NARA M320, reel 032; M818, reel 04
New Orleans, LA, Directories, 1890–1891
US Census 1860

BROOKS, Aaron C.

RECORD OF SERVICE

CSA ENLISTMENT	Apr. 1862/Tupelo, MS/Duration of the war
ORLEANS LIGHT HORSE TRANSFER DATA	
INBOUND	Apr. 1862/Private
OUTBOUND	June 1862/Private
SERVICE RÉSUMÉ	
Apr. 1862	Tupelo, MS/Received into the Orleans Light Horse
May–June 1862	Present

SOURCES
Booth, 2:127
NARA M320, reel 032

BROWN, John B.

| BIRTH | ca. 1832/Louisiana |

RECORD OF SERVICE

CSA ENLISTMENT	29 May 1863/Shelbyville, TN/Duration of the war
ORLEANS LIGHT HORSE TRANSFER DATA	
INBOUND	29 May 1863/Private
OUTBOUND	1 May 1865/Private
SERVICE RÉSUMÉ	
29 May 1863	Shelbyville, TN/Received into the Orleans Light Horse; enlistment bounty, $50
May–June 1863	Present
July 1863–June 1864	Present
9 Sept. 1863	Atlanta, GA/Admitted to Fairgrounds Hospital for acute dysentery
26 Apr. 1865	Durham Station, NC/Surrendered
SEPARATION	1 May 1865/Greensboro, NC/Parole, released from military service

PERSONAL NARRATIVE

| OCCUPATION | Fire department captain |

RESIDENCES   1860, New Orleans, LA
                          1891, New Orleans, LA

SOURCES
Appendix C (CD-ROM), in Welsh, *Two Confederate Hospitals*
Booth, 2:146
Gardner's New Orleans Directory, 1861
NARA M320, reel 032; M1781, reel 006
New Orleans, LA, Directories, 1890–1891
US Census 1860

BRYAN, Courtland A.

BIRTH   1840/Thomas County, GA
DEATH   1909/Thomasville, GA

RECORD OF SERVICE
CSA ENLISTMENT   22 Mar. 1862/New Orleans, LA/90 days
ORLEANS LIGHT HORSE TRANSFER DATA
    INBOUND   22 Mar. 1862/Private
    OUTBOUND   22 Apr. 1863/Private
SERVICE RÉSUMÉ
    22 Mar. 1862   New Orleans, LA/Mustered into service of CSA with the
                              Orleans Light Horse
    Mar.–Apr. 1863   Present
SEPARATION   22 Apr. 1863/Shelbyville, TN/Discharge, acceptable
                              substitute (William O. Bickle)

PERSONAL NARRATIVE
OCCUPATION   Clerk, merchant
GENEALOGY   Son of William Hardy and Maria (Wyche) Bryan,
                              Natchitoches, LA
                          Brother of William Hardy Bryan Jr.
                          Married, ca. 1867, Mary E. —— (b. ca. 1838, Alabama)
RESIDENCES   1850, Thomas County, GA
                          1860, Natchitoches, LA

SOURCES
NARA M320, reel 032
US Census 1850, 1860

BRYAN, T.

RECORD OF SERVICE
CSA ENLISTMENT   22 Mar. 1862/New Orleans, LA/90 days
                          25 July 1862/Tupelo, MS/Duration of the war
ORLEANS LIGHT HORSE TRANSFER DATA
    INBOUND   22 Mar. 1862/Private
    OUTBOUND   Apr. 1863/Private

22 Mar. 1862	New Orleans, LA/Mustered into service of CSA with the Orleans Light Horse
Sept.–Oct. 1862	Present
Nov.–Dec. 1862	Absent with leave
Jan.–Feb. 1863	Absent, furlough

PERSONAL NARRATIVE

RESIDENCES   1861, New Orleans, LA

SOURCES

Gardner's New Orleans Directory, 1861
NARA M320, reel 032

BRYAN, William Hardy, Jr.

BIRTH   ca. 1839/Thomas County, GA
DEATH   Louisiana

RECORD OF SERVICE

CSA ENLISTMENT   22 Mar. 1862/New Orleans, LA/90 days
                    25 July 1862/Tupelo, MS/Duration of the war

ORLEANS LIGHT HORSE TRANSFER DATA
  INBOUND   22 Mar. 1862/Private
  OUTBOUND   June 1862/Private

SERVICE RÉSUMÉ

22 Mar. 1862	New Orleans, LA/Mustered into service of CSA with the Orleans Light Horse
22 Mar.–25 May 1862	Present

PERSONAL NARRATIVE

OCCUPATION   Planter
GENEALOGY   Son of William Hardy and Maria (Wyche) Bryan,
                        Natchitoches, LA
                    Brother of Courtland A. Bryan
RESIDENCES   1850, Thomas County, GA
                    1860, Natchitoches, LA
                    1861, New Orleans, LA

SOURCES

Gardner's New Orleans Directory, 1861
NARA M320, reel 032
US Census 1850, 1860

BUORD, Louis A.

BIRTH   ca. 1820/Haiti
DEATH   2 Nov. 1868/New Orleans, LA

RECORD OF SERVICE

CSA ENLISTMENT   22 Mar. 1862/New Orleans, LA/90 days
                    25 July 1862/Tupelo, MS/Duration of the war

ORLEANS LIGHT HORSE TRANSFER DATA
    INBOUND   22 Mar. 1862/Private
    OUTBOUND   Aug. 1864/Private
SERVICE RÉSUMÉ

22 Mar. 1862	New Orleans, LA/Mustered into service of CSA with the Orleans Light Horse
22 Mar.–25 May 1862	Present
6 June 1862	Camp Williamson, Tupelo, MS/Absent, sick
Sept.–Dec. 1862	Present
Jan.–Feb. 1863	Absent, furlough
Mar.–Apr. 1863	Reported as deserter
May–June 1863	Present, returned from desertion with surgeon's certificate of inability
July–Dec. 1863	Present
May–June 1864	Present

PERSONAL NARRATIVE

OCCUPATION   Drayman
GENEALOGY   Married, ca. 1845, New Orleans, LA, Marie Roueche
                    (b. ca. 1822, France; d. 5 July 1894, New Orleans, LA)

RESIDENCES   1850, New Orleans, LA
                    1860, New Orleans, LA

SOURCES

NARA M320, reel 032
New Orleans, LA, Death Records Index, 1804–1949
US Census 1850, 1860
US Naturalization Record Indexes, 1791–1992

BUTLER, James M.

BIRTH   ca. 1840/South Carolina

RECORD OF SERVICE

CSA ENLISTMENT   22 Apr. 1864/Demopolis, AL/Duration of the war
ORLEANS LIGHT HORSE TRANSFER DATA
    INBOUND   22 Apr. 1864/Private
    OUTBOUND   1 May 1865/Private
SERVICE RÉSUMÉ

22 Apr. 1864	Demopolis, AL/Received into the Orleans Light Horse
May–June 1864	Absent, sick
20 July 1864	Macon, GA/Admitted to the hospital for typhoid, emaciation, and debility
4 Sept. 1864	Placed on medical leave
26 Apr. 1865	Durham Station, NC/Surrendered
SEPARATION	1 May 1865/Greensboro, NC/Parole, released from military service

PERSONAL NARRATIVE

OCCUPATION   Farm laborer
GENEALOGY   Son of Bennett B. and Mary F. (Criddle) Butler, Houston, MS

RESIDENCES   1850, Chickasaw County, MS
                              1860, Chickasaw County, MS

SOURCES
NARA M320, reel 032; M1781, reel 006
US Census 1850, 1860

BYRD, John Grayson

BIRTH   1845/New Orleans, LA
DEATH   21 Aug. 1898/New Orleans, LA

RECORD OF SERVICE

CSA ENLISTMENT   29 May 1863/Mobile, AL/Duration of the war

ORLEANS LIGHT HORSE TRANSFER DATA

    INBOUND   29 May 1863/Private
    OUTBOUND   Dec. 1864/Private

SERVICE RÉSUMÉ

    29 May 1863   Mobile, AL/Received into the Orleans Light Horse;
                                  enlistment bounty, $50

    May–June 1863   Present
    July–Dec. 1863   Present
    May–June 1864   Absent, sick
    June 1864   Received clothing issue
    Oct. 1864   Received clothing issue

PERSONAL NARRATIVE

OCCUPATION   Insurance representative, cotton broker

GENEALOGY   Son of Orran T. and Evelina (Hopkins) Byrd,
                                  New Orleans, LA
                              Brother-in-law of Frederick G. Freret
                              Nephew of Aristide R. Hopkins
                              Married, 6 Apr. 1869, Ascension, LA, Olive McCall (b. 1845,
                                  Ascension, LA; d. 23 Nov. 1886, New Orleans, LA)

RESIDENCES   1860, Mobile, AL
                              1870, New Orleans, LA
                              1880, New Orleans, LA
                              1890, New Orleans, LA

SOURCES
Louisiana Marriages, 1718–1925
NARA M320, reel 032
New Orleans, LA, Death Records Index, 1804–1949
New Orleans, LA, Directories, 1890–1891
Obituary: *New Orleans Daily Picayune*, 22 Aug. 1898
US Census 1860, 1870, 1880

BYRNE, Thomas K.

BIRTH	3 Feb. 1814/Inverkip, Scotland
DEATH	Oct. 1844/Lancashire, England

RECORD OF SERVICE

CSA ENLISTMENT	22 Mar. 1862/New Orleans, LA/90 days
	25 July 1862/Tupelo, MS/Duration of the war

ORLEANS LIGHT HORSE TRANSFER DATA

INBOUND	22 Mar. 1862/Private
OUTBOUND	12 Apr. 1862/Private

SERVICE RÉSUMÉ

22 Mar. 1862	New Orleans, LA/Mustered into service of CSA with the Orleans Light Horse
22 Mar.–12 Apr. 1862	Present
SEPARATION	12 Apr. 1862/Tupelo, MS/Honorable discharge, unspecified

PERSONAL NARRATIVE

OCCUPATION	Cotton factor, merchant
GENEALOGY	Married, 1846, New Orleans, LA, Coralie Delphine Byrne (b. 1827, New Orleans, LA; d. Jan. 1893, Lancashire, England)
RESIDENCES	1850, New Orleans, LA
	1860, New Orleans, LA
	1881, Liverpool, Lancashire, England

SOURCES

1881 England Census
NARA M320, reel 032
US Census 1850, 1860

CAMMACK, Thomas Dixon

BIRTH	1831/New Orleans, LA
DEATH	25 Sept. 1876/Mandeville, LA

RECORD OF SERVICE

ORLEANS LIGHT HORSE TRANSFER DATA

INBOUND	Apr. 1865/Private
OUTBOUND	11 May 1865/Private

SERVICE RÉSUMÉ

26 Apr. 1865	Newbern, NC/Surrendered
SEPARATION	11 May 1865/Newbern, NC/Parole, released from military service

PERSONAL NARRATIVE

GENEALOGY	Son of Horace Claiborne Chew and Amelia J. (Saul) Cammack, New Orleans, LA
RESIDENCES	1861, New Orleans, LA
	1875, New Orleans, LA

SOURCES

NARA M320, reel 032; M1781, reel 006

Obituary: *New Orleans Daily Picayune*, 27 Sept. and 1 Oct. 1876

Soards' New Orleans City Directory, 1875

CAMPBELL, James

RECORD OF SERVICE

CSA ENLISTMENT   11 Aug. 1862/Chattanooga, TN/Duration of the war

ORLEANS LIGHT HORSE TRANSFER DATA

    INBOUND   11 Aug. 1862/Private

    OUTBOUND   Aug. 1864/Private

SERVICE RÉSUMÉ

    11 Aug. 1862   Chattanooga, TN/Received into the Orleans Light Horse

    Sept.–Dec. 1862   Present

    Jan.–June 1863   Shelbyville, TN/Present

    July–Dec. 1863   Present

    Jan.–June 1864   Present

SOURCES

NARA M320, reel 032

CAMPBELL, Martin Gordon

BIRTH   6 Oct. 1843/New Orleans, LA

RECORD OF SERVICE

CSA ENLISTMENT   22 Mar. 1862/New Orleans, LA/90 days

ORLEANS LIGHT HORSE TRANSFER DATA

    INBOUND   22 Mar. 1862/Private

    OUTBOUND   16 July 1862/Private

SERVICE RÉSUMÉ

    22 Mar. 1862   New Orleans, LA/Mustered into service of CSA with the
                                     Orleans Light Horse

    22 Mar.–25 May 1862   Present

    6 June 1862   Camp Williamson, Tupelo, MS/Present

SEPARATION   16 July 1862/Tupelo, MS/Discharge, under age

PERSONAL NARRATIVE

GENEALOGY   Son of George Washington and Martha (Gordon) Campbell,
                                     New Orleans, LA

RESIDENCES   1850, New Orleans, LA

                      1860, New Orleans, LA

                      1870, New Orleans, LA

SOURCES

NARA M320, reel 032

New Orleans, LA, Birth Records Index, 1790–1899

US Census 1850, 1860, 1870

CAREY, Henry Shields

BIRTH	1837/East Pascagoula, MS
DEATH	17 Aug. 1869/New Orleans, LA

RECORD OF SERVICE

CSA ENLISTMENT	22 Mar. 1862/New Orleans, LA/90 days
	25 July 1862/Tupelo, MS/Duration of the war

ORLEANS LIGHT HORSE TRANSFER DATA

INBOUND	22 Mar. 1862/Private
OUTBOUND	5 July 1862/Private

SERVICE RÉSUMÉ

22 Mar. 1862	New Orleans, LA/Mustered into service of CSA with the Orleans Light Horse
22 Mar.–25 May 1862	Present
6 June 1862	Camp Williamson, Tupelo, MS/Present
SEPARATION	5 July 1862/Tupelo, MS/Discharge, wounded, disabled

PERSONAL NARRATIVE

OCCUPATION	Grocer
GENEALOGY	Son of Dr. Orson and Martha (Monroe) Carey, New Orleans, LA
RESIDENCES	1860, New Orleans, LA

SOURCES

Gardner's New Orleans Directory, 1861
NARA M320, reel 032
New Orleans, LA, Death Records Index, 1804–1949
Obituary: *New Orleans Daily Picayune*, 18 Aug. 1896
US Census 1860

CAREY, R. S.

RECORD OF SERVICE

CSA ENLISTMENT	1 July 1861/Memphis, TN/One year
	1 Sept. 1863/Chattanooga, TN/Duration of the war

ORLEANS LIGHT HORSE TRANSFER DATA

INBOUND	1 Sept. 1863/Private
OUTBOUND	Feb. 1864/Private

SERVICE RÉSUMÉ

1 Sept. 1863	Chattanooga, TN/Received into the Orleans Light Horse from the Twelfth Tennessee Regiment (dismounted)
Sept.–Oct. 1863	Present
Nov.–Dec. 1863	Absent, furlough to resettle family

SOURCES

NARA M320, reel 032

CARRÉ, Walter William

BIRTH	6 June 1829/Gainesville, MS
DEATH	31 Jan. 1877/New Orleans, LA

RECORD OF SERVICE

MILITIA SERVICE	23 Nov. 1861/Absent without leave

ORLEANS LIGHT HORSE TRANSFER DATA

INBOUND	1861/Private
OUTBOUND	22 Mar. 1862/Private

SERVICE RÉSUMÉ

23 Nov. 1861	New Orleans, LA/Militia service with the Orleans Light Horse; absent without leave
SEPARATION	22 Mar. 1862/New Orleans, LA/Declined enlistment

PERSONAL NARRATIVE

OCCUPATION	Lumber merchant
GENEALOGY	Son of Henry and Amelia (Wingate) Carré, Pearl River, MS
	Married, 26 Apr. 1862, New Orleans, LA, Elvira Adams Beach (b. 31 Mar. 1842, Lockland, OH; d. 28 May 1924, New Orleans, LA)
RESIDENCES	1830, Gainesville, MS
	1860, New Orleans, LA
	1870, New Orleans. LA

SOURCES

NARA M320, reel 032

New Orleans, LA, Death Records Index, 1804–1949

Obituary: *New Orleans Daily Picayune*, 1 and 4 Feb. 1877

US Census 1860, 1870

US IRS Tax Assessment Lists, 1862–1918

www.findagrave.com, 89704881

CASSADY, B.

RECORD OF SERVICE

CSA ENLISTMENT	1 July 1861/Memphis, TN/One year
	1 Sept. 1863/Chattanooga, TN/Duration of the war

ORLEANS LIGHT HORSE TRANSFER DATA

INBOUND	1 Sept. 1863/Private
OUTBOUND	1 May 1865/Private

SERVICE RÉSUMÉ

1 Sept. 1863	Chattanooga, TN/Received into the Orleans Light Horse from the Twelfth Tennessee Regiment (dismounted)
Sept.–Dec. 1863	Present
May–June 1864	Present
16 Apr. 1865	West Point, GA/Captured
23 Apr. 1865	Macon, GA/Transferred to US military prison

SEPARATION   1 May 1865/Macon, GA/Parole, released from military service
SOURCES
NARA M320, reel 032

CENAS, Edgar Henry

BIRTH   13 Apr. 1844/New Orleans, LA
DEATH   30 July 1866/New Orleans, LA

RECORD OF SERVICE
CSA ENLISTMENT   7 Aug. 1862/Chattanooga, TN/Duration of the war
ORLEANS LIGHT HORSE TRANSFER DATA
   INBOUND   7 Aug. 1862/Private
   OUTBOUND   13 May 1865/Private
SERVICE RÉSUMÉ
   7 Aug. 1862   Chattanooga, TN/Received into the Orleans Light Horse
   18 Sept. 1862   Detailed at Col. William K. Beard's office, inspector general,
      Army of Tennessee
   Nov. 1862–Apr. 1863   Absent, detached
   May–June 1863   Absent, detailed on special duty
   July–Oct. 1863   Absent, detailed at office of Col. Beard, inspector general
   Nov.–Dec. 1863   Present
   Feb.–Mar. 1864   Demopolis, AL/Employed on extra duty as clerk
   May–June 1864   Absent, sick
   25 Aug. 1864   Macon, GA/Admitted to hospital
   4 Sept. 1864   Placed on medical leave
   4 May 1865   Citronelle, AL/Surrendered
SEPARATION   13 May 1865/Meridian, MS/Parole, released from
      military service

PERSONAL NARRATIVE
GENEALOGY   Son of Dr. Auguste Henri and Minerve Charlotte (Carmick)
      Cenas, New Orleans, LA
RESIDENCES   1850, New Orleans, LA
      1860, New Orleans, LA

SOURCES
NARA M320, reel 032
New Orleans, LA, Birth Records Index, 1790–1899
New Orleans, LA, Death Records Index, 1804–1949
Obituary: *New Orleans Bee*, 31 July 1866
US Census 1850, 1860
www.findagrave.com, 39830162

CHAILLÉ, Stanford Emerson

BIRTH   9 July 1830/Natchez, MS
DEATH   27 May 1911/New Orleans, LA

RECORD OF SERVICE

MILITIA SERVICE   23 Nov. 1861/Active

ORLEANS LIGHT HORSE TRANSFER DATA
   INBOUND   Oct. 1861/Private
   OUTBOUND   17 Feb. 1862/Private

SERVICE RÉSUMÉ
   Oct. 1861–16 Feb. 1862 New Orleans, LA/Militia service with the Orleans Light
                             Horse; present
     17 Feb. 1862   Released from enlistment; appointed acting surgeon general
                             of Louisiana

PERSONAL NARRATIVE

OCCUPATION   Physician

GENEALOGY   Son of William Hamilton and Mary (Stanford) Chaillé,
                      New Orleans, LA
                      Married (1), 23 Feb. 1857, New Orleans, LA, Laura Ellena
                        Mountfort (b. 1832, New Orleans, LA; d. 17 Aug. 1858,
                        New Orleans, LA)
                      Married (2), 1863, New Orleans, LA, Mary Louisa Napier
                        (b. ca. 1843, Macon, GA; d. 5 July 1873, New Orleans, LA)

RESIDENCES   1850, Cambridge, MA
                      1860, New Orleans, LA
                      1890, New Orleans, LA
                      1900, New Orleans, LA
                      1910, New Orleans, LA

SOURCES

Directory of Deceased American Physicians, 1804–1929
Gardner's New Orleans Directory, 1861
NARA M320, reel 032
New Orleans, LA, Death Records Index, 1804–1949
Obituary: *New Orleans Daily Picayune*, 28 May 1911
US Census 1850, 1900, 1910
Welsh, 28, 29, 155–56
www.findagrave.com, 11713493

CHARVET, Lucien

BIRTH	1826/Franklin, LA
DEATH	20 Nov. 1878/New Orleans, LA

RECORD OF SERVICE

CSA ENLISTMENT	1 Nov. 1862/Knoxville, TN/Duration of the war

ORLEANS LIGHT HORSE TRANSFER DATA

INBOUND	1 Nov. 1862/Private
OUTBOUND	1 May 1865/Private

SERVICE RÉSUMÉ

Nov. 1862	Knoxville, TN/Received into the Orleans Light Horse
Nov.–Dec. 1862	Present
Jan.–June 1863	Present
July–Dec. 1863	Present
19 Sept. 1863	Chickamauga, GA/On duty as headquarters courier; involved in controversy that caused Lt. Gen. Leonidas Polk to be relieved of command
May–June 1864	Present
26 Apr. 1865	Durham Station, NC/Surrendered
SEPARATION	1 May 1865/Greensboro, NC/Parole, released from military service

PERSONAL NARRATIVE

OCCUPATION	Attorney
GENEALOGY	Son of Jacob Charvet, Franklin, LA
	Brother-in-law of Yves R. Le Monnier Jr.
	Married, 1865, New Orleans, LA, Marie Amire Le Monnier (b. 26 June 1817, New Orleans, LA, d. 12 June 1882, New Orleans, LA)
RESIDENCES	1830, Franklin, LA
	1860, New Orleans, LA
	1870, New Orleans, LA

SOURCES

Gardner's New Orleans Directory, 1861
Louisiana, Compiled Census and Census Substitutes Index, 1791–1890
NARA M320, reel 032; M1781, reel 006
New Orleans, LA, Death Records Index, 1804–1949
Obituary: *New Orleans Daily Picayune*, 21, 22, and 24 Nov. 1878
OR, ser. 1, vol. 30, pt. 2:58–59
US Census 1830, 1860, 1870

CHEW, ——

RECORD OF SERVICE
ORLEANS LIGHT HORSE TRANSFER DATA
    INBOUND   June 1862/Private
    OUTBOUND   Aug. 1862/Private
SERVICE RÉSUMÉ
    6 June 1862   Camp Williamson, Tupelo, MS/Present with the
                         Orleans Light Horse
ADDITIONAL INFORMATION   Available archives provide only the surname shown, with no
given name or amplifying data. While no identification can be
made with certainty, it is possible that this is Morris Robinson
Chew, who was born in New Orleans, LA, in 1829 to Beverly
and Maria (Duer) Chew. Morris Robinson Chew was a
cousin of Thomas Dixon Cammack. He went to California
for the 1850 gold rush; in 1860 he was in Davenport, IA, and
subsequently returned to Louisiana.

SOURCES
NARA M320, reel 032
US Census 1850, 1860, 1870

CHRISTIAN, Paul John

BIRTH   Apr. 1829/Pennsylvania
DEATH   15 Dec. 1913/New Orleans, LA

RECORD OF SERVICE
CSA ENLISTMENT   22 Mar. 1862/New Orleans, LA/90 days
                         25 July 1862/Tupelo, MS/Duration of the war
ORLEANS LIGHT HORSE TRANSFER DATA
    INBOUND   22 Mar. 1862/Private
    OUTBOUND   3 Aug. 1863/Private
SERVICE RÉSUMÉ
    22 Mar. 1862   New Orleans, LA/Mustered into service of CSA with the
                         Orleans Light Horse
    22 Mar.–25 May 1862 Present
    6 June 1862   Camp Williamson, Tupelo, MS/Absent, sick
    Sept.–Dec. 1862   Present
    Jan.–June 1863   Present
    July–Aug. 1863   Present
    3 Aug. 1863   Chattanooga, TN/Transferred to Co. E, First Tennessee
                         Cavalry

PERSONAL NARRATIVE
OCCUPATION   Clerk in stationery store, wood and coal dealer
GENEALOGY   Married, 25 Sept. 1877, New Orleans, LA, Corinne Lawrence
                         Catlett (b. Feb. 1850, East Feliciana Parish, LA;
                         d. 10 Aug. 1913, New Orleans, LA)

RESIDENCES	1850, New Orleans, LA
	1860, New Orleans, LA
	1870, New Orleans, LA
	1880, New Orleans, LA
	1890, New Orleans, LA
	1900, New Orleans, LA
	1910, New Orleans, LA

SOURCES

Gardner's New Orleans Directory, 1861
Louisiana, Compiled Census and Census Substitutes Index, 1791–1890
NARA M320, reel 032
New Orleans, LA, Death Records Index, 1804–1949
Obituary: *New Orleans Daily Picayune*, 13 Dec. 1913
US Census 1850, 1860, 1880, 1900, 1910
www.findagrave.com, 78227228

CLAIBORNE, Archibald Junius

| BIRTH | 1836/Adams County, MS |
| DEATH | 28 Apr. 1896/New Orleans, LA |

RECORD OF SERVICE

| CSA ENLISTMENT | 22 Mar. 1862/New Orleans, LA/90 days |
| | 25 July 1862/Tupelo, MS/Duration of the war |

ORLEANS LIGHT HORSE TRANSFER DATA

| INBOUND | 22 Mar. 1862/Private |
| OUTBOUND | 3 Nov. 1863/Private |

SERVICE RÉSUMÉ

22 Mar. 1862	New Orleans, LA/Mustered into service of CSA with the Orleans Light Horse
22 Mar.–25 May 1862	Present
6 June 1862	Camp Williamson, Tupelo, MS/Absent, sick
Sept.–Dec. 1862	Absent, detailed
Jan.–June 1863	Present
2 May 1863	Appointed assistant surgeon, CSA
3 Nov. 1863	Meridian, MS/Discharged to other service

PERSONAL NARRATIVE

OCCUPATION	Physician
GENEALOGY	Son of Ferdinand Leigh and Courtney Ann (Terrell) Claiborne
	Married, 9 Sept. 1890, Yazoo, MS, Lena Maie Brown
	(b. 7 Sept. 1865, Hazelhurst, MS; d. 4 Oct. 1958, Alameda, CA)
RESIDENCES	1861, New Orleans, LA
	1890, Yazoo, MS

SOURCES

California Death Index, 1940–1997
Gardner's New Orleans Directory, 1861
Mississippi Marriages, 1776–1935

NARA M320, reel 032
New Orleans, LA, Death Records Index, 1804–1949
Obituary: *New Orleans Daily Picayune*, 29 and 30 Apr. and 3 May 1896
US Military and Naval Academies Cadet Records and Applications, 1805–1908

CLARKE, Thomas L.

BIRTH	1830/Kentucky
DEATH	18 Feb. 1874/New Orleans, LA

RECORD OF SERVICE

MILITIA SERVICE	23 Nov. 1861/Active

ORLEANS LIGHT HORSE TRANSFER DATA

INBOUND	1861/Private
OUTBOUND	22 Mar. 1862/Private

SERVICE RÉSUMÉ

23 Nov. 1861	New Orleans, LA/Militia service with the Orleans Light Horse; present
SEPARATION	22 Mar. 1862/New Orleans, LA/Declined enlistment

PERSONAL NARRATIVE

OCCUPATION	Teamster, coffee merchant
GENEALOGY	Son of James and Martha (Holloway) Clarke, New Orleans, LA
	Married, ca. 1869, Louisiana, Elizabeth McWilliams (b. ca. 1846, St. Mary Parish, LA; d. 30 Apr. 1924, New Orleans, LA)
RESIDENCES	1850, Louisville, KY
	1860, New Orleans, LA
	1870, New Orleans, LA

SOURCES

Gardner's New Orleans Directory, 1861
NARA M320, reel 032
New Orleans, LA, Death Records Index, 1804–1949
US Census 1850, 1860, 1870
www.findagrave.com, 11893910

CLAUDEN, Edmon

RECORD OF SERVICE

MILITIA SERVICE	23 Nov. 1861/Active

ORLEANS LIGHT HORSE TRANSFER DATA

INBOUND	1861/Private
OUTBOUND	22 Mar. 1862/Private

SERVICE RÉSUMÉ

23 Nov. 1861	New Orleans, LA/Militia service with the Orleans Light Horse; present, detailed to duty, facilities maintenance custodian, troop headquarters

22 Mar. 1862/New Orleans, LA/Declined enlistment

SOURCES
NARA M320, reel 032

CLOUGH, John Adolphus

BIRTH | ca. 1840/Canada
DEATH | 9 Nov. 1897/Amite, LA

RECORD OF SERVICE

CSA ENLISTMENT | 22 Mar. 1862/New Orleans, LA/90 days
| 25 July 1862/Tupelo, MS/Duration of the war

ORLEANS LIGHT HORSE TRANSFER DATA
  INBOUND | 22 Mar. 1862/Private
  OUTBOUND | Aug. 1864/Private

SERVICE RÉSUMÉ

22 Mar. 1862 | New Orleans, LA/Mustered into service of CSA with the Orleans Light Horse

22 Mar.–25 May 1862 | Present
6 June 1862 | Camp Williamson, Tupelo, MS/Present
Sept.–Oct. 1862 | Knoxville, TN/Present, detailed on duty
Nov.–Dec. 1862 | Murfreesboro, TN/Present
Jan.–June 1863 | Shelbyville, TN/Present
July–Dec. 1863 | Present
28 Nov. 1863 | Enterprise, MS/Application for 30-day leave of absence (forwarded to corps headquarters for approval)

May–June 1864 | Present

PERSONAL NARRATIVE

OCCUPATION | Butcher
GENEALOGY | Married, 23 Apr. 1867, St. Helena Parish, LA, Brenda M. Sharkey (b. England, ca. 1840; emigrated to New Orleans, LA, with family, Mar. 1849; d. 14 Oct. 1897, Amite, LA)

RESIDENCES | 1861, New Orleans, LA
| 1865, Amite, LA
| 1870, Amite, LA

SOURCES
Gardner's New Orleans Directory, 1861
NARA M320, reel 032
US Census 1870
US IRS Tax Assessment Lists, 1862–1918
www.findagrave.com, 64965435

CONVERSE, Ephraim Kingsbury

BIRTH	23 June 1823/Lyme, NH
DEATH	6 Mar. 1904/New Orleans, LA

RECORD OF SERVICE

MILITIA SERVICE	23 Nov. 1861/Active
CSA ENLISTMENT	22 Mar. 1862/New Orleans, LA/90 days
	25 July 1862/Tupelo, MS/Duration of the war

ORLEANS LIGHT HORSE TRANSFER DATA

INBOUND	1861/Corporal
OUTBOUND	16 July 1862/Sergeant

SERVICE RÉSUMÉ

23 Nov. 1861	New Orleans, LA/Militia service with the Orleans Light Horse; present, in rank of corporal
22 Mar. 1862	New Orleans, LA/Mustered into service of CSA in position of orderly sergeant
22 Mar.–25 May 1862	Present, in position of orderly sergeant
6 June 1862	Absent with leave, in position of orderly sergeant
SEPARATION	16 July 1862/Tupelo, MS/Discharge, over age

PERSONAL NARRATIVE

OCCUPATION	Wholesale merchant
GENEALOGY	Son of Otis and Clarissa (Porter) Converse, Grafton, NH
	Married, 1845, New Orleans, LA, Marguerite Anais Deneufbourg (b. 12 Mar. 1825, New Orleans, LA; d. 17 Aug. 1915, New Orleans, LA)
RESIDENCES	1840, Plainfield, NH
	1845, Orleans Parish, LA
	1850, New Orleans, LA
	1861, New Orleans, LA
	1870, New Orleans, LA
	1880, New Orleans, LA
	1890, New Orleans, LA
	1900, New Orleans, LA

SOURCES

Gardner's New Orleans Directory, 1861
NARA M320, reel 032
New Orleans, LA, Death Records Index, 1804–1949
New Orleans, LA, Directories, 1890–1891
Obituaries: *New Orleans Daily Picayune*, 7, 8, and 13 Mar. 1904; *New Orleans Times-Democrat*, 7 and 13 Mar. 1904
US Census 1840, 1850, 1870, 1880, 1900

COWARDEN, Samuel Lynch

BIRTH	ca. 1823/Virginia
DEATH	20 Nov. 1880/New Orleans, LA

RECORD OF SERVICE

CSA ENLISTMENT	26 Feb. 1864/Demopolis, AL/Duration of the war

ORLEANS LIGHT HORSE TRANSFER DATA

INBOUND	26 Feb. 1864/Private
OUTBOUND	June 1865/Private

SERVICE RÉSUMÉ

26 Feb. 1864	Demopolis, AL/Received into the Orleans Light Horse
May–June 1864	Present
4 May 1865	Citronelle, AL/Surrendered
SEPARATION	June 1865/Gainesville, AL/Parole, released from military service

PERSONAL NARRATIVE

OCCUPATION	Steamboat crewman, contractor
GENEALOGY	Married, ca. 1857, St. Louis, MO, Louisa Amelia —— (b. ca. 1834, Norway; d. 23 June 1874, New Orleans, LA)
RESIDENCES	ca. 1855, St. Louis, MO
	1860, St. Louis, MO
	1866, Mobile, AL
	1880, New Orleans, LA

SOURCES

Civil War Prisoner of War Records, 1861–1865
Directory of the City of Mobile for the Year 1866
NARA M320, reel 032
New Orleans, LA, Death Records Index, 1804–1949
Obituary: Mrs. S. L. Cowarden, *New Orleans Daily Picayune*, 24 and 28 June 1874
Soards' New Orleans City Directory, 1874, 1879
US Census 1860, 1880

CRAIN, Peter Wood

BIRTH	ca. 1840/Fauquier County, VA
DEATH	11 Oct. 1863/Stevensburg, VA

RECORD OF SERVICE

CSA ENLISTMENT	11 Mar. 1861/New Orleans, LA/90 days
	24 Oct. 1862/Chattanooga, TN/Duration of the war

ORLEANS LIGHT HORSE TRANSFER DATA

INBOUND	1 July 1862/Private
OUTBOUND	20 Apr. 1863/Private

SERVICE RÉSUMÉ

1 July 1862	Tupelo, MS/Received into Orleans Light Horse from Co. K, Crescent Regiment, Twenty-Fourth Louisiana Infantry
Sept.–Oct.	Jackson, TN/Absent, sick

Nov.–Dec. 1862	Present
Jan.–Apr. 1863	Present
20 Apr. 1863	Transferred by order of secretary of war to Fourth Virginia (Black Horse) Cavalry Regiment

PERSONAL NARRATIVE

OCCUPATION	Retail store clerk
GENEALOGY	Son of Bailey and Huldah (Cockerill) Crain, Fauquier County, VA
RESIDENCES	1850, Fauquier County, VA
	1860, Alexandria, VA

SOURCES

NARA M320, reels 032, 0382; M324, reel 039
US Census 1850, 1860

CRAIN, Robert A.

| BIRTH | ca. 1819/Virginia |

RECORD OF SERVICE

| CSA ENLISTMENT | 22 Mar. 1862/New Orleans, LA/90 days |
| | 25 July 1862/Tupelo, MS/Duration of the war |

ORLEANS LIGHT HORSE TRANSFER DATA

| INBOUND | 22 Mar. 1862/Private |
| OUTBOUND | Dec. 1862/Private |

SERVICE RÉSUMÉ

| 22 Mar. 1862 | New Orleans, LA/Mustered into service of CSA with the Orleans Light Horse |
| Sept.–Oct. 1862 | Present |

PERSONAL NARRATIVE

OCCUPATION	Oyster fisherman
RESIDENCES	1850, Morgan, KY
	1860, St Bernard Parish, LA

SOURCES

NARA M320, reel 032
US Census 1850, 1860

CRUMHORN, Harvey Nicholas

| BIRTH | 1837/New Orleans, LA |
| DEATH | 18 Apr. 1899/New Orleans, LA |

RECORD OF SERVICE

| CSA ENLISTMENT | 22 Mar. 1862/New Orleans, LA/90 days |
| | 25 July 1862/Tupelo, MS/Duration of the war |

ORLEANS LIGHT HORSE TRANSFER DATA

| INBOUND | 22 Mar. 1862/Private |
| OUTBOUND | 1 May 1865/Private |

SERVICE RÉSUMÉ

22 Mar. 1862	New Orleans, LA/Mustered into service of CSA with the Orleans Light Horse
22 Mar.–25 May 1862	Present
6 June 1862	Camp Williamson, Tupelo, MS/Present
Sept.–Dec. 1862	Present, detailed on duty at Maj. Gen. Leonidas Polk's headquarters
Jan.–Apr. 1863	Present
19 June 1863	Detailed as baker with Maj. John J. Murphy, chief commissary of Polk's Corps, effective 1 May 1863
23 June–7 Aug. 1862	Superintendent of building ovens and baking bread for Polk's Corps, under direction of Maj. Murphy
Sept.–Dec. 1863	Absent, detailed at government bakery, Marietta, GA
May–June 1864	Present
26 Apr. 1865	Durham Station, NC/Surrendered
SEPARATION	1 May 1865/Greensboro, NC/Parole, released from military service

PERSONAL NARRATIVE

OCCUPATION	Plantation overseer
GENEALOGY	Son of Niklas Carl Gustave and Elizabeth (Meyers) Crumhorn, New Orleans, LA
	Married, 31 Mar. 1858, East Feliciana, LA, Sarah Elizabeth Templeton (b. 1842, East Feliciana, LA; d. 18 May 1914, New Orleans, LA)
RESIDENCES	1868, New Orleans, LA
	1870, St. John the Baptist Parish, LA
	1878, New Orleans, LA
	1891, New Orleans, LA

SOURCES

Confederate Pension Applications Collection, Louisiana State Archives
Gardner's New Orleans Directory, 1868
Louisiana Marriages, 1718–1925
NARA M320, reel 032; M1781, reel 006
New Orleans, LA, Death Records Index, 1804–1949
Obituaries: *New Orleans Times-Democrat*, 19 Apr. and Apr. 1899; *New Orleans States*, 23 Apr. 1899; *New Orleans Daily Picayune*, 19 and 23 Apr. 1899
Soards' New Orleans City Directory, 1877–78, 1891
US Census 1870

D'AQUIN, Thomas Albert

BIRTH	18 June 1838/New Orleans, LA
DEATH	2 May 1891/New Orleans, LA

RECORD OF SERVICE

CSA ENLISTMENT	1 Oct. 1862/Bardstown, KY/Duration of the war

ORLEANS LIGHT HORSE TRANSFER DATA

INBOUND	1 Oct. 1862/Private
OUTBOUND	Aug. 1864/Private

SERVICE RÉSUMÉ

1 Oct. 1862	Bardstown, KY/Received into the Orleans Light Horse
Sept.–Dec. 1862	Present
Jan.–June 1863	Present
July–Oct. 1863	Present
9 Aug. 1863	Detailed in charge of stock in pasture
7 Dec. 1863	Enterprise, MS/Application for 20-day furlough to visit family
Nov.–Dec. 1863	Absent, furlough
May–June 1864	Absent, detailed to Army of Mississippi (clerk in inspector general's department) by order of Lt. Gen. Leonidas Polk

PERSONAL NARRATIVE

OCCUPATION	Sugar broker
GENEALOGY	Son of François Adolphe and Emilie (Webre) D'Aquin, New Orleans, LA
RESIDENCES	1840, St. James Parish, LA
	1850, Jefferson Parish, LA
	1850, Mobile, AL (at school)
	1860, New Orleans, LA
	1870, New Orleans, LA
	1890, New Orleans, LA

SOURCES

NARA M320, reel 032
New Orleans, LA, Birth Records Index, 1790–1899
New Orleans, LA, Death Records Index, 1804–1949
New Orleans, LA, Directories, 1890–1891
US Census 1840, 1850, 1860, 1870

DAVIS, R. H.

RECORD OF SERVICE

CSA ENLISTMENT	22 Mar. 1862/New Orleans, LA/90 days

ORLEANS LIGHT HORSE TRANSFER DATA

INBOUND	22 Mar. 1862/Private
OUTBOUND	10 May 1862/Private

SERVICE RÉSUMÉ

Mar. 1862	New Orleans, LA/Mustered into service of CSA with the Orleans Light Horse
22 Mar.–25 May 1862	Present
SEPARATION	10 May 1862/Tupelo, MS/Discharge, unspecified

PERSONAL NARRATIVE

OCCUPATION	Western Union telegraph operator
RESIDENCES	1861, New Orleans, LA
	1903, New Orleans, LA

SOURCES
NARA, M320, reel 032
Soards' New Orleans City Directory, 1903

DELGADO, Alexander

BIRTH	8 Mar. 1844/Jamaica, British West Indies
DEATH	21 Jan. 1920/Houston, TX

RECORD OF SERVICE

CSA ENLISTMENT	5 Mar. 1862/New Orleans, LA/90 days
	11 Sept. 1862/Mumfordsville, TN/Duration of the war

ORLEANS LIGHT HORSE TRANSFER DATA

INBOUND	11 Sept. 1862/Private
OUTBOUND	4 May 1865/Private

SERVICE RÉSUMÉ

11 Sept. 1862	Mumfordsville, TN/Received into the Orleans Light Horse from the Crescent Regiment, Twenty-Fourth Louisiana Infantry
Nov.–Dec. 1862	Present
Jan.–June 1863	Present
July–Aug. 1863	Present, detailed at headquarters of Lt. Gen. Leonidas Polk
1 Aug. 1863	Detailed at office of chief of artillery
Sept.–Oct. 1863	Present
Nov.–Dec. 1863	Absent, detailed at headquarters of Lt. Gen. Polk
May–June 1864	Absent, detailed at engineer depot by order of Lt. Gen. Polk
Sept.–Dec. 1864	Clerk with Maj. Wilbur F. Foster, senior engineer, Stewart's Corps
30 Nov. 1864	Franklin, TN/Wounded
4 May 1865	Citronelle, AL/Surrendered

SEPARATION	8 May 1865/Meridian, MS/Parole, released from military service

PERSONAL NARRATIVE

OCCUPATION	Accountant, merchant
GENEALOGY	Son of Henry and Sophia (Brett) Delgado, Jamaica, British West Indies
	Arrived in New Orleans, LA, from Jamaica, Oct. 1859
	Married, 1872, New Orleans, LA, Ann Howard Bridges (b. Oct. 1855, Alabama; d. 30 Dec. 1901, Houston, TX)
RESIDENCES	1850, Jamaica, British West Indies
	1860, New Orleans, LA
	1870, New Orleans, LA
	1880, Montgomery County, TX
	1900, Houston, TX
	1910, Houston, TX

SOURCES
NARA M320, reel 032
New Orleans Passenger Lists, 1813–1945
Texas Death Index, 1903–2000
US Census 1870, 1880, 1900, 1910
www.findagrave.com, 39160403

DELRIEU, Leon Raymond

BIRTH	ca. 1824
DEATH	15 Apr. 1879/New Orleans, LA

RECORD OF SERVICE

MILITIA SERVICE	23 Nov. 1861/Active

ORLEANS LIGHT HORSE TRANSFER DATA

INBOUND	1861/Veterinary surgeon
OUTBOUND	22 Mar. 1862/Veterinary surgeon

SERVICE RÉSUMÉ

23 Nov. 1861	New Orleans, LA/Militia service with the Orleans Light Horse; present, in position of veterinary surgeon
SEPARATION	22 Mar. 1862/New Orleans, LA/Declined enlistment

PERSONAL NARRATIVE

OCCUPATION	Veterinary physician
RESIDENCES	1860, New Orleans, LA
	1879, New Orleans, LA

SOURCES
Gardner's New Orleans Directory, 1861
Louisiana, Compiled Census and Census Substitutes Index, 1791–1890
NARA M320, reel 032
New Orleans, LA, Death Records Index, 1804–1949
US Census 1860

DE MAHY, Henry J.

BIRTH	ca. 1832/Louisiana
DEATH	27 Sept. 1877/New Orleans, LA

RECORD OF SERVICE

MILITIA SERVICE	23 Nov. 1861/Absent without leave

ORLEANS LIGHT HORSE TRANSFER DATA

INBOUND	1861/Private
OUTBOUND	22 Mar. 1862/Private

SERVICE RÉSUMÉ

23 Nov. 1861	New Orleans, LA/Militia service with the Orleans Light Horse; absent without leave; failed to fulfill duties
SEPARATION	22 Mar. 1862/New Orleans, LA/Declined enlistment

PERSONAL NARRATIVE

OCCUPATION   Builder

RESIDENCES   1861, New Orleans, LA

                          1870, New Orleans, LA

SOURCES

Gardner's New Orleans Directory, 1861

NARA M320, reel 032

New Orleans, LA, Death Records Index, 1804–1949

US Census 1870

DENIS, Henri William

BIRTH   12 Jan. 1828/New Orleans, LA

DEATH   Aug. 1916/Pass Christian, MS

RECORD OF SERVICE

MILITIA SERVICE   23 Nov. 1861/Active

ORLEANS LIGHT HORSE TRANSFER DATA

    INBOUND   1861/Private

    OUTBOUND   22 Mar. 1862/Private

SERVICE RÉSUMÉ

    23 Nov. 1861   New Orleans, LA/Militia service with the

                               Orleans Light Horse; present

SEPARATION   22 Mar. 1862/New Orleans, LA/Declined enlistment

PERSONAL NARRATIVE

OCCUPATION   Attorney

GENEALOGY   Son of Henri Raphael and Marie Aimée (Derbigny) Denis,

                               New Orleans, LA

                             Married, 1872, New Orleans, LA, Arabella Harlan Bell

                                 (b. Feb. 1844, New Orleans, LA; d. 19 Mar. 1918,

                                 New Orleans, LA)

RESIDENCES   1830, New Orleans, LA

                          1850, New Orleans, LA

                          1860, New Orleans, LA

                          1880, New Orleans, LA

                          1900, New Orleans, LA

                          1910, New Orleans, LA

ADDITIONAL INFORMATION   Alternate spelling: Henry Denis

SOURCES

Gardner's New Orleans Directory, 1861

Louisiana, Compiled Census and Census Substitutes Index, 1791–1890

NARA M320, reel 032

US Census 1830, 1850, 1860, 1880, 1900, 1910

www.findagrave.com, 50789346

DILLON, J. W.

RECORD OF SERVICE

CSA ENLISTMENT	1 July 1861/Memphis, TN/90 days
	1 Sept. 1863/Chattanooga, TN/Duration of the war

ORLEANS LIGHT HORSE TRANSFER DATA

INBOUND	1 Sept. 1863/Private
OUTBOUND	28 Apr. 1865/Private

SERVICE RÉSUMÉ

1 Sept. 1863	Chattanooga, TN/Received into the Orleans Light Horse from the Twelfth Tennessee Regiment (dismounted)
Sept.–Oct. 1863	Present
Nov.–Dec. 1863	Enterprise, MS/Absent, sick, Forney's Division Hospital
18 Jan. 1864	Receipt for clothing issue
May–June 1864	Dalton, GA/Wounded, in hospital
26 Apr. 1865	Durham Station, NC/Surrendered
SEPARATION	1 May 1865/Greensboro, NC/Parole, released from military service

SOURCES

NARA M320, reel 032; M1781, reel 006

DOWSING, Jonathan Wesley

BIRTH	9 Mar. 1830/Lowndes County, MS
DEATH	29 May 1895/Birmingham, AL

RECORD OF SERVICE

CSA ENLISTMENT	22 Mar. 1862/New Orleans, LA/90 days
	25 July 1862/Tupelo, MS/Duration of the war

ORLEANS LIGHT HORSE TRANSFER DATA

INBOUND	22 Mar. 1862/Private
OUTBOUND	10 May 1865/Private

SERVICE RÉSUMÉ

22 Mar. 1862	New Orleans, LA/Mustered into service of CSA with the Orleans Light Horse
22 Mar.–25 May 1862	Present, detailed to medical staff, Surgeon William Lyles
6 June 1862	Camp Williamson, Tupelo, MS/Absent, detailed
20 June 1862	Appointed acting surgeon, Forty-First Georgia Infantry Regiment; paid for said services from 2 Aug. to 16 Dec. 1862
Nov.–Dec. 1862	Absent without leave
Jan.–Feb. 1863	Absent, sick
Mar.–Apr. 1863	Reported as a deserter
May–June 1863	Present, returned from desertion 12 June 1863 in accordance with Gen. Braxton Bragg's amnesty order; bounty for reenlisting, $50
July–Oct. 1863	Rome, GA/Absent, sick in hospital

Nov.–Dec. 1863	Present
May–June 1864	Absent, detailed to hospital per order of
	Lt. Gen. Alexander P. Stewart
SEPARATION	10 May 1865/Memphis, TN/Parole, released from
	military service

PERSONAL NARRATIVE

OCCUPATION	Physician
GENEALOGY	Son of William and Ellen V. Dowsing, New Orleans, LA
	Married, about 1869, Rio de Janeiro, Brazil, Louisa ——
	(b. ca. 1836, Brazil; d. ca. 1930, Birmingham, AL)
RESIDENCES	1850, Lowndes County, MS
	1860, Washington, DC
	1861, New Orleans, LA
	1867–72, Rio de Janeiro, Brazil
	1888, Birmingham, AL

SOURCES

Antunes de Oliveira, 183–90
Birmingham, AL, Directories, 1888–1890
NARA M320, reel 032
New York Passenger Lists, 1820–1957
US and Canada, Passenger and Immigration Lists Index, 1500s–1900s
US Census 1850; 1860
www.findagrave.com, 15296988

DUBOSE, F. M.

RECORD OF SERVICE

CSA ENLISTMENT	7 May 1864/Demopolis, AL/Duration of the war
ORLEANS LIGHT HORSE TRANSFER DATA	
INBOUND	7 May 1864/Private
OUTBOUND	Aug. 1864/Private
SERVICE RÉSUMÉ	
7 May 1864	Demopolis, AL/Received into the Orleans Light Horse
May–June 1864	Absent, sick

SOURCES

NARA M320, reel 032

DUBOSE, N. W.

RECORD OF SERVICE

CSA ENLISTMENT	7 May 1864/Demopolis, AL/Duration of the war
ORLEANS LIGHT HORSE TRANSFER DATA	
INBOUND	7 May 1864/Private
OUTBOUND	8 May 1865/Private
SERVICE RÉSUMÉ	
7 May 1864	Demopolis, AL/Received into the Orleans Light Horse

May–June 1864	Absent, sick
4 May 1865	Citronelle, AL/Surrendered
SEPARATION	8 May 1865/Meridian, MS/Parole, released from military service

SOURCES
NARA M320, reel 032

DUNCAN, Samuel P.

| BIRTH | ca. 1809/Maine |

RECORD OF SERVICE

| MILITIA SERVICE | 23 Nov. 1861/Absent without leave |

ORLEANS LIGHT HORSE TRANSFER DATA

| INBOUND | 1861/Private |
| OUTBOUND | 22 Mar. 1862/Private |

SERVICE RÉSUMÉ

| 23 Nov. 1861 | New Orleans, LA/Militia service with the Orleans Light Horse; absent without leave; failed to fulfill duties |
| SEPARATION | 22 Mar. 1862/New Orleans, LA/Declined enlistment |

PERSONAL NARRATIVE

OCCUPATION	Riverboat captain
GENEALOGY	Married, ca. 1855, Mary E. —— (b. ca. 1829, District of Columbia)
RESIDENCES	1850, Orleans Parish, LA
	1860, Tensas Parish, LA

SOURCES
Louisiana, Compiled Census and Census Substitutes Index, 1791–1890
NARA M320, reel 032
US Census 1850, 1860

EBERLE, G.

RECORD OF SERVICE

| CSA ENLISTMENT | 22 Mar. 1862/New Orleans, LA/90 days |

ORLEANS LIGHT HORSE TRANSFER DATA

| INBOUND | 22 Mar. 1862/Private |
| OUTBOUND | 23 June 1862/Saddler |

SERVICE RÉSUMÉ

22 Mar. 1862	New Orleans, LA/Mustered into service of CSA with the Orleans Light Horse
22 Mar.–25 May 1862	Present
6 June 1862	Camp Williamson, Tupelo, MS/Approved for discharge
SEPARATION	23 June 1862/Tupelo, MS/Discharge, unspecified

SOURCES
NARA M320, reel 032

EGELLY, Charles Robert

BIRTH   25 Apr. 1845/Louisiana
DEATH   23 Feb. 1903/Lake Providence, LA

RECORD OF SERVICE

CSA ENLISTMENT   1 Oct. 1862/Bardstown, KY/Duration of the war
ORLEANS LIGHT HORSE TRANSFER DATA
     INBOUND   1 Oct. 1862/Private
     OUTBOUND   Aug. 1864/Sergeant
SERVICE RÉSUMÉ
     1 Oct. 1862   Bardstown, KY/Received into the Orleans Light Horse
     Sept.–Dec. 1862   Present
     Jan.–June 1863   Present
     July–Oct. 1863   Present
     Nov.–Dec. 1863   Present, in position of commissary sergeant
     May–June 1864   Present, in position of commissary sergeant

PERSONAL NARRATIVE

OCCUPATION   Merchant, collections agent
GENEALOGY   Married, 3 Jan. 1868, East Carroll Parish, LA, Nancy
                                Houghton Green (b. 13 Jan. 1849, East Carroll Parish,
                                LA; d. 11 Dec. 1903, New Orleans, LA)
RESIDENCES   1870, Lake Providence, LA
                                1880, East Carroll Parish, LA
                                1900, East Carroll Parish, LA

SOURCES

NARA M320, reel 032
Obituaries: Mrs. C. R. Egelley, *New Orleans Daily Picayune*, 12 Dec. 1903; *New Orleans Times-Democrat*, 12 Dec. 1903
US Census 1870, 1880, 1900
www.findagrave.com, 43664679

ELENTERIUS, Louis C.

RECORD OF SERVICE

CSA ENLISTMENT   2 June 1862/Baldwyn, MS/Duration of the war
ORLEANS LIGHT HORSE TRANSFER DATA
     INBOUND   2 June 1862/Private
     OUTBOUND   Feb. 1864/Private
SERVICE RÉSUMÉ
     2 June 1862   Baldwyn, MS/Received into the Orleans Light Horse
     Sept.–Dec. 1862   Present
     Jan.–June 1863   Present
     19 June 1863   Detailed as company cook
     July–Dec. 1863   Present

PERSONAL NARRATIVE

OCCUPATION   Retail merchant
RESIDENCES   1861, New Orleans, LA
                      1865, New Orleans, LA

SOURCES

NARA M320, reel 032; M711, reel 081
US IRS Tax Assessment Lists, 1862–1918

FAZENDE, Leon Jacques

BIRTH   Oct. 1827/Louisiana
DEATH   26 Mar. 1907/New Orleans, LA

RECORD OF SERVICE

CSA ENLISTMENT   22 Mar. 1862/New Orleans, LA/90 days
                      25 July 1862/Tupelo, MS/Duration of the war

ORLEANS LIGHT HORSE TRANSFER DATA

  INBOUND   22 Mar. 1862/Private
  OUTBOUND   June 1862/Private

SERVICE RÉSUMÉ

  22 Mar. 1862   New Orleans, LA/Mustered into service of CSA with the
                        Orleans Light Horse
  22 Mar.–25 May 1862 Present
  6 June 1862   Camp Williamson, Tupelo, MS/Approved for discharge
SEPARATION   June 1862/Tupelo, MS/Discharge, unspecified

PERSONAL NARRATIVE

OCCUPATION   Clerk, conveyance office
GENEALOGY   Son of Rene and Eulalia (Villeré) Fazende, New Orleans, LA
                      Married, 12 Mar. 1853, New Orleans, LA, Pauline Cousin
                        (b. 16 Aug. 1833, New Orleans, LA; d. 14 Nov. 1917,
                        New Orleans, LA)
RESIDENCES   1860, New Orleans, LA
                      1890, New Orleans, LA
                      1900, New Orleans, LA

SOURCES

Louisiana, Compiled Census and Census Substitutes Index, 1791–1890
NARA M320, reel 032
New Orleans, LA, Death Records Index, 1804–1949
New Orleans, LA, Directories, 1890–1891
US Census 1850, 1860, 1900
www.findagrave.com, 103052044

FISHER, John Henry

BIRTH   26 June 1841/Chattanooga, TN
DEATH   1 Mar. 1892/Greenville, MS

RECORD OF SERVICE

CSA ENLISTMENT   1 July 1861/Memphis, TN/One year
                     1 Sept. 1863/Chattanooga, TN/Duration of the war

ORLEANS LIGHT HORSE TRANSFER DATA
    INBOUND   1 Sept. 1863/Private
    OUTBOUND   4 May 1865/Private

SERVICE RÉSUMÉ
    1 Sept. 1863   Chattanooga, TN/Received into the Orleans Light Horse
                         from the Twelfth Tennessee Regiment (dismounted)
    Sept.–Dec. 1863 Present
    19 Sept. 1863   Chickamauga, GA/On duty as headquarters courier;
                         involved in controversy that caused Lt. Gen. Leonidas
                         Polk to be relieved of command
    May–June 1864   Present
    26 Apr. 1865   Durham Station, NC/Surrendered

SEPARATION   4 May 1865/Greensboro, NC/Parole, released from
                         military service

PERSONAL NARRATIVE

OCCUPATION   Carpenter
GENEALOGY   Son of Louis and Sarah (Stanley) Fisher, St. Mary Parish, LA
                     Married, 11 May 1881, Tensas Parish, LA, Lucinda J. Roy
                         (b. 1 Apr. 1853, Tensas Parish, LA; d. 3 Oct. 1929,
                         Greenville, MS)
RESIDENCES   1850, St. Mary Parish, LA
                     1860, St. Mary Parish, LA
                     1890, New Orleans, LA

SOURCES

Louisiana Marriages, 1718–1925
NARA M320, reel 032; M1781, reel 006
New Orleans, LA, Directories, 1890–1891
OR, ser. 1, vol. 30, pt. 2:57–58
US Census 1850, 1860
www.findagrave.com, 31873163

FLEITAS, Jean Baptiste

BIRTH   1836/Louisiana
DEATH   27 May 1866/New Orleans, LA

RECORD OF SERVICE

MILITIA SERVICE   23 Nov. 1861/Active
CSA ENLISTMENT   22 Mar. 1862/New Orleans, LA/90 days
                     25 July 1862/Tupelo, MS/Duration of the war

ORLEANS LIGHT HORSE TRANSFER DATA
INBOUND	1861/Private
OUTBOUND	Aug. 1863/Private

SERVICE RÉSUMÉ
23 Nov. 1861	New Orleans, LA/Militia service with the Orleans Light Horse; present
22 Mar. 1862	New Orleans, LA/Mustered into service of CSA
22 Mar.–25 May 1862	Present
6 June 1862	Camp Williamson, Tupelo, MS/Absent, sick
25 May 1862	Tupelo, MS/Sick in camp
Sept.–Oct. 1862	Absent, sick
Nov.–Dec. 1862	Absent without leave
Jan.–Feb. 1863	Absent without leave
Mar.–Apr. 1863	Reported as deserter
May–June 1863	Present, returned from desertion with surgeon's certificate of inability

PERSONAL NARRATIVE
OCCUPATION	Farmer
GENEALOGY	Son of Paulin Joseph and Celestine (Jumonville deVilliers) Fleitas, New Orleans, LA
	Married, 1855, Louisiana, Jeanne Louise Troxler (b. ca. 1840, Louisiana; d. 25 Mar. 1895, New Orleans, LA)
RESIDENCES	1850, New Orleans, LA
	1860, St. Charles Parish, LA

SOURCES
NARA M320, reel 032
New Orleans, LA, Death Records Index, 1804–1949
US Census 1850, 1860

FLOYD, Thomas M.

BIRTH	ca. 1843/Virginia
DEATH	ca. 1880/Louisiana

RECORD OF SERVICE
CSA ENLISTMENT	1 June 1861/Memphis, TN/One year
	1 Sept. 1863/Chattanooga, TN/Duration of the war

ORLEANS LIGHT HORSE TRANSFER DATA
INBOUND	1 Sept. 1863/Private
OUTBOUND	6 June 1864/Private

SERVICE RÉSUMÉ
1 Sept. 1863	Chattanooga, TN/Received into the Orleans Light Horse from the Twelfth Tennessee Regiment
Sept.–Dec. 1863	Present
May–June 1864	Marietta, GA/Deserted
SEPARATION	6 June 1864/Marietta, GA/Deserter, dropped from rolls

OCCUPATION · Rail splitter

GENEALOGY · Married, ca. 1869, Louisiana, Odilla —— (b. ca. 1851, Louisiana)

RESIDENCES · 1870, Iberia Parish, LA
1880, Lafayette Parish, LA

SOURCES

Civil War Prisoner of War Records, 1861–1865

NARA M320, reel 032

US Census 1870, 1880

FOLEY, Thomas William Pierre

BIRTH · 5 Apr. 1837/Plattenville, LA

DEATH · 10 Feb. 1866/New Orleans, LA

RECORD OF SERVICE

CSA ENLISTMENT · 22 Mar. 1862/New Orleans, LA/90 days
25 July 1862/Tupelo, MS/Duration of the war

ORLEANS LIGHT HORSE TRANSFER DATA

    INBOUND · 22 Mar. 1862/Private

    OUTBOUND · Aug. 1862/Private

SERVICE RÉSUMÉ

    22 Mar. 1862 · New Orleans, LA/Mustered into service of CSA with the Orleans Light Horse

    22 Mar.–25 May 1862 · Present

    6 June 1862 · Camp Williamson, Tupelo, MS/Absent, detailed

PERSONAL NARRATIVE

OCCUPATION · Physician

GENEALOGY · Son of Arthur Morgan and Marcelite (Blanchard) Foley, Napoleonville, LA
Brother-in-law of James John and Samuel Robert Stewart Jr.
Married, 24 Dec. 1860, New Orleans, LA, Terese Ophelia Stewart (b. 10 Jan. 1839, New Orleans, LA; d. 9 Dec. 1923, Louisville, KY)

RESIDENCES · 1850, Assumption Parish, LA
1860, Assumption Parish, LA
1866, New Orleans, LA

SOURCES

NARA M320, reel 032

New Orleans, LA, Death Records Index, 1804–1949

US Census 1850, 1860

www.findagrave.com, 94569836

FOSTER, George

BIRTH 1822/Boston, MA
DEATH 26 Nov. 1877/New Orleans, LA

RECORD OF SERVICE

MILITIA SERVICE 23 Nov. 1861/Active
CSA ENLISTMENT 22 Mar. 1862/New Orleans, LA/90 days
ORLEANS LIGHT HORSE TRANSFER DATA
 INBOUND 1861/Sergeant
 OUTBOUND 28 June 1862/Lieutenant
SERVICE RÉSUMÉ
 23 Nov. 1861 New Orleans, LA/Militia service with the Orleans Light
     Horse; present, in position of orderly sergeant
 22 Mar. 1862 New Orleans, LA/Mustered into service of CSA,
     in position of second lieutenant
 25 May 1862 Tupelo, MS/Present, in position of second lieutenant
SEPARATION 28 June 1862/Tupelo, MS/Honorable discharge in position of
     first lieutenant, unspecified

PERSONAL NARRATIVE

OCCUPATION Dry goods merchant
GENEALOGY Married, 1862, New Orleans, LA, Katte —— (b. 1840,
     Louisiana; d. 24 Dec. 1894, New Orleans, LA)
RESIDENCES 1850, New Orleans, LA
     1860, New Orleans, LA
     1870, New Orleans, LA

SOURCES

NARA M320, reel 032
Obituaries: *New Orleans Daily Picayune*, 27 Nov. 1877; Mrs. George Foster,
 New Orleans Daily Picayune, 26 Dec. 1894
US Census 1850, 1860, 1870

FOX, W. H.

RECORD OF SERVICE

CSA ENLISTMENT 11 Apr. 1864/Demopolis, AL/Duration of the war
ORLEANS LIGHT HORSE TRANSFER DATA
 INBOUND 11 Apr. 1864/Private
 OUTBOUND June 1864/Private
SERVICE RÉSUMÉ
 11 Apr. 1864 Demopolis, AL/Received into the Orleans Light Horse
 May–June 1864 Present
SOURCES
NARA M320, reel 032

FREDERIC, S.

BIRTH   ca. 1815/Germany
RECORD OF SERVICE
ORLEANS LIGHT HORSE TRANSFER DATA
    INBOUND   25 Oct. 1862/Private
    OUTBOUND   25 Oct. 1862/Private
SERVICE RÉSUMÉ
    25 Oct. 1862   On a list of prisoners of war leaving Cairo, IL, for
                    Vicksburg, MS, for exchange

PERSONAL NARRATIVE
GENEALOGY   Arrived in New Orleans, LA, 1835
RESIDENCES   1860, Bonnet Carré, LA
SOURCES
Louisiana, Compiled Census and Census Substitutes Index, 1791–1890
NARA M320, reel 032
New Orleans Passenger List Quarterly Abstracts, 1820–1875
US Census 1860

FRERET, Frederick George

BIRTH   Dec. 1839/Louisiana
DEATH   14 Mar. 1904/New Orleans, LA
RECORD OF SERVICE
CSA ENLISTMENT   22 Mar. 1862/New Orleans, LA/90 days
                             25 July 1862/Tupelo, MS/Duration of the war
ORLEANS LIGHT HORSE TRANSFER DATA
    INBOUND   22 Mar. 1862/Sergeant
    OUTBOUND   Aug. 1862/Sergeant
SERVICE RÉSUMÉ
    22 Mar. 1862   New Orleans, LA/Mustered into service of CSA with the
                    Orleans Light Horse
    22 Mar.–25 May 1862   Present, in rank of sergeant
    6 June 1862   Camp Williamson, Tupelo, MS/Present, in rank
                    of sergeant

PERSONAL NARRATIVE
OCCUPATION   Insurance executive
GENEALOGY   Son of William Alfred and Frances (Salkeld) Freret,
                    New Orleans, LA
                    Brother of William A. Freret II; brother-in-law of
                    John G. Byrd
                    Married, 1861, Ascension Parish, LA, Lise Jones McCall
                    (b. 30 Sept. 1842, Louisiana; d. 30 May 1914,
                    New Orleans, LA)

RESIDENCES   1850, New Orleans, LA
                           1861, New Orleans, LA
                           1880, New Orleans, LA
                           1900, New Orleans, LA

SOURCES

NARA M320, reel 032

New Orleans, LA, Death Records Index, 1804–1949

Obituaries: *New Orleans Daily Picayune*, 15, 16, and 20 Mar. 1904; *New Orleans Times-Democrat*, 15 and 30 Mar. 1904

US Census 1850, 1880, 1900

US and International Marriage Records, 1560–1900

www.findagrave.com, 11894153

FRERET, William Alfred, II

BIRTH   19 Jan. 1833/New Orleans, LA
DEATH   5 Dec. 1911/New Orleans, LA

RECORD OF SERVICE

MILITIA SERVICE   23 Nov. 1861/Active
CSA ENLISTMENT   22 Mar. 1862/New Orleans, LA/90 days

ORLEANS LIGHT HORSE TRANSFER DATA

  INBOUND   1861/Corporal
  OUTBOUND   June 1862/Private

SERVICE RÉSUMÉ

  23 Nov. 1861   New Orleans, LA/Militia service with the Orleans Light
                           Horse; present, in rank of corporal
  22 Mar. 1862   New Orleans, LA/Mustered into service of CSA, in rank
                           of corporal
  25 May 1862   Tupelo, MS/Permitted by Capt. Thomas L. Leeds to
                           accompany Washington Artillery, in rank of private
                           (possibly an exchange with Robert W. Simmons, received
                           from the Washington Artillery)
  6 June 1862   Camp Williamson, Tupelo, MS/Transferred to Fifth Co.,
                           Washington Artillery

PERSONAL NARRATIVE

OCCUPATION   Architect
GENEALOGY   Son of William Alfred and Frances (Salkeld) Freret,
                           New Orleans, LA
                           Brother of Frederick G. Freret
                           Married, 23 Dec. 1865, Yalobusha County, MS, Caroline C.
                           Lewis (b. 16 Aug. 1839, Louisiana; d. 18 Dec. 1923,
                           New Orleans, LA)
RESIDENCES   1850, New Orleans, LA
                           1862, New Orleans, LA
                           1880, New Orleans, LA
                           1910, New Orleans, LA

SOURCES
Confederate Applications for Presidential Pardons, 1865–1867
Confederate Pension Applications Collection, Louisiana State Archives
Mississippi Marriages, 1776–1935
NARA M320, reel 032
New Orleans, LA, Death Records Index, 1804–1949
Obituary: *New Orleans Daily Picayune*, 6 Dec. 1911
US Census 1850, 1880, 1910
www.findagrave.com, 70632843

FRERICHS, Adolph

BIRTH	28 Feb. 1834/Germany
DEATH	29 Sept. 1885/Bremen, Germany

RECORD OF SERVICE

MILITIA SERVICE	23 Nov. 1861/Active

ORLEANS LIGHT HORSE TRANSFER DATA

INBOUND	1861/Private
OUTBOUND	22 Mar. 1862/Private

SERVICE RÉSUMÉ

23 Nov. 1861	New Orleans, LA/Militia service with the Orleans Light Horse; present
SEPARATION	22 Mar. 1862/New Orleans, LA/Declined enlistment

PERSONAL NARRATIVE

OCCUPATION	Cotton factor
GENEALOGY	Son of Hermann and Wilhelmina (Kleine) Frerichs, Bremen, Germany
	Married, 15 Oct. 1862, New Orleans, LA, Marie Josephine Althée D'Aquin (b. 12 Aug. 1841, New Orleans, LA; d. 21 May 1912, New Orleans, LA)
RESIDENCES	1861, New Orleans, LA
	1865, New Orleans, LA
	1866, New Orleans, LA
	1869, New Orleans, LA
	1872, New Orleans, LA
	1875, New Orleans, LA
ADDITIONAL INFORMATION	Alternate spelling: A. Freriche

SOURCES
Edwards' Annual Director, 1872
Gardner's New Orleans Directory, 1861, 1869
NARA M320, reel 032
New Orleans, LA, Justices of the Peace Index to Marriage Records, 1846–1880
Obituary: *New York Times*, 30 Sept. 1885
Soards' New Orleans City Directory, 1875
US IRS Tax Assessment Lists, 1862–1918

GALLIER, James, Jr.

BIRTH	25 Sept. 1827/Huntingdonshire, England
DEATH	16 May 1868/New Orleans, LA

RECORD OF SERVICE

MILITIA SERVICE	23 Nov. 1861/Active

ORLEANS LIGHT HORSE TRANSFER DATA

INBOUND	1861/Private
OUTBOUND	22 Mar. 1862/Private

SERVICE RÉSUMÉ

23 Nov. 1861	New Orleans, LA/Militia service with the Orleans Light Horse; present
SEPARATION	22 Mar. 1862/New Orleans, LA/Declined enlistment

PERSONAL NARRATIVE

OCCUPATION	Architect, builder
GENEALOGY	Son of James and Elizabeth (Tyler) Gallier
	Arrived in New York, 27 Mar. 1832
	Married, 29 Jan. 1853, St. Bernard, LA, Josephine Aglae Villavaso (b. 1835, St. Bernard, LA; d. 9 Dec. 1906, New Orleans, LA)
RESIDENCES	1834, New Orleans, LA
	1840, New Orleans, LA
	1850, New Orleans, LA
	1860, New Orleans, LA
	1865, New Orleans, LA

SOURCES

Gallier, 10–18
NARA M320, reel 032; M237, reel 016
New Orleans, LA, Death Records Index, 1804–1949
US Census 1840, 1850, 1860
US IRS Tax Assessment Lists, 1862–1918
Van Zante, www.knowla.org/entry/815
www.findagrave.com, 94570013

GALLWEY, Charles

BIRTH	1838/New Orleans, LA
DEATH	23 Nov. 1884/New Orleans, LA

RECORD OF SERVICE

CSA ENLISTMENT	22 Mar. 1862/New Orleans, LA/90 days
	25 July 1862/Tupelo, MS/Duration of the war

ORLEANS LIGHT HORSE TRANSFER DATA

INBOUND	22 Mar. 1862/Private
OUTBOUND	Aug. 1864/Sergeant

22 Mar. 1862	New Orleans, LA/Mustered into service of CSA with the Orleans Light Horse
22 Mar.–25 May 1862	Present, in rank of private
6 June 1862	Camp Williamson, Tupelo, MS/Absent, detailed in rank of private
Sept.–Oct. 1862	Knoxville, TN/Present, promoted to sergeant
Nov.–Dec. 1862	Absent, duty in rank of sergeant
Jan.–Feb. 1863	Absent, furlough in rank of sergeant
Mar.–Apr. 1863	Shelbyville, TN/Present, in rank of sergeant
May–Jun. 1863	Present, promoted orderly sergeant 31 May 1863
July–Dec. 1863	Present, in position of orderly sergeant
May–June 1864	Resaca, GA/Present, in position of orderly sergeant

PERSONAL NARRATIVE

OCCUPATION	Clerk, cotton brokerage
GENEALOGY	Son of Patrice Henry and Zoe (Vienne) Gallwey, New Orleans, LA
RESIDENCES	1840, New Orleans, LA
	1850, New Orleans, LA
	1860, New Orleans, LA
	1870, New Orleans, LA
	1880, New Orleans, LA

SOURCES

NARA M320, reel 032
Obituary: *New Orleans Daily Picayune*, 24 and 30 Nov. 1884
US Census 1840, 1850, 1860, 1870, 1880

GARDNER, Livingston Hall, Sr.

BIRTH	7 Nov. 1836/Louisiana
DEATH	23 Nov. 1910/New Orleans, LA

RECORD OF SERVICE

CSA ENLISTMENT	22 Mar. 1862/New Orleans, LA/90 days

ORLEANS LIGHT HORSE TRANSFER DATA

INBOUND	22 Mar. 1862/Private
OUTBOUND	6 June 1862/Private

SERVICE RÉSUMÉ

22 Mar. 1862	New Orleans, LA/Mustered into service of CSA with the Orleans Light Horse
22 Mar.–25 May 1862	Present
SEPARATION	6 June 1862/Tupelo, MS/Discharge, unspecified

PERSONAL NARRATIVE

OCCUPATION	Cotton factor

GENEALOGY	Son of Phineas and Eliza Jane (Hall) Gardner, Warren County, MS
	Married, 11 Mar. 1858, Baldwin County, AL, Elizabeth Hudson (b. June 1840, LA; d. 1 Jan. 1927, St. Mary Parish, LA)
RESIDENCES	1858, New Orleans, LA
	1860, New Orleans, LA
	1870, New Orleans, LA
	1880, New Orleans, LA
	1900, New Orleans, LA
	1910, New Orleans, LA

SOURCES

Alabama Marriage Collection, 1800–1969
Alabama Marriages, 1809–1920 (Selected Counties)
NARA M320, reel 032
New Orleans, LA, Death Records Index, 1804–1949
US Census 1860, 1870, 1880, 1900, 1900, 1910
www.findagrave.com, 77926395

GATCH, Joseph A. R.

BIRTH	ca. 1836/Maryland
RECORD OF SERVICE	
CSA ENLISTMENT	19 Feb. 1863/Shelbyville, TN/Duration of the war
ORLEANS LIGHT HORSE TRANSFER DATA	
INBOUND	19 Feb. 1863/Private
OUTBOUND	31 May 1863/Private
SERVICE RÉSUMÉ	
19 Feb. 1863	Shelbyville, TN/Received into the Orleans Light Horse
13 May 1863	Received clothing issue
SEPARATION	31 May 1863/Shelbyville, TN/Deserter, dropped from rolls
PERSONAL NARRATIVE	
OCCUPATION	Harness maker
RESIDENCES	1870, Baltimore, MD
	1880, Howard County, MD

SOURCES

NARA M320, reel 032
US Census 1870, 1880

GLYNN, Michael

BIRTH	6 Nov. 1838/Ireland
DEATH	24 Apr. 1918/Franklin, LA
RECORD OF SERVICE	
CSA ENLISTMENT	1 July 1861/Memphis, TN/One year
	1 Sept. 1863/Chattanooga, TN/Duration of the war

ORLEANS LIGHT HORSE TRANSFER DATA
INBOUND 1 Sept. 1863/Private
OUTBOUND 1 May 1865/Private
SERVICE RÉSUMÉ
1 Sept. 1863 Chattanooga, TN/Received into the Orleans Light Horse
from the Twelfth Tennessee Regiment (dismounted)
Sept.–Oct. 1863 Present
Nov.–Dec. 1863 Enterprise, MS/Absent, sick, Forney's Division Hospital
May–June 1864 Present
26 Apr. 1865 Durham Station, NC/Surrendered
SEPARATION 1 May 1865/Greensboro, NC/Parole, released from
military service

PERSONAL NARRATIVE
OCCUPATION Retail grocer
GENEALOGY Arrived in Boston, MA, 6 Apr. 1850 (age 11)
Married, ca. 1865, St. Mary Parish, LA, Mary Verret (b. 8 July
1842, New Orleans, LA; d. 19 Mar. 1896, Franklin,
St. Mary Parish, LA)
RESIDENCES 1850, Boston, MA
1861, Memphis, TN
1865, Louisiana
1870, Franklin, LA
1910, Franklin, LA

SOURCES
Boston, 1821–1850, Passenger and Immigration Lists
Confederate Pension Applications Collection, Louisiana State Archives
Louisiana Statewide Death Index, 1900–1949
NARA M320, reel 032; M1781, reel 006
US Census 1870, 1910
www.findagrave.com, 61292303

GORDON, William Alexander

BIRTH 1828/Ross, Scotland
DEATH 1 Mar. 1885/Chatawa, MS
RECORD OF SERVICE
MILITIA SERVICE 23 Nov. 1861/Active
CSA ENLISTMENT 22 Mar. 1862/New Orleans, LA/90 days
25 July 1862/Tupelo, MS/Duration of the war
ORLEANS LIGHT HORSE TRANSFER DATA
INBOUND 1861/Lieutenant
OUTBOUND 7 Mar. 1864/Lieutenant
SERVICE RÉSUMÉ
1 July 1861 Letter to Maj. Gen. Leonidas Polk; application for staff
appointment
23 Nov. 1861 New Orleans, LA/Militia service with the Orleans Light
Horse; present, in position of second lieutenant

22 Mar. 1862	New Orleans, LA/Mustered into service of CSA, in position of first lieutenant
1 May 1862	Detailed for court, in position of first lieutenant
16 Apr.–23 Oct. 1862	First lieutenant, acting commander, Orleans Light Horse
25 May 1862	Corinth, MS/Present, in position of first lieutenant
24 Oct. 1862	Detailed
26 Jan. 1863	Detailed, assistant inspector general, Mississippi seacoast and eastern Louisiana
29 Jan. 1864	Requested for conscription duty in Mobile, AL
5 Mar. 1864	Medical evaluation: unfit for field service, congenital presbyopia
7 Mar. 1864	Demopolis, AL/Transferred to Conscript Bureau, CSA headquarters, Mobile, AL

PERSONAL NARRATIVE

OCCUPATION	Attorney, partner in the firm of Gordon and Castile, New Orleans, LA
GENEALOGY	Son of Alexander and Ann (Bakewell) Gordon, Ross, Scotland
	Arrived in New York, NY, 11 Nov. 1831 (age 3)
	Married, ca. 1853, New Orleans, LA, Mary Cartwright (b. June 1836, Philadelphia, PA; d. July 1889, Philadelphia, PA)
RESIDENCES	1850, New Orleans, LA
	1860, New Orleans, LA
	1870, Pike County, MS
	1880, New Orleans, LA
	1885, Chatawa, MS

SOURCES

Gardner's New Orleans Directory, 1861
NARA M320, reel 032
New York Passenger and Immigration Lists, 1820–1850
New York Passenger Lists, 1820–1957
Obituary: *New Orleans Daily Picayune*, 2 and 8 Mar. 1885
US Census 1850, 1860, 1870, 1880
www.findagrave.com, 26065033

GREENLEAF, James Leeds

| BIRTH | 6 Mar. 1834/New Orleans, LA |
| DEATH | 13 June 1894/New Orleans, LA |

RECORD OF SERVICE

MILITIA SERVICE	23 Nov. 1861/Active
CSA ENLISTMENT	22 Mar. 1862/New Orleans, LA/90 days
	25 July 1862/Tupelo, MS/Duration of the war
ORLEANS LIGHT HORSE TRANSFER DATA	
INBOUND	1861/Sergeant
OUTBOUND	1 May 1865/Captain

23 Nov. 1861	New Orleans, LA/Militia service with the Orleans Light Horse; present, in rank of sergeant
22 Mar. 1862	New Orleans, LA/Mustered into service of CSA in position of third lieutenant
25 May 1862	Tupelo, MS/Present, in position of third lieutenant
24 Oct. 1862	Knoxville, TN/Acting commander, in position of first lieutenant
1 Nov. 1862	Murfreesboro, TN/Promoted to rank of captain; confirmed as commander
Jan.–Apr. 1863	Present, in rank of captain
July–Dec. 1863	Present, in rank of captain
17 Jan. 1864	Meridian, MS/Absent, furlough
May–June 1864	Present, in rank of captain
Sept. 1864	Commended by Lt. Gen. Alexander P. Stewart in dispatches as a result of action at Peachtree Creek in the battle for Atlanta, GA
Oct. 1864	Executed pay voucher
26 Apr. 1865	Durham Station, NC/Surrendered
SEPARATION	1 May 1865/Greensboro, NC/Parole, released from military service

PERSONAL NARRATIVE

OCCUPATION   Cashier (Leeds Foundry, New Orleans, LA)

GENEALOGY   Son of James and Sara (Leeds) Greenleaf
Cousin of Thomas L. Leeds
Married, 21 Dec. 1865, New Orleans, LA, Josephine Skinner
(b. 1834, New Orleans, LA; d. 27 Dec. 1909,
New Orleans, LA)

ADDITIONAL INFORMATION   Obituary data: "Born in New Orleans . . . but soon removed to Connecticut, in which state he was reared and educated. . . [later] he came to New Orleans and engaged in business with the Leeds foundry . . . Soon after going to the front, he was promoted to a captaincy and was assigned to duty upon the staff of General Leonidas Polk, with whom he served till the death of that general. He did staff duty during the remainder of the war. When hostilities had ceased [he] returned to New Orleans and became the cashier of the Leeds foundry, a position he held acceptably till his death."

SOURCES
Greenleaf, 175, 225
NARA M320, reel 032; M1781, reel 006
New Orleans, LA, Death Records Index, 1804–1949
Obituary: *New Orleans Daily Picayune*, 14 and 17 June 1894
OR, ser. 1, v. 38:872
US Census 1840, 1860
Wildey, 419

GRIBBLE, William Carroll

BIRTH	Jan. 1831/Tennessee
DEATH	7 Nov. 1910/Warren County, TN

RECORD OF SERVICE

CSA ENLISTMENT	17 Aug. 1863/Chattanooga, TN/Duration of the war

ORLEANS LIGHT HORSE TRANSFER DATA

INBOUND	17 Aug. 1863/Private
OUTBOUND	9 June 1864/Private

SERVICE RÉSUMÉ

17 Aug. 1863	Chattanooga, TN/Received into the Orleans Light Horse
Nov.–Dec. 1863	Newman, GA/Detailed to duty at quartermaster depot
May–June 1864	Absent, detailed to Army of Mississippi by order of Lt. Gen. Leonidas Polk
3 June 1864	Medical evaluation: unfit for field service; dyspepsia and debility with emaciation
9 June 1864	Greenville, AL/Assigned to duty at commissary depot, by reason of surgeon's certificate of disability

PERSONAL NARRATIVE

OCCUPATION	Farmer
GENEALOGY	Son of John Carmack and Susan (Roberts) Gribble, Warren County, TN
	Married (1), 8 June 1855, Warren County, TN, Mary J. Campaigne (b. 1822, North Carolina; d. ca. 1869, Warren County, TN)
	Married (2), 1904, Van Buren County, TN, Annie —— (b. ca. 1871, Tennessee)
RESIDENCES	1840, Warren County, TN
	1850, Warren County, TN
	1860, Warren County, TN
	1870, Warren County, TN
	1880, Warren County, TN
	1900, Van Buren County, TN
	1910, Van Buren County, TN

SOURCES

NARA M320, reel 032
US Census 1840, 1850, 1860, 1870, 1880, 1900, 1910
Tennessee State Marriages, 1780–2002
Tennessee Marriages, 1851–1900
www.findagrave.com, 37543873

GRIFFITH, Robert S.

RECORD OF SERVICE

CSA ENLISTMENT   22 Mar. 1862/New Orleans, LA/90 days

25 July 1862/Tupelo, MS/Duration of the war

ORLEANS LIGHT HORSE TRANSFER DATA

INBOUND   22 Mar. 1862/Private

OUTBOUND   Aug. 1864/Corporal

SERVICE RÉSUMÉ

22 Mar. 1862	New Orleans, LA/Mustered into service of CSA with the Orleans Light Horse
25 May 1862	Holly Springs, MS/Absent, sick
6 June 1862	Camp Williamson, Tupelo, MS/Absent, sick, in rank of corporal
Sept.–Oct. 1862	Present, in rank of corporal
Nov.–Dec. 1862	Present, in rank of corporal
Jan.–Apr. 1863	Present, in rank of corporal
May–June 1863	Absent, sick, in rank of corporal
July–Aug. 1863	Present, in rank of corporal
Sept.–Oct. 1863	Rome, GA/Absent, sick in hospital, in rank of corporal
Nov.–Dec. 1863	Absent, furlough, in rank of corporal
May–June 1864	Absent, detailed in Trans-Mississippi Department by Lt. Gen. Leonidas Polk

SOURCES

NARA M320, reel 032

GRISWOLD, Arthur Breese

BIRTH   9 Sept. 1829/Utica, NY

DEATH   30 May 1877/Poughkeepsie, NY

RECORD OF SERVICE

MILITIA SERVICE   23 Nov. 1861/Active

ORLEANS LIGHT HORSE TRANSFER DATA

INBOUND   1861/Private

OUTBOUND   22 Mar. 1862/Private

SERVICE RÉSUMÉ

23 Nov. 1861   New Orleans, LA/Militia service with the Orleans Light Horse; present

SEPARATION   22 Mar. 1862/New Orleans, LA/Declined enlistment

PERSONAL NARRATIVE

OCCUPATION   Jeweler

GENEALOGY   Son of Samuel Birdsill and Catherine (Breese) Griswold, Poughkeepsie, NY

Married, 18 Apr. 1858, New Orleans, LA, Frances Susan Newman (b. ca. 1838, Adams County, MS; d. 28 Mar. 1915, New Orleans, LA)

RESIDENCES
1830, Oneida, NY
1840, Saratoga, NY
1860, New Orleans, LA
1870, Boston, MA

SOURCES
NARA M320, reel 032
New Orleans, LA, Death Records Index, 1804–1949
New Orleans Passenger Lists, 1820–1945
US Census 1830, 1840, 1850, 1860, 1870
US IRS Tax Assessment Lists, 1862–1918
US Passport Applications, 1795–1925
www.findagrave.com, 6589311

GUBERNATOR, John L.

BIRTH
17 June 1821/Berwick, PA
DEATH
6 Feb. 1895/New Orleans, LA

RECORD OF SERVICE
MILITIA SERVICE
23 Nov. 1861/Active
ORLEANS LIGHT HORSE TRANSFER DATA
INBOUND
1861/Private
OUTBOUND
22 Mar. 1862/Private
SERVICE RÉSUMÉ
23 Nov. 1861
New Orleans, LA/Militia service with the
Orleans Light Horse; present
SEPARATION
22 Mar. 1862/New Orleans, LA/Declined enlistment

PERSONAL NARRATIVE
OCCUPATION
Hauling heavy materials
GENEALOGY
Son of John Laurentius and Anna Margaret (Shanefelter)
Gubernator, Adams County, PA
RESIDENCES
1840, Adams County, PA
1861, New Orleans, LA
1865, New Orleans, LA
1870, New Orleans, LA
1890–91, New Orleans, LA

SOURCES
NARA M320, reel 032
New Orleans, LA, Directories, 1890–1891
US Census 1840, 1870
US IRS Tax Assessment Lists, 1862–1918
www.findagrave.com, 11894561

GUILFANT, A. J.

BIRTH   1822

RECORD OF SERVICE

CSA ENLISTMENT   1 July 1862/Tupelo, MS/Duration of the war

ORLEANS LIGHT HORSE TRANSFER DATA

    INBOUND   1 July 1862/Private

    OUTBOUND   1 May 1865/Private

SERVICE RÉSUMÉ

    1 July 1862   Tupelo, MS/Received into the Orleans Light Horse

    Sept.–Dec. 1862   Present

    Jan.–June 1863   Present

    July–Dec. 1863   Present

    May–June 1864   Absent, sick

    25 Mar. 1865   Macon, GA/Admitted for surgery, Polk Hospital
        (recuperating well)

SEPARATION   1 May 1865/Macon, GA/Parole, released from
        military service

ADDITIONAL INFORMATION   Alternate spelling: Gilfant, A.

SOURCES

NARA M320, reel 032; M1781, reel 006

GUNNISON, Amos B.

BIRTH   10 May 1839/Sullivan County, NH

DEATH   8 Mar. 1885/New Orleans, LA

RECORD OF SERVICE

CSA ENLISTMENT   22 Mar. 1862/New Orleans, LA/90 days
        25 July 1862/Tupelo, MS/Duration of the war

ORLEANS LIGHT HORSE TRANSFER DATA

    INBOUND   22 Mar. 1862/Private

    OUTBOUND   1 May 1865/Corporal

SERVICE RÉSUMÉ

    22 Mar. 1862   New Orleans, LA/Mustered into service of CSA with the
        Orleans Light Horse

    25 May 1862   Absent, in camp sick

    6 June 1862   Camp Williamson, Tupelo, MS/Present

    Sept.–Oct. 1862   Present, detached on duty, in rank of corporal

    Nov.–Dec. 1862   Present, in rank of corporal

    Jan.–June 1863   Present, in rank of corporal

    July–Aug. 1863   Absent, sick in hospital, in rank of corporal

    9 Aug. 1863   Detailed to drive stock to Georgia

    Sept.–Oct. 1863   Present, in rank of corporal

    Nov.–Dec. 1863   Absent, furlough, in rank of corporal

    May–June 1864   Present, in rank of corporal

10 June 1864	Selma, AL/Received clothing issue at quartermaster depot
26 Apr. 1865	Durham Station, NC/Surrendered
SEPARATION	1 May 1865/Greensboro, NC/Parole, released from military service

PERSONAL NARRATIVE

OCCUPATION	Oil mill worker
GENEALOGY	Son of Vinal and Eliza (Baker) Gunnison, Sullivan County, NH
	Married, 15 May 1879, New Orleans, LA, Marie Eva Pelle (b. Dec. 1859, New Orleans, LA; d. 31 Aug. 1937, New Orleans, LA)
RESIDENCES	1850, Goshen, NH
	1862, New Orleans, LA
	1880, New Orleans, LA

SOURCES

NARA M320, reel 032; M1781, reel 006
New Hampshire Births and Christenings Index, 1714–1904
New Orleans, LA, Death Records Index, 1804–1949
New Orleans, LA, Marriage Records Index, 1831–1925
US Census 1850, 1880
www.findagrave.com, 11894570

HAMILTON, William Brownlow

| BIRTH | 22 Nov. 1843/McMinn, TN |

RECORD OF SERVICE

| CSA ENLISTMENT | 1 July 1861/Memphis, TN/One year |
| | 1 Sept. 1863/Chattanooga, TN/Duration of the war |

ORLEANS LIGHT HORSE TRANSFER DATA

| INBOUND | 1 Sept. 1863/Private |
| OUTBOUND | 12 Sept. 1864/Private |

SERVICE RÉSUMÉ

1 Sept. 1863	Chattanooga, TN/Received into the Orleans Light Horse from the Twelfth Tennessee Regiment
Sept.–Dec. 1863	Present
May–June 1864	Absent, sick in hospital
12 Sept. 1864	Jonesboro, GA/Transfer to Invalid Corps, Provisional Army of the Confederate States
SEPARATION	12 Sept. 1864/Jonesboro, GA/Discharge, physical disability

PERSONAL NARRATIVE

OCCUPATION	Farmer
GENEALOGY	Son of Jonathan and Margaret Melissa (Williams) Hamilton, Athens, TN
RESIDENCES	1860, McMinn, TN
	1870, McMinn, TN

SOURCES
NARA M320, reel 032
US Census 1860, 1870

HANEY, Martin

BIRTH	July 1842/County Tipperary, Ireland
DEATH	1 Aug. 1906/New Orleans, LA

RECORD OF SERVICE

CSA ENLISTMENT	22 Mar. 1862/New Orleans, LA/90 days

ORLEANS LIGHT HORSE TRANSFER DATA

INBOUND	22 Mar. 1862/Private
OUTBOUND	20 May 1862/Private

SERVICE RÉSUMÉ

22 Mar. 1862	New Orleans, LA/Mustered into service of CSA with the Orleans Light Horse
22 Mar.–25 May 1862	Present
SEPARATION	20 May 1862/Tupelo, MS/Honorable discharge, unspecified

PERSONAL NARRATIVE

OCCUPATION	Plantation owner
	Member, Tangipahoa Parish Police Jury, 1873–85
	Member, Louisiana Legislature, 1888–92
GENEALOGY	Son of John and Julia (Foley) Haney, County Tipperary, Ireland
	Arrived in New York, NY, 1847; migrated to Louisiana, 1859
	Married, 28 Mar. 1865, St. Helena Parish, LA, Eliza Hulda (Morse) Parham (b. 1827, Vicksburg, MS; d. 5 Apr. 1889, Amite, LA)
RESIDENCES	1860, Greensburg, LA
	1870, Tangipahoa Parish, LA
	1880, Tangipahoa Parish, LA
	1900, Tangipahoa Parish, LA
ADDITIONAL INFORMATION	Alternate spelling: Hayne

SOURCES
Biographical and Historical Memoirs of Louisiana, 1:458–59.
Louisiana Marriages, 1718–1925
NARA M320, reel 032
New Orleans Daily Picayune, 12 Jan. 1873; 8 Apr. 1889; 2, 3, 5 Aug. 1906
New Orleans, LA, Death Records Index, 1804–1949
US Census 1860, 1870, 1880, 1900
www.findagrave.com, 94670501

HANKINS, C. D.

RECORD OF SERVICE

CSA ENLISTMENT   1 July 1861/Memphis, TN/One year
                            1 Sept. 1863/Chattanooga, TN/Duration of the war

ORLEANS LIGHT HORSE TRANSFER DATA

    INBOUND   1 Sept. 1863/Private
    OUTBOUND   Feb. 1864/Private

SERVICE RÉSUMÉ

    1 Sept. 1863   Chattanooga, TN/Received into the Orleans Light Horse
                            from the Twelfth Tennessee Regiment
    Sept.–Oct. 1863   Present
    Nov.–Dec. 1863   Absent, furlough

SOURCES

NARA M320, reel 032; M231, reel 018

HARDIN, James Otey

BIRTH   18 May 1837/Pittsboro, NC
DEATH   24 Apr. 1924/Spring Hill, TN

RECORD OF SERVICE

CSA ENLISTMENT   22 Mar. 1862/New Orleans, LA/90 days
                            25 July 1862/Tupelo, MS/Duration of the war

ORLEANS LIGHT HORSE TRANSFER DATA

    INBOUND   22 Mar. 1862/Private
    OUTBOUND   20 May 1865/Private

SERVICE RÉSUMÉ

    22 Mar. 1862   New Orleans, LA/Mustered into service of CSA with the
                            Orleans Light Horse
    22 Mar.–25 May 1862 Present
    6 June 1862   Camp Williamson, Tupelo, MS/Present
    Sept.–Oct. 1862   Absent, duty
    Nov.–Dec. 1862   Present
    Jan.–June 1863   Present
    July–Oct. 1863   Present
    Nov.–Dec. 1863   Absent, furlough
    May–June 1864   Present

SEPARATION   20 May 1865/Atlanta, GA/Parole, released from
                            military service

PERSONAL NARRATIVE

OCCUPATION   Physician

GENEALOGY   Son of William Hill and Maria Rhett (Hill) Hardin, Maury
                            County, TN
                            Married, 27 Oct. 1870, Maury, TN, Margaret Eliza White
                            (b. 23 July 1850, Maury, TN; d. 21 Apr. 1880, Maury, TN)

RESIDENCES	1850, Cumberland County, NC
	1870, Maury County, TN
	1880, Maury County, TN
	1900, Maury County, TN
	1910, Maury County, TN
	1920, Maury County, TN

SOURCES
Directory of Deceased American Physicians, 1804–1929
NARA M320, reel 032; M1781, reel 006
Tennessee Civil War Confederate Pension Applications Index
Tennessee State Marriages, 1780–2002
US Census 1850, 1870, 1880, 1900, 1910, 1920
www.findagrave.com, 14327995

HARRISON, Frederick W.

RECORD OF SERVICE

| CSA ENLISTMENT | 22 Mar. 1862/New Orleans, LA/90 days |
| | 25 July 1862/Tupelo, MS/Duration of the war |

ORLEANS LIGHT HORSE TRANSFER DATA

| INBOUND | 22 Mar. 1862/Private |
| OUTBOUND | Apr. 1863/Private |

SERVICE RÉSUMÉ

22 Mar. 1862	New Orleans, LA/Mustered into service of CSA with the Orleans Light Horse
22 Mar.–25 May 1862	Present
6 June 1862	Camp Williamson, Tupelo, MS/Present
Sept.–Dec. 1862	Absent without leave
Jan.–Feb. 1863	Absent without leave
SEPARATION	Apr. 1863/Shelbyville, TN/Deserter, dropped from rolls

SOURCES
NARA M320, reel 032

HARTIGAN, J.

RECORD OF SERVICE

| CSA ENLISTMENT | 27 Aug. 1863/Chattanooga, TN/Duration of the war |

ORLEANS LIGHT HORSE TRANSFER DATA

| INBOUND | 27 Aug. 1863/Private |
| OUTBOUND | Aug. 1864/Private |

SERVICE RÉSUMÉ

27 Aug. 1863	Chattanooga, TN/Received into the Orleans Light Horse
July–Dec. 1863	Absent, detailed with Maj. Lawrence Louis Butler
May–June 1864	Absent, detailed with Maj. Butler

SOURCES
NARA M320, reel 032

HAYDEL, Edouard C.

BIRTH   1835/St. Charles Parish, LA
DEATH   1875/New Orleans, LA

RECORD OF SERVICE
CSA ENLISTMENT   7 Mar. 1862/New Orleans, LA/One year
                                25 Dec. 1862/Murfreesboro, TN/Duration of the war
ORLEANS LIGHT HORSE TRANSFER DATA
     INBOUND   25 Dec. 1862/Private
     OUTBOUND   1 May 1865/Private
SERVICE RÉSUMÉ
     25 Dec. 1862   Murfreesboro, TN/Received into the Orleans Light Horse
                                  from the Orleans Guard Battery, Louisiana Artillery
     Jan.–June 1863   Present
     July–Dec. 1863   Present
     May–June 1864   Present
     16 Apr. 1865   West Point, GA/Captured
     23 Apr. 1865   Transferred to US military prison, Macon, GA
SEPARATION   1 May 1865/Macon, GA/Parole, released from military service

PERSONAL NARRATIVE
OCCUPATION   Teacher
GENEALOGY   Son of Marcien Belfort and Marguerite Adele Haydel,
                                  Edgard, LA
RESIDENCES   1850, St. John the Baptist Parish, LA
                                  1870, New Orleans, LA

SOURCES
Booth, 2:229
NARA M320, reel 032
US Census 1850, 1870

HEARN, E. O.

RECORD OF SERVICE
CSA ENLISTMENT   22 Mar. 1862/New Orleans, LA/90 days
ORLEANS LIGHT HORSE TRANSFER DATA
     INBOUND   22 Mar. 1862/Private
     OUTBOUND   June 1862/Private
SERVICE RÉSUMÉ
     22 Mar. 1862   New Orleans, LA/Mustered into service of CSA with the
                                  Orleans Light Horse
     22 Mar.–25 May 1862   Present

SOURCES
NARA M320, reel 032

HÉBERT, Jules A.

BIRTH	Apr. 1840/St. Mary Parish, LA
DEATH	9 Feb. 1905/New Orleans, LA

RECORD OF SERVICE

CSA ENLISTMENT	1 July 1861/Memphis, TN/One year
	1 Sept. 1863/Chattanooga, TN/Duration of the war

ORLEANS LIGHT HORSE TRANSFER DATA

INBOUND	1 Sept. 1863/Private
OUTBOUND	1 May 1865/Private

SERVICE RÉSUMÉ

1 Sept. 1863	Chattanooga, TN/Received into the Orleans Light Horse from Co. C, Twenty-Second Tennessee Cavalry Regiment
Sept.–Oct. 1863	Present
Nov.–Dec. 1863	Enterprise, MS/Absent, sick; admitted to Forney's Division Hospital
May–June 1864	Present
26 Apr. 1865	Durham Station, NC/Surrendered
SEPARATION	1 May 1865/Greensboro, NC/Parole, released from military service

PERSONAL NARRATIVE

OCCUPATION	Bartender, riverboatman
GENEALOGY	Son of Alexis Seraphin and Anne Arsenne (Langlinais) Hébert, Assumption Parish, LA
	Married, 27 July 1891, New Orleans, LA, Caroline Grenair (b. May 1840, St. Malo, France; d. 10 Jan. 1915, New Orleans, LA)
RESIDENCES	1850, Assumption Parish, LA
	1860, Berwick, LA
	1880, New Orleans, LA
	1900, New Orleans, LA

SOURCES

Confederate Pension Applications Collection, Louisiana State Archives
Louisiana Marriages, 1718–1925
NARA M320, reel 032; M1781, reel 006
New Orleans, LA, Death Records Index, 1804–1949
New Orleans, LA, Marriage Records Index, 1831–1925
Obituary: *New Orleans Daily Picayune*, 17 July 1907
US Census 1850, 1860, 1880, 1900
www.findagrave.com, 70632921

HILDRETH, Charles Allen

BIRTH   Dec. 1841/Lynn, MA
DEATH   ca. 1902/Galveston, TX

RECORD OF SERVICE

CSA ENLISTMENT   22 Mar. 1862/New Orleans, LA/90 days
     25 July 1862/Tupelo, MS/Duration of the war

ORLEANS LIGHT HORSE TRANSFER DATA
     INBOUND   22 Mar. 1862/Private
     OUTBOUND   1 May 1865/Private

SERVICE RÉSUMÉ

22 Mar. 1862	New Orleans, LA/Mustered into service of CSA with the Orleans Light Horse
22 Mar.–24 May 1862	Present
6 June 1862	Camp Williamson, Tupelo, MS/Absent, sick
25 Mar. 1862	Corinth, MS/Sick in hospital
Sept.–Dec. 1862	Present
Jan.–Apr. 1863	Present
May–June 1863	Absent, sick
July–Oct. 1863	Rome, GA/Absent, sick in hospital
Nov.–Dec. 1863	Absent, sick
May–June 1864	Absent, sick in hospital
16 Sept. 1864	Received clothing issue
26 Apr. 1865	Durham Station, NC/Surrendered

SEPARATION   1 May 1865/Durham Station, NC/Parole, released from military service

PERSONAL NARRATIVE

OCCUPATION   Stockbroker, real estate

GENEALOGY   Son of David Morgan and Elizabeth (Washburn) Hildreth, Lynn, MA
     Married, 1892, San Antonio, TX, Nancy Ann Moore (b. 19 Feb. 1854, Linn County, OR; d. 1 June 1929, Travis County, TX)

RESIDENCES   1850, Lynn, MA
     1860, New Orleans, LA
     1870, New York, NY
     1900, Galveston, TX

SOURCES

Boston Passenger and Crew Lists, 1820–1954
Morrison and Fourmy's General Directory of the City of Galveston, 1896–97
NARA M320, reel 032; M1781, reel 006
US Census 1850, 1860, 1870, 1900

HITE, Cadwalader M.

BIRTH	11 June 1836/Kentucky
DEATH	22 Apr. 1882/Houston, TX

RECORD OF SERVICE

CSA ENLISTMENT	22 Mar. 1862/New Orleans, LA/90 days

ORLEANS LIGHT HORSE TRANSFER DATA

INBOUND	22 Mar. 1862/Private
OUTBOUND	4 July 1862/Private

SERVICE RÉSUMÉ

22 Mar. 1862	New Orleans, LA/Mustered into service of CSA with the Orleans Light Horse
22 Mar.–25 May 1862	Present
6 June 1862	Camp Williamson, Tupelo, MS/Absent, sick
SEPARATION	4 July 1862/Tupelo, MS/Discharge, physical disability

PERSONAL NARRATIVE

OCCUPATION	Clerk, railroad agent
GENEALOGY	Married, ca. 1868, Fannie Belle —— (b. 26 Nov. 1840, Maryland; d. 4 June 1915, Houston, TX)
RESIDENCES	1860, New Orleans, LA
	1880, Dallas, TX

SOURCES

NARA M320, reel 032
US Census 1860, 1880
www.findagrave.com, 83905638

HOBART, Edward

BIRTH	26 June 1825/Bridgewater, MA
DEATH	18 Feb. 1885/New York

RECORD OF SERVICE

MILITIA SERVICE	23 Nov. 1861/Active
CSA ENLISTMENT	22 Mar. 1862/New Orleans, LA/90 days
	25 July 1862/Tupelo, MS/Duration of the war

ORLEANS LIGHT HORSE TRANSFER DATA

INBOUND	1861/Private
OUTBOUND	Aug. 1862/Private

SERVICE RÉSUMÉ

23 Nov. 1861	New Orleans, LA/Militia service with the Orleans Light Horse; present, in rank of private
22 Mar. 1862	New Orleans, LA/Mustered into service of CSA
22 Mar.–23 May 1862	Present
24 May 1862	Detailed by Gen. Mansfield Lovell
6 June 1862	Camp Williamson, Tupelo, MS/Absent, detailed

PERSONAL NARRATIVE

OCCUPATION	Merchant

GENEALOGY	Son of Aaron and Maria (Leach) Hobart III, Bridgewater, MA
RESIDENCES	1850, New Orleans, LA
	1860, New Orleans, LA

SOURCES

Massachusetts, Town Birth Records, 1620–1850
Massachusetts, Town and Vital Records, 1620–1988
NARA M320, reel 032
New York, Death Newspaper Extracts, 1801–1890 (Barber Collection)
US Census 1850, 1860
US Passport Applications, 1795–1925
www.findagrave.com, 108699275

HOPKINS, Aristide R.

| BIRTH | 10 Nov. 1839/New Orleans, LA |
| DEATH | 27 June 1925/Biloxi, MS |

RECORD OF SERVICE

MILITIA SERVICE	23 Nov. 1861/Active
CSA ENLISTMENT	22 Mar. 1862/New Orleans, LA/90 days
	25 July 1862/Tupelo, MS/Duration of the war

ORLEANS LIGHT HORSE TRANSFER DATA

| INBOUND | 1861/Private |
| OUTBOUND | 1 May 1865/Lieutenant |

SERVICE RÉSUMÉ

23 Nov. 1861	New Orleans, LA/Militia service with the Orleans Light Horse; present, in rank of private
22 Mar. 1862	New Orleans, LA/Mustered into service of CSA, in rank of corporal
22 Mar.–25 May 1862	Present, in rank of corporal
6 June 1862	Tupelo, MS/Present, in rank of sergeant
Sept.–Dec. 1862	Present, in rank of sergeant
Jan.–Apr. 1863	Shelbyville, TN/Present, in position of ordnance sergeant
May–June 1863	Shelbyville, TN/Elected junior second lieutenant, effective 31 May 1863
July–Dec. 1863	Present, in position of junior second lieutenant
May–June 1864	Present, in position of junior second lieutenant
23 May 1864	Designated aide-de-camp to the commanding general
Sept. 1864	Commended by Lt. Gen. Alexander P. Stewart in dispatches as a result of action at Peachtree Creek in the battle for Atlanta, GA
16 Jan. 1865	Leave of absence, 30 days
26 Apr. 1865	Durham Station, NC/Surrendered
SEPARATION	1 May 1865/Greensboro, NC/Parole, released from military service

PERSONAL NARRATIVE

| OCCUPATION | Customs weigher |

GENEALOGY	Son of James Alexis and Nellie (Miltenberger) Hopkins, New Orleans, LA
	Uncle of John G. Byrd
	Married, 1867, New Orleans, LA, Mary McNeil (b. Sept. 1849, Louisiana; d. 13 Mar. 1908, New Orleans, LA)
RESIDENCES	1860, New Orleans, LA
	1870, New Orleans, LA
	1880, New Orleans, LA
	1900, New Orleans, LA
	1920, New Orleans, LA

SOURCES

Mississippi Marriages, 1776–1935
NARA M320, reel 032; M1781, reel 006
New Orleans, LA, Death Records Index, 1804–1949
Obituaries: *New Orleans Times-Picayune*, 28 and 29 June 1925; Mary McNeil Hopkins, *New Orleans Daily Picayune*, 13 Mar. 1908
OR, ser. 1, v. 38:872
US Census 1860, 1870, 1880, 1900, 1920
www.findagrave.com, 8584395

HOSMER, Charles H.

BIRTH	ca. 1845/Louisiana

RECORD OF SERVICE

CSA ENLISTMENT	1 June 1864/Meridian, MS/Duration of the war

ORLEANS LIGHT HORSE TRANSFER DATA

INBOUND	1 June 1864/Private
OUTBOUND	1 May 1865/Private

SERVICE RÉSUMÉ	
1 June 1864	Meridian, MS/Received into the Orleans Light Horse
May–June 1864	Present
Jan. 1865	West Point, GA/Admitted, St. Mary's Hospital
26 Apr. 1865	Durham Station, NC/Surrendered
SEPARATION	1 May 1865/Greensboro, NC/Parole, released from military service

PERSONAL NARRATIVE

OCCUPATION	Bookkeeper
GENEALOGY	Son of William B. and Mary Jane (Jones) Hosmer, Covington, LA
	Married, 9 Sept. 1884, Summit, MS, Ida Bell Matthews (b. 13 July 1853, Pike County, MS; d. 21 Oct. 1949, St. Tammany Parish, LA)
RESIDENCES	1850, St. Tammany Parish, LA
	1860, St. Tammany Parish, LA
	1880, Summit, MS

SOURCES
Confederate Pension Applications Collection, Louisiana State Archives
Mississippi Marriages, 1776–1935
NARA M320, reel 032; M1781, reel 006
US Census 1850, 1860, 1880

HOUSE, John A.

BIRTH	Nov. 1845/Mississippi
DEATH	16 Aug. 1916/Madera County, CA

RECORD OF SERVICE

CSA ENLISTMENT	1 July 1862/Tupelo, MS/Duration of the war

ORLEANS LIGHT HORSE TRANSFER DATA

INBOUND	1 July 1862/Private
OUTBOUND	Feb. 1864/Private

SERVICE RÉSUMÉ

1 July 1862	Tupelo, MS/Received into the Orleans Light Horse
Sept.–Dec. 1862	Present
Jan.–June 1863	Present
July–Dec. 1863	Rome, GA/Absent, sick in hospital

PERSONAL NARRATIVE

OCCUPATION	Farmer
GENEALOGY	Son of Elisha and Nancy House, Banner, MS
	Married, 1878, Fresno County, CA, Sarah Lewis (b. 25 Oct. 1859, Fresno, CA; d. 8 Mar. 1930, Madera, CA)
RESIDENCES	1860, Banner, MS
	1880, Fresno County, CA
	1900, Madera County, CA
	1910, Madera County, CA

SOURCES
NARA M320, reel 032
US Census 1850, 1860, 1880, 1900, 1910

HUGHES, Edward A.

BIRTH	ca. 1844/New York
DEATH	ca. 1890/New Orleans, LA

RECORD OF SERVICE

CSA ENLISTMENT	1 July 1862/Tupelo, MS/Duration of the war

ORLEANS LIGHT HORSE TRANSFER DATA

INBOUND	1 July 1862/Private
OUTBOUND	14 June 1864/Private

SERVICE RÉSUMÉ

1 July 1862	Tupelo, MS/Received into the Orleans Light Horse
Sept.–Oct. 1862	Absent without leave

Jan. 1863	Captured and paroled by US forces during Sept.–Nov. 1862; exchanged and transferred to CSA (Army of Tennessee) at Chattanooga, TN
Jan.–Feb. 1863	Present
Mar.–Apr. 1863	Absent, one month stoppage in pay ($12) for overstaying furlough 30 days
May–Aug. 1863	Present, dismounted
9 July 1863	Detailed at Lt. Gen. Leonidas Polk's stables
Sept.–Oct. 1863	Present
Nov.–Dec. 1863	Absent without leave
14 June 1864	Transferred to First Louisiana Cavalry (Department of Alabama, Mississippi, and East Louisiana) by order of Gen. Joseph E. Johnston

PERSONAL NARRATIVE

OCCUPATION	Streetcar driver
GENEALOGY	Son of George and Ellen Hughes
	Married, 26 Aug. 1872, New Orleans, LA, Louisiana Nafe (b. Dec. 1849, Louisiana; d. 5 June 1909, New Orleans, LA)
RESIDENCES	1870, New Orleans, LA
	1880, New Orleans, LA

SOURCES

Louisiana Marriages, 1718–1925
NARA M320, reel 032
New Orleans, LA, Marriage Records Index, 1831–1920
Soards' New Orleans City Directory, 1891
US Census 1880

HULBURT, B. M.

RECORD OF SERVICE

CSA ENLISTMENT	22 Apr. 1864/Demopolis, AL/Duration of the war
ORLEANS LIGHT HORSE TRANSFER DATA	
INBOUND	22 Apr. 1864/Private
OUTBOUND	19 May 1865/Private
SERVICE RÉSUMÉ	
22 Apr. 1864	Demopolis, AL/Received into the Orleans Light Horse
May–June 1864	Present
14 May 1865	Citronelle, AL/Surrendered
SEPARATION	19 May 1865/Jackson, MS/Parole, released from military service

SOURCES

NARA M320, reel 032
Civil War Prisoner of War Records, 1861–1865

HUNTINGTON, Benjamin Wolcott

BIRTH   16 July 1822/Norwich CT
DEATH   9 Jan. 1887/Natchez, MS

RECORD OF SERVICE

MILITIA SERVICE   23 Nov. 1861/Active
CSA ENLISTMENT   25 May 1862/Tupelo, MS/Duration of the war
ORLEANS LIGHT HORSE TRANSFER DATA
     INBOUND   25 May 1862/Private
     OUTBOUND   Aug. 1862/Private
SERVICE RÉSUMÉ

23 Nov. 1861	New Orleans, LA/Militia service with the Orleans Light Horse; present
22 Mar. 1862	New Orleans, LA/Dropped from rolls prior to muster; enlisted in another unit
25 May 1862	Tupelo, MS/Received into the Orleans Light Horse from the Twentieth Louisiana Regiment
6 June 1862	Camp Williamson, Tupelo, MS/Present

PERSONAL NARRATIVE

OCCUPATION   Merchant grocer
GENEALOGY   Son of Alfred Isham and Caroline (Sims) Huntington, New Orleans, LA

Married, 24 Dec. 1851, Natchez, MS, Eliza W. Wade (b. 16 May 1829, Natchez, MS; d. 18 Feb. 1894, Natchez, MS)

RESIDENCES   1850, New Orleans, LA
                 1860, New Orleans, LA
                 1870, Natchez, MS
                 1880, Natchez, MS

SOURCES

Mississippi Marriages, 1776–1935
NARA M320, reel 032
US Census 1850, 1860, 1870, 1880
www.findagrave.com, 102355749

HUNTINGTON, Samuel

BIRTH   1832/Adams County, MS
DEATH   16 Jan. 1870/New Orleans, LA

RECORD OF SERVICE

CSA ENLISTMENT   1 July 1862/Tupelo, MS/Duration of the war
ORLEANS LIGHT HORSE TRANSFER DATA
     INBOUND   1 July 1862/Sergeant
     OUTBOUND   1 Aug. 1864/Lieutenant
SERVICE RÉSUMÉ
     1 July 1862   Tupelo, MS/Received into the Orleans Light Horse

Sept.–Oct. 1862	Knoxville, TN/Present, in rank of sergeant
Nov.–Dec. 1862	Present, in rank of sergeant
Jan.–June 1863	Shelbyville, TN/Present, in rank of sergeant
July–Aug. 1863	Chattanooga, TN/Present, in rank of sergeant
17 July 1863	Detailed (with six men) to drive cattle to government pasture
9 Aug. 1863	Detailed in charge of stock in pasture
Sept.–Oct. 1863	Present, in rank of sergeant
Nov.–Dec. 1863	Meridian, MS/Present, in position of second lieutenant
May–June 1864	Present, in position of second lieutenant

PERSONAL NARRATIVE

OCCUPATION	Riverboat pilot
GENEALOGY	Son of Henry William and Helen (Dunbar) Huntington, Catahoula Parish, LA
RESIDENCES	1830, Adams County, MS
	1840, Catahoula Parish, LA
	1850, Catahoula Parish, LA
	1860, Concordia Parish, LA

SOURCES
NARA M320, reel 032
Obituaries: *New Orleans Daily Picayune*, 19 and 23 Jan. 1870; *New Orleans Bee*, 20 Jan. 1870
US Census 1830, 1840, 1850, 1860
US Federal Census Mortality Schedules Index, 1850–1885

HURD, J. H.

BIRTH	ca. 1830/Kentucky

RECORD OF SERVICE

CSA ENLISTMENT	1 July 1861/Memphis, TN/One year
	1 Sept. 1863/Memphis, TN/Duration of the war

ORLEANS LIGHT HORSE TRANSFER DATA

INBOUND	1 Sept. 1863/Private
OUTBOUND	1 May 1865/Private

SERVICE RÉSUMÉ

1 Sept. 1863	Memphis, TN/Received into the Orleans Light Horse from the Twelfth Tennessee Regiment
Sept.–Oct. 1863	Rome, GA/Absent, detailed as mechanic
Nov.–Dec. 1863	Absent, detached by order of Gen. Braxton Bragg
May–June 1864	Absent, sick in hospital
10 Nov. 1864	Jackson, MS/Admitted, First Mississippi CSA Hospital; returned to duty
26 Apr. 1865	Durham Station, NC/Surrendered
SEPARATION	1 May 1865/Greensboro, NC/Parole, released from military service

SOURCES
NARA M320, reel 032; M1781, reel 006

JACKSON, John Norman

BIRTH	1821/Easton, PA
DEATH	New Orleans, LA

RECORD OF SERVICE

MILITIA SERVICE	23 Nov. 1861/Active
CSA ENLISTMENT	22 Mar. 1862/New Orleans, LA/90 days
	25 July 1862/Tupelo, MS/Duration of the war

ORLEANS LIGHT HORSE TRANSFER DATA

INBOUND	1861/Private
OUTBOUND	June 1862/Sergeant

SERVICE RÉSUMÉ

23 Nov. 1861	New Orleans/Militia service with the Orleans Light Horse; present
22 Mar. 1862	Mustered into service of CSA at New Orleans, in rank of private
25 May 1862	Tupelo, MS/Present, in rank of sergeant

PERSONAL NARRATIVE

OCCUPATION	Commercial broker
GENEALOGY	Son of Francis and Mary (Miller) Jackson, Easton, PA
	Married, ca. 1862, New Orleans, LA, Anna Mercer Cartwright (b. 23 July 1845, Natchez, MS; d. New Orleans, LA)
RESIDENCES	1860, New Orleans, LA
	1867, New Orleans, LA
	1895, New Orleans, LA

SOURCES

Gardner's New Orleans Directory, 1867
NARA M320, reel 032
Obituaries: Norman Jackson, infant son, *New Orleans Daily Picayune*, 23 Aug. 1865; *New Orleans Times*, 23 Aug. 1865
Soards' New Orleans City Directory, 1895
US Census 1860
US IRS Tax Assessment Lists, 1862–1918

JOHNSON, Charles Andrew

BIRTH	ca. 1815/Connecticut

RECORD OF SERVICE

MILITIA SERVICE	23 Nov. 1861/Active

ORLEANS LIGHT HORSE TRANSFER DATA

INBOUND	1861/Private
OUTBOUND	22 Mar. 1862/Private

SERVICE RÉSUMÉ

23 Nov. 1861	New Orleans, LA/Militia service with the Orleans Light Horse; present

SEPARATION	22 Mar. 1862/New Orleans, LA/Declined enlistment

PERSONAL NARRATIVE

OCCUPATION	Attorney
RESIDENCES	1850, Ascension Parish, LA

SOURCES
NARA M320, reel 032
US Census 1850

JONAS, Julian J.

BIRTH	12 Aug. 1836/Kentucky
DEATH	27 Feb. 1872/New Orleans, LA

RECORD OF SERVICE

CSA ENLISTMENT	1 July 1862/Tupelo, MS/Duration of the war

ORLEANS LIGHT HORSE TRANSFER DATA

INBOUND	1 July 1862/Private
OUTBOUND	1 May 1865/Sergeant

SERVICE RÉSUMÉ

1 July 1862	Tupelo, MS/Received into the Orleans Light Horse
19 Sept. 1862	Promoted to quartermaster sergeant
Sept.–Oct. 1862	Present, in position of quartermaster sergeant
Nov.–Dec. 1862	Absent with leave
Jan.–June 1863	Present, in position of quartermaster sergeant
July–Oct. 1863	Present, in position of quartermaster sergeant
May–June 1864	Present, in position of quartermaster sergeant
28 June 1864	Received clothing issue
26 Apr. 1865	Durham Station, NC/Surrendered
SEPARATION	1 May 1865/Greensboro, NC/Parole, released from military service

PERSONAL NARRATIVE

GENEALOGY	Son of Abraham and Louisa (Block) Jonas, Quincy, IL
RESIDENCES	1840, Adams County, IL
	1850, Quincy, IL
	1860, New Orleans, LA

SOURCES
JewishGen Online Worldwide Burial Registry
NARA M320, reel 032; M1781, reel 006
Obituary: *New Orleans Daily Picayune*, 2 and 3 Mar. 1872
US Census 1840, 1850, 1860
www.findagrave.com, 71341439

JORDAN, J. Dillon, III

BIRTH   ca. 1830/Cumberland County, NC

RECORD OF SERVICE

CSA ENLISTMENT   25 Feb. 1864/Demopolis, AL/Duration of the war

ORLEANS LIGHT HORSE TRANSFER DATA

   INBOUND   25 Feb. 1864/Private

   OUTBOUND   10 May 1865/Private

SERVICE RÉSUMÉ

   25 Feb. 1864   Demopolis, AL/Received into the Orleans Light Horse

   May–June 1864   Absent, detailed with Maj. Richard Mason, assistant
                                     quartermaster, by order of Lt. Gen. Leonidas Polk

   11 June 1864   Commended by the chief quartermaster, Army of
                                     Mississippi, and recommended for field commission as
                                     assistant quartermaster for Polk's Corps

   4 May 1865   Citronelle, AL/Surrendered

SEPARATION   10 May 1865/Gainesville, AL/Parole, released from
                                     military service

PERSONAL NARRATIVE

OCCUPATION   Surveyor

GENEALOGY   Son of J. Dillon and Elizabeth Ann (McRacken) Jordan,
                                     Pensacola, FL

RESIDENCES   1840, Escambia, Florida Territory
                                     1850, Pensacola, FL
                                     1860, Pensacola, FL

SOURCES

NARA M320, reel 032; M1781, reel 006
US Census 1840, 1850, 1860

KEEBLE, Richard Cheatham

BIRTH   12 Dec. 1840/Maury County, TN

DEATH   14 July 1885/Dallas County, AL

RECORD OF SERVICE

CSA ENLISTMENT   10 May 1861/Nashville, TN/One year
                                     1 Jan. 1863/Shelbyville, TN/Duration of the war

ORLEANS LIGHT HORSE TRANSFER DATA

   INBOUND   1 Jan. 1863/Private

   OUTBOUND   1 Feb. 1864/Private

SERVICE RÉSUMÉ

   1 Jan. 1863   Shelbyville, TN/Received into the Orleans Light Horse
                                     from Co. B, First Tennessee Infantry

   Jan.–June 1863   Present

   July–Dec. 1863   Present

| 1 Feb. 1864 | Meridian, MS/Application approved for transfer (exchange) with Maj. Gen. Nathan Bedford Forrest's Escort (Jackson's Co., Tennessee Cavalry) |

PERSONAL NARRATIVE

OCCUPATION	Wholesale grocer
GENEALOGY	Son of Martha W. Keeble, Maury County, TN
	Married, 25 Nov. 1868, Perry County, AL, Mary M. Tutt (b. 1845, Perry County, AL; d. 1 Oct. 1871, Perry County, AL)
RESIDENCES	1850, Maury County, TN
	1860, Nashville, TN
	1870, Selma, AL
	1880, Selma, AL

SOURCES

Alabama, Deaths and Burials Index, 1881–1974
Alabama Marriage Collection, 1800–1969
NARA M320, reel 032
US Census 1850, 1860, 1870, 1880
www.findagrave.com, 76996724

KENNEDY, John M.

| BIRTH | ca. 1829/Kentucky |

RECORD OF SERVICE

| CSA ENLISTMENT | 22 Mar. 1862/New Orleans, LA/90 days |
| | 25 July 1862/Tupelo, MS/Duration of the war |

ORLEANS LIGHT HORSE TRANSFER DATA

| INBOUND | 22 Mar. 1862/Private |
| OUTBOUND | 1 May 1865/Sergeant |

SERVICE RÉSUMÉ

22 Mar. 1862	New Orleans, LA/Mustered into service of CSA with the Orleans Light Horse
22 Mar.–25 May 1862	Present, in rank of private
6 June 1862	Present, in rank of private
Sept.–Dec. 1862	Present, in rank of corporal
Jan.–Feb. 1863	Absent, furlough, in rank of corporal
Mar.–Apr. 1863	Reported as deserter
May–June 1863	Present, in rank of corporal
July–Aug. 1863	Present
1 Aug. 1863	Promoted sergeant
Sept.–Dec. 1863	Present, in rank of sergeant
May–June 1864	Present, in rank of sergeant
16 Apr. 1865	West Point, GA/Captured
23 Apr. 1865	Transferred to US military prison, Macon, GA
SEPARATION	1 May 1865/Macon, GA/Parole, released from military service

PERSONAL NARRATIVE
OCCUPATION   Printer

GENEALOGY   Son of Sarah Kennedy

                      Married, ca. 1849, Josephine —— (b. 1831, Alabama)

RESIDENCES   1850, New Orleans, LA

                      1860, New Orleans, LA

SOURCES

NARA M320, reel 032

US Census 1850, 1860

KENNEDY, Thomas Seilles

BIRTH   1 Mar. 1844/New Orleans, LA

DEATH   20 Oct. 1917/New Orleans, LA

RECORD OF SERVICE

CSA ENLISTMENT   7 Mar. 1862/New Orleans, LA/90 days

                      1 July 1862/Tupelo, MS/Duration of the war

ORLEANS LIGHT HORSE TRANSFER DATA

   INBOUND   1 July 1862/Private

   OUTBOUND   17 May 1865/Private

SERVICE RÉSUMÉ

   1 July 1862   Tupelo, MS/Received into the Orleans Light Horse from
                          the Orleans Guards Artillery

   Sept.–Oct. 1862   Present, detailed on duty

   Nov.–Dec. 1862   Present

   Jan.–June 1863   Present

   6 Mar. 1863   Commended by Brig. Gen. Stephen D. Lee and recommended
                          for field commission as lieutenant of artillery

   July–Oct. 1863   Present

   9 Aug. 1863   Detailed in charge of stock in pasture

   Nov.–Dec. 1863   Absent, furlough

   May–June 1864   Present

   4 May 1865   Citronelle, AL/Surrendered

SEPARATION   17 May 1865/Meridian, MS/Parole, released from
                          military service

PERSONAL NARRATIVE

OCCUPATION   Physician

GENEALOGY   Son of Thomas Hall and Catherine Alexander (Chew)
                          Kennedy, New Orleans, LA

                      Married, 1882, Ruby Angela Mallory (b. Apr. 1856, Florida;
                          d. 17 Jan. 1902, New Orleans, LA), daughter of Navy
                          Secretary Stephen Russell Mallory and Angela Sylvania
                          Moreno

RESIDENCES   1850, New Orleans, LA
1860, New Orleans, LA
1870, New Orleans, LA
1900, New Orleans, LA
1910, New Orleans, LA

SOURCES
Directory of Deceased American Physicians, 1804–1929
NARA M320, reel 032
New Orleans, LA, Birth Records Index, 1790–1899
New Orleans, LA, Death Records Index, 1804–1949
New Orleans, LA, Directories, 1890–1891
US Census 1850, 1860, 1870, 1900, 1910
www.findagrave.com, 105643915

KENNER, Philip Minor

BIRTH	21 July 1833/Jefferson Parish, LA
DEATH	14 July 1903/New Orleans, LA

RECORD OF SERVICE

CSA ENLISTMENT	22 Mar. 1862/New Orleans, LA/90 days
	25 July 1862/Tupelo, MS/Duration of the war

ORLEANS LIGHT HORSE TRANSFER DATA

INBOUND	22 Mar. 1862/Private
OUTBOUND	1 May 1865/Lieutenant

SERVICE RÉSUMÉ

22 Mar. 1862	New Orleans, LA/Mustered into service of CSA with the Orleans Light Horse, in rank of corporal
22 Mar.–25 May 1862	Present, in rank of corporal
6 June 1862	Camp Williamson, Tupelo, MS/In charge of sick or dismissed men, in rank of sergeant
Sept.–Oct. 1862	Present, in position of first sergeant
18 Dec. 1862	Elected junior second lieutenant
Nov.–Dec. 1862	Present, in position of junior second lieutenant
Jan.–June 1863	Present, in position of junior second lieutenant
19 June 1863	Present, in position of first lieutenant
July–Dec. 1863	Present, in position of first lieutenant
May–June 1864	Present, in position of first lieutenant
21 Jan. 1865	Leave of absence, 60 days
SEPARATION	1 May 1865/Greensboro, NC/Parole, released from military service

PERSONAL NARRATIVE

OCCUPATION	Planter
GENEALOGY	Son of William Butler and Rumahah (Riske) Kenner, Jefferson Parish, LA
	Married, ca. 1866, Louisiana, Ella Eulalie Humphreys (b. 1836, Louisiana; d. 13 Feb. 1897, New Orleans, LA)

RESIDENCES	1840, Jefferson Parish, LA
	1850, Jefferson Parish, LA
	1860, Jefferson Parish, LA
	1880, St. Charles Parish, LA
	1900, New Orleans, LA

SOURCES

NARA M320, reel 032; M1781, reel 006

New Orleans, LA, Death Records Index, 1804–1949

US Census 1840, 1850, 1860, 1880, 1900

LALLANDE, Charles D.

| BIRTH | Feb. 1840/New Orleans, LA |
| DEATH | ca. 1902/New Orleans, LA |

RECORD OF SERVICE

MILITIA SERVICE	23 Nov. 1861/Active
CSA ENLISTMENT	22 Mar. 1862/New Orleans, LA/90 days
	25 July 1862/Tupelo, MS/Duration of the war

TRANSFER DATA

| INBOUND | 1861/Corporal |
| OUTBOUND | 9 June 1863/Lieutenant |

SERVICE RÉSUMÉ

23 Nov. 1861	New Orleans, LA/Militia service with the Orleans Light Horse; present, in rank of corporal
22 Mar. 1862	New Orleans, LA/Mustered into service of CSA, in position of first sergeant
22 Mar.–25 May 1862	Present, in position of first sergeant
6 June 1862	Camp Williamson, Tupelo, MS/Present, in position of first sergeant
Nov.–Dec. 1862	Present, in position of first lieutenant
Jan.–Feb. 1863	Shelbyville, TN/Absent, sick, in position of first lieutenant
Mar.–June 1863	Shelbyville, TN/Present, in position of first lieutenant
9 June 1863	Shelbyville, TN/Transfer to Capt. Taylor's Co., First Louisiana Cavalry

PERSONAL NARRATIVE

OCCUPATION	Clerk, grocer
GENEALOGY	Son of Joseph Gustave and Marie Caroline (Roche) Lallande deFerriere, New Orleans, LA
	Brother of John B. Lallande
	Married, ca. 1865, Virginia, Suzanne —— (b. ca. 1845, Virginia)
RESIDENCES	1840, New Orleans, LA
	1860, New Orleans, LA
	1870, Fredericksburg, VA
	1880, New Orleans, LA
	1900, New Orleans, LA

SOURCES

NARA M320, reel 032

Soards' New Orleans City Directory, 1895

US Census 1840, 1860, 1870, 1880, 1900

LALLANDE, John Berkeley

BIRTH	27 Dec. 1840/New Orleans, LA
DEATH	10 Dec. 1911/New Orleans, LA

RECORD OF SERVICE

MILITIA SERVICE	23 Nov. 1861/Absent without leave

ORLEANS LIGHT HORSE TRANSFER DATA

INBOUND	1861/Private
OUTBOUND	22 Mar. 1862/Private

SERVICE RÉSUMÉ

23 Nov. 1861	New Orleans, LA/Militia service with the Orleans Light Horse; absent without leave
SEPARATION	22 Mar. 1862/New Orleans, LA/Declined enlistment

PERSONAL NARRATIVE

OCCUPATION	Commercial traveler, cotton merchant
GENEALOGY	Son of Joseph Gustave and Marie Caroline (Roche) Lallande deFerriere, New Orleans, LA
	Brother of Charles D. Lallande
	Married, 1 Aug. 1871, New Orleans, LA, Marie Celeste Emma Rathbone (b. Dec. 1860, New Orleans, LA)
RESIDENCES	1860, New Orleans, LA
	1880, New Orleans, LA
	1890, New Orleans, LA
	1900, New Orleans, LA

SOURCES

New Orleans, LA, Directories, 1890–1891

New Orleans, LA, Marriage Records Index, 1831–1920

NARA M320, reel 032

US Census 1860, 1880, 1890, 1900

US Passport Applications, 1795–1925

LANDREAUX, Pierre Frederick

BIRTH	1832/New Orleans, LA

RECORD OF SERVICE

CSA ENLISTMENT	22 Mar. 1862/New Orleans, LA/90 days
	25 July 1862/Tupelo, MS/Duration of the war

ORLEANS LIGHT HORSE TRANSFER DATA

INBOUND	22 Mar. 1862/Private
OUTBOUND	30 Apr. 1863/Private

SERVICE RÉSUMÉ
22 Mar. 1862	New Orleans, LA/Mustered into service of CSA with the Orleans Light Horse
22 Mar.–25 May 1862	Present
14 Apr. 1862	Corinth, MS/Dismounted, horse commandeered to carry wounded from Battle of Shiloh; application made for replacement horse
6 June 1862	Camp Williamson, Tupelo, MS/Absent with leave
Sept.–Oct. 1862	Absent without leave
Nov.–Dec. 1862	Absent without leave
Jan.–Feb. 1863	Absent without leave
SEPARATION	30 Apr. 1863/Shelbyville, TN/Deserter, dropped from rolls

PERSONAL NARRATIVE

OCCUPATION	Attorney
GENEALOGY	Son of Honoré and Rose Josephine (Armand) Landreaux, New Orleans, LA
RESIDENCES	1850, New Orleans, LA
	1860, New Orleans, LA
	1870, New Orleans, LA

SOURCES

Booth, 3:636
NARA M320, reel 032
US Census 1850, 1860, 1870
US IRS Tax Assessment Lists, 1862–1918
US Passport Applications, 1795–1925

LANGE, Leopold

BIRTH	1840/New Orleans, LA
DEATH	1921/Havana, Cuba

RECORD OF SERVICE

CSA ENLISTMENT	22 Mar. 1862/New Orleans, LA/90 days
	25 July 1862/Tupelo, MS/Duration of the war

ORLEANS LIGHT HORSE TRANSFER DATA

INBOUND	22 Mar. 1862/Private
OUTBOUND	25 May 1862/Private

SERVICE RÉSUMÉ

22 Mar. 1862	New Orleans, LA/Mustered into service of CSA with the Orleans Light Horse
22 Mar.–25 May 1862	Present
6 June 1862	Tupelo, MS/Transferred to Co. H, Twentieth Louisiana Infantry

PERSONAL NARRATIVE

OCCUPATION	Merchant
GENEALOGY	Son of Louis Cherrie and Susanne Gabrielle Aurore (Santo Domingo) Lange, New Orleans, LA

RESIDENCES   1850, New Orleans, LA
1860, New Orleans, LA
1892–95, New Orleans, LA

SOURCES
NARA M320, reels 032 and 311
New Orleans City Directory, 1892–1895
New Orleans Passenger Lists, 1820–1945
US Census 1850, 1860

LAWLER, John W.

BIRTH   Dec. 1836/Missouri
DEATH   1910/Riverside, CA

RECORD OF SERVICE
CSA ENLISTMENT   1 July 1861/Memphis, TN/One year
                     1 Sept. 1863/Chattanooga, TN/Duration of the war

ORLEANS LIGHT HORSE TRANSFER DATA
   INBOUND   1 Sept. 1863/Private
   OUTBOUND   1 May 1865/Private
SERVICE RÉSUMÉ
   1 Sept. 1863   Chattanooga, TN/Received into the Orleans Light Horse
                      from the Twelfth Tennessee Regiment

   Sept.–Dec. 1863   Present
   May–June 1864   Present
   27 Mar. 1865   Macon, GA/Admitted, Ocmulgee Hospital
   1 Apr. 1865   Returned to duty
   26 Apr. 1865   Macon, GA/Surrendered
SEPARATION   1 May 1865/Macon, GA/Parole, released from
                      military service

PERSONAL NARRATIVE
OCCUPATION   Grocer, cotton factor
GENEALOGY   Son of Timothy and Mary Lawler, Cooper County, MO
                     Married, 1878, Shelby, TN, Jennie Barron Taylor (b. 16 Mar.
                        1855, Mississippi; d. 17 Mar. 1943, Riverside, CA)
RESIDENCES   1870, Memphis, TN
                     1880, Memphis, TN
                     1900, Riverside, CA
                     1910, Riverside, CA

SOURCES
California Death Index, 1940–1997
NARA M320, reel 032
US Census 1870, 1880, 1900, 1910
www.findagrave.com, 7129066

LEEDS, Thomas Lafayette

BIRTH   1825/New Orleans, LA
DEATH   23 Apr. 1862/Jackson, MS

RECORD OF SERVICE

MILITIA SERVICE   23 Nov. 1861/Active
CSA ENLISTMENT   22 Mar. 1862/New Orleans, LA/90 days
ORLEANS LIGHT HORSE TRANSFER DATA
    INBOUND   1861/Lieutenant
    OUTBOUND   24 Apr. 1862/Captain
SERVICE RÉSUMÉ
    1 Feb. 1861   New Orleans, LA/Militia service with the Orleans Light Horse; present, in position of first lieutenant
    1 June 1861   Elected captain on resignation of Capt. John McDonald Taylor
    23 Nov. 1861   New Orleans, LA/Active, in rank of captain
    22 Mar. 1862   New Orleans, LA/Mustered into service of CSA with the Orleans Light Horse
    16–23 Apr. 1862   Tupelo, MS/Absent, sick
SEPARATION   24 Apr. 1862/Jackson, MS/Death

PERSONAL NARRATIVE

OCCUPATION   Partner in Leeds Foundry, New Orleans, LA
GENEALOGY   Son of Jedediah and Mary Rossiter (Stanton) Leeds, New Orleans, LA

Brother of Charles J. Leeds, mayor of New Orleans, LA, 1874–76 (b. 1823; d. 1898)

Cousin of J. Leeds Greenleaf

Married, ca. 1848, New Orleans, LA, Olivia Barbarin Horne (b. July 1826, New Orleans, LA; d. 17 June 1900, New Orleans, LA)

RESIDENCES   1840, New Orleans, LA
1850, New Orleans, LA
1860, New Orleans, LA

SOURCES

Gardner's New Orleans Directory, 1861
NARA M320, reel 032
New Orleans, LA, Death Records Index, 1804–1949
Obituaries: *New Orleans Daily Picayune*, 24 Apr. 1862; Mrs. Olivia B. Leeds, *New Orleans States*, 24 June 1900; *New Orleans Daily Picayune*, 18 June 1900; *New Orleans Times-Democrat*, 18 and 24 June 1900
US Census 1840, 1850, 1860
Wildey, 417

LE MONNIER, Yves René "Paul," Jr.

BIRTH   29 Jan. 1843/Paris, France
DEATH   14 Jan. 1928/New Orleans, LA

RECORD OF SERVICE

CSA ENLISTMENT   5 Mar. 1862/New Orleans, LA/90 days
     1 July 1862/Tupelo, MS/Duration of the war

ORLEANS LIGHT HORSE TRANSFER DATA
  INBOUND   1 July 1862/Private
  OUTBOUND   1 May 1865/Private

SERVICE RÉSUMÉ
  1 July 1862   Tupelo, MS/Received into the Orleans Light Horse from Co. B, Crescent Regiment, Twenty-Fourth Louisiana Infantry
  Sept.–Oct. 1862   Present, detailed for duty
  Nov.–Dec. 1862   Present
  Jan.–June 1863   Present
  July–Oct. 1863   Present
  Nov.–Dec. 1863   Absent, furlough
  May–June 1864   Present
  26 Apr. 1865   Durham Station, NC/Surrendered
SEPARATION   1 May 1865/Greensboro, NC/Parole, released from military service

PERSONAL NARRATIVE

OCCUPATION   Physician
GENEALOGY   Son of Yves René and Adele Marie (Communy) Le Monnier, New Orleans, LA
     Brother-in-law of Lucien Charvet and Benjamin F. Peters
     Cousin of John and René Macready
     Married, 6 Feb. 1873, Eulalie LeBreton DesChapelles (b. Apr. 1850, New Orleans, LA; d. 27 Apr. 1906, New Orleans, LA)
RESIDENCES   1850, New Orleans, LA
     1860, New Orleans, LA
     1870, New Orleans, LA
     1880, New Orleans, LA
     1900, New Orleans, LA
     1910, New Orleans, LA
     1920, New Orleans, LA

SOURCES

Directory of Deceased American Physicians, 1804–1929
NARA M320, reels 032, 0384; M1781, reel 006
New Orleans, LA, Death Records Index, 1804–1949
New Orleans, LA, Marriage Records Index, 1831–1920
Notes on the Louisiana troops at the Battle of Chickamauga, box 5, folder 4, p. 10, Chalaron Papers, Tulane

OR, ser. 1, vol. 10, pt. 1:525
US Census 1850, 1860, 1870, 1880, 1900, 1910, 1920
US Passport Applications, 1795–1925

LE SASSIER, George

BIRTH	1 July 1839/St. Tammany Parish, LA
DEATH	11 Mar. 1908/New Orleans, LA

RECORD OF SERVICE

CSA ENLISTMENT	22 Sept. 1862/Mobile, AL/Duration of the war

ORLEANS LIGHT HORSE TRANSFER DATA

INBOUND	22 Sept. 1862/Private
OUTBOUND	Aug. 1864/Private

SERVICE RÉSUMÉ

22 Sept. 1862	Mobile, AL/Received into the Orleans Light Horse
Sept.–Oct. 1862	Present
Nov.–Dec. 1862	Absent, sick
Jan.–Feb. 1863	Absent, sick
Mar.–Apr. 1863	Absent, detached for duty, effective 3 Mar. 1863
May–June 1863	Chattanooga, TN/Absent, detached on special duty at hospital
July–Aug. 1863	Chattanooga, TN/Absent, detailed to hospital duty
Sept.–Dec. 1863	Rome, GA/Absent, detailed to duty at hospital
Feb. 1864	Rome, GA/Present for duty, Polk Hospital
May–June 1864	Rome, GA/Absent, detailed in hospital by order of Gen. Braxton Bragg
11 June 1864	Received clothing issue

PERSONAL NARRATIVE

OCCUPATION	Stockbroker
GENEALOGY	Son of Louis and Carmelite (Baham) Le Sassier, Madisonville, LA
RESIDENCES	1890, New Orleans, LA
	1891, New Orleans, LA
	1900, New Orleans, LA

SOURCES

NARA M320, reel 032
New Orleans, LA, Death Records Index, 1804–1949
New Orleans, LA, Directories, 1890–1891
US Census 1900
www.findagrave.com, 70785786

LONSDALE, Fitzwilliam

BIRTH — 1832/Kentucky
DEATH — 12 Aug. 1875/New Orleans, LA

RECORD OF SERVICE

MILITIA SERVICE — 23 Nov. 1861/Active

ORLEANS LIGHT HORSE TRANSFER DATA
   INBOUND — 1861/Private
   OUTBOUND — 22 Mar. 1862/Private

SERVICE RÉSUMÉ
   23 Nov. 1861 — New Orleans, LA/Militia service with the Orleans Light Horse; present

SEPARATION — 22 Mar. 1862/New Orleans, LA/Declined enlistment

PERSONAL NARRATIVE

OCCUPATION — Coffee merchant

GENEALOGY — Son of Henry T. and Jane (Holloway) Lonsdale, New Orleans, LA
Married, 3 Feb. 1858, New Orleans, LA, Nannie Johnson (b. 27 Dec. 1839, Kentucky; d. 11 Feb. 1886, New Orleans, LA)

RESIDENCES — 1850, New Orleans, LA
1860, New Orleans, LA
1866, New Orleans, LA
1870, Havana, Cuba
1872, New Orleans, LA

ADDITIONAL INFORMATION — Alternate spelling: Fitz Londale

SOURCES

NARA M320, reel 032
New Orleans Passenger Lists, 1820–1945
US Census 1850, 1860
www.findagrave.com, 12326515

LOTSPEICH, James T.

BIRTH — Dec. 1830/Kentucky
DEATH — 11 Dec. 1907/Corsicana, TX

RECORD OF SERVICE

CSA ENLISTMENT — 1 Feb. 1863/Shelbyville, TN/Duration of the war

ORLEANS LIGHT HORSE TRANSFER DATA
   INBOUND — 1 Feb. 1863/Private
   OUTBOUND — 10 May 1865/Private

SERVICE RÉSUMÉ
   1 Feb. 1863 — Shelbyville, TN/Received into the Orleans Light Horse
   13 Feb. 1863 — Shelbyville, TN/On roster of quartermasters, commissaries, and assistants, Polk's Corps, Army of Tennessee

15 July 1863	Chattanooga, TN/Received pay as clerk, quartermaster department
Oct. 1863	Chickamauga, GA/Received pay as clerk, quartermaster department
May–June 1864	Absent, detailed to Maj. Richard Mason, assistant quartermaster, by order of Lt. Gen. Leonidas Polk
4 May 1865	Citronelle, AL/Surrendered
SEPARATION	10 May 1865/Gainesville, AL/Parole, released from military service

PERSONAL NARRATIVE

OCCUPATION	Cotton broker
GENEALOGY	Son of David and Nancy (Western) Lotspeich, Hopkinsville, KY
	Married, 15 Mar. 1868, Margaret E. Kennedy (b. 9 Feb. 1849, Dallas County, AL; d. 1 Aug. 1932, Navarro County, TX)
RESIDENCES	1840, Christian County, KY
	1850, Christian County, KY
	1860, Jefferson Parish, LA
	1870, Selma, AL
	1880, Selma, AL
	1900, Corsicana, TX

SOURCES

Alabama State Census, 1820–1866
NARA M320, reel 032
US Census 1840, 1850, 1860, 1870, 1880, 1900
US Confederate Pensions, 1884–1958
www.findagrave.com, 104362920

LOUIS, ——

RECORD OF SERVICE

ORLEANS LIGHT HORSE TRANSFER DATA

INBOUND	June 1862/Private
OUTBOUND	Aug. 1862/Private

SERVICE RÉSUMÉ

6 June 1862	Camp Williamson, Tupelo, MS/Orleans Light Horse; present

SOURCES

NARA M320, reel 032

LOVE, William Dickson

BIRTH	1837/Hardin County, KY
DEATH	23 Jan. 1879/Memphis, TN

RECORD OF SERVICE

CSA ENLISTMENT	1 Sept. 1862/Richmond, VA/One year
	1 Sept. 1863/Chattanooga, TN/Duration of the war

ORLEANS LIGHT HORSE TRANSFER DATA
    INBOUND   1 Sept. 1863/Private
    OUTBOUND   10 May 1865/Private
SERVICE RÉSUMÉ
    1 Sept. 1863   Chattanooga, TN/Received into the Orleans Light Horse
                           from the Eighteenth Virginia Infantry (Longstreet's Corps)
    Sept.–Dec. 1863   Absent, detailed with quartermaster department
    May–June 1864   Absent, detailed with quartermaster department
    4 May 1865   Citronelle, AL/Surrendered
SEPARATION   10 May 1865/Gainesville, AL/Parole, released from
                           military service

PERSONAL NARRATIVE
OCCUPATION   Corporate secretary
GENEALOGY   Son of Madison and Mary Love, Vernon, IN
                       Married, 8 Oct. 1865, St. Louis, MO, Eliza Jane Switzer (b. 17
                           Mar. 1841, Utica, IN; d. 30 Oct. 1933, Maplewood, MO)
RESIDENCES   1840, Jackson County, IN
                       1860, Vernon, Jackson County, IN
                       1870, St. Louis, MO

SOURCES
Missouri Marriage Records, 1805–2002
NARA M320, reel 032
US Census 1840, 1860, 1870

LYND, Sav.

RECORD OF SERVICE
CSA ENLISTMENT   1 Oct. 1862/Bardstown, KY/Duration of the war
ORLEANS LIGHT HORSE TRANSFER DATA
    INBOUND   1 Oct. 1862/Private
    OUTBOUND   Aug. 1864/Private
SERVICE RÉSUMÉ
    1 Oct. 1862   Bardstown, KY/Received into the Orleans Light Horse
    Sept.–Dec. 1862   Absent, left sick at Bardstown, KY
    Jan.–June 1863   Absent, sick
    July–Dec. 1863   Absent, left sick at Bardstown, KY
    May–June 1864   Absent, left sick at Bardstown, KY
SOURCES
NARA M320, reel 032

MACREADY, John

BIRTH	7 Dec. 1837/New Orleans, LA

RECORD OF SERVICE

CSA ENLISTMENT	1 Nov. 1862/Knoxville, TN/Duration of the war

ORLEANS LIGHT HORSE TRANSFER DATA

INBOUND	1 Nov. 1862/Private
OUTBOUND	Aug. 1864/Private

SERVICE RÉSUMÉ

1 Nov. 1862	Knoxville, TN/Received into the Orleans Light Horse
Nov.–Dec. 1862	Present
Jan.–June 1863	Present
July–Dec. 1863	Present
May–June 1864	Present

PERSONAL NARRATIVE

OCCUPATION	Teacher
GENEALOGY	Son of John and Marie Amire (Le Monnier) Macready
	Brother of René Macready
	Cousin of Yves R. Le Monnier Jr.
RESIDENCES	1860, New Orleans, LA
	1870, Colerain, OH
	1900, Colerain, OH

SOURCES

NARA M320, reel 032
New Orleans, LA, Birth Records Index, 1790–1899
New Orleans Passenger Lists, 1813–1945
US Census 1860, 1870, 1900

MACREADY, René

BIRTH	1840/New Orleans, LA
DEATH	30 Dec. 1881/New Orleans, LA

RECORD OF SERVICE

CSA ENLISTMENT	5 Mar. 1862/New Orleans, LA/90 days
	1 July 1862/Tupelo, MS/Duration of the war

ORLEANS LIGHT HORSE TRANSFER DATA

INBOUND	1 July 1862/Private
OUTBOUND	1 May 1865/Private

SERVICE RÉSUMÉ

1 July 1862	Tupelo, MS/Received into the Orleans Light Horse from the Crescent Regiment, Twenty-Fourth Louisiana Infantry
Sept.–Oct. 1862	Present
Nov.–Dec. 1862	Present, detailed at Lt. Gen. Leonidas Polk's headquarters, effective 22 Dec. 1862
Jan.–June 1863	Present, detailed at Lt. Gen. Polk's headquarters
July–Dec. 1863	Present, detailed at Lt. Gen. Polk's headquarters

1–31 Jan. 1864	Meridian, MS/Receipt for pay
May–June 1864	Present, detailed at Lt. Gen. Polk's headquarters
24 June 1864	Received clothing issue
26 Apr. 1865	Durham Station, NC/Surrendered
SEPARATION	1 May 1865/Greensboro, NC/Parole, released from military service

PERSONAL NARRATIVE

OCCUPATION	Purser
GENEALOGY	Son of John and Marie Amire (Le Monnier) Macready
	Brother of John Macready
	Cousin of Yves R. Le Monnier Jr.
RESIDENCES	1860, New Orleans, LA
	1870, Brashear, LA
	1880, New Orleans, LA

SOURCES

Louisiana, Compiled Census and Census Substitutes Index, 1791–1890
NARA M320, reel 032; M1781, reel 006
New Orleans, LA, Death Records Index, 1804–1949
US Census 1860, 1870, 1880

MALLEN, J. B.

| BIRTH | ca. 1844/New Orleans, LA |

RECORD OF SERVICE

| CSA ENLISTMENT | 1 July 1861/Memphis, TN/One year |
| | 1 Sept. 1863/Chattanooga, TN/Duration of the war |

ORLEANS LIGHT HORSE TRANSFER DATA

| INBOUND | 1 Sept. 1863/Private |
| OUTBOUND | Aug. 1864/Private |

SERVICE RÉSUMÉ

1 Sept. 1863	Chattanooga, TN/Received into the Orleans Light Horse from the Twelfth Tennessee Regiment (dismounted)
Sept.–Dec. 1863	Present
May–June 1864	Present
ADDITIONAL INFORMATION	Alternate spelling: J. Mallon

SOURCES

NARA M320, reel 032
US Census 1860

MANDEVILLE, T.

RECORD OF SERVICE

| CSA ENLISTMENT | 1 July 1862/Tupelo, MS/Duration of the war |

ORLEANS LIGHT HORSE TRANSFER DATA

| INBOUND | 1 July 1862/Private |
| OUTBOUND | Feb. 1863/Private |

| 1 July 1862 | Tupelo, MS/Received into the Orleans Light Horse |
| Sept.–Dec. 1862 | Present |

SOURCES

NARA M320, reel 032

MANSFIELD, Richard

BIRTH   ca. 1832/Ireland
DEATH   2 Dec. 1863/Mobile, AL

RECORD OF SERVICE

CSA ENLISTMENT   1 July 1861/Memphis, TN/One year
                       1 Sept. 1863/Chattanooga, TN/Duration of the war

ORLEANS LIGHT HORSE TRANSFER DATA

    INBOUND   1 Sept. 1863/Private
    OUTBOUND   2 Dec. 1863/Private

SERVICE RÉSUMÉ

    1 Sept. 1863   Chattanooga, TN/Received into the Orleans Light Horse from the Twelfth Tennessee Regiment

    Sept.–Oct. 1863   Rome, GA/Absent, sick in hospital

SEPARATION   2 Dec. 1863/Mobile, AL/Death

PERSONAL NARRATIVE

GENEALOGY   Arrived in New Orleans, LA, from Liverpool, England, 2 Aug. 1850

RESIDENCES   1860, New Orleans, LA

SOURCES

Confederate Pension Applications Collection, Louisiana State Archives
NARA M320, reel 032
New Orleans Passenger Lists, 1813–1945
US Census 1860
www.findagrave.com, 70944272

MARTINDALE, Fenelon Beardsly

BIRTH   Sept. 1835/New York
DEATH   10 Feb. 1906/Covington, LA

RECORD OF SERVICE

CSA ENLISTMENT   18 Sept. 1862/Munfordville, KY/Duration of the war

ORLEANS LIGHT HORSE TRANSFER DATA

    INBOUND   18 Sept. 1862/Private
    OUTBOUND   20 May 1865/Private

SERVICE RÉSUMÉ

    18 Sept. 1862   Munfordville, KY/Received into the Orleans Light Horse
    Nov.–Dec. 1862   Present
    Jan.–Feb. 1863   Present
    Mar.–June 1863   Present, detached at headquarters of Lt. Gen. Leonidas Polk

17 Apr. 1863	Detailed at stable of Lt. Gen. Polk and staff
July–Oct. 1863	Present
9 Aug. 1863	Detailed to drive stock to Georgia
Nov.–Dec. 1863	Absent, furlough
May–June 1864	Present
26 Apr. 1865	Durham Station, NC/Included in surrender terms of Gen. Joseph E. Johnston
SEPARATION	20 May 1865/Atlanta, GA/Parole, released from military service

PERSONAL NARRATIVE

OCCUPATION	Wood dealer
GENEALOGY	Married, 23 Apr. 1867, Covington, LA, Hester G. Thompson (b. Oct. 1847, Louisiana; d. 11 Mar. 1914, Covington, St. Tammany Parish, LA)
RESIDENCES	1850, Batavia, NY
	1870, Covington, LA
	1880, Covington, LA
	1900, Covington, LA

SOURCES

Confederate Pension Applications Collection, Louisiana State Archives
NARA M320, reel 032; M1781, reel 006
US Census 1850, 1870, 1880, 1900
US IRS Tax Assessment Lists, 1862–1918
www.findagrave.com, 86565118

MAY, Thomas Paine

| BIRTH | 17 July 1842/New Orleans, LA |
| DEATH | 10 Jan. 1887/London, England |

RECORD OF SERVICE

CSA ENLISTMENT	22 Mar. 1862/New Orleans, LA/90 days
ORLEANS LIGHT HORSE TRANSFER DATA	
INBOUND	22 Mar. 1862/Private
OUTBOUND	23 May 1862/Private
SERVICE RÉSUMÉ	
22 Mar. 1862	New Orleans, LA/Mustered into service of CSA with the Orleans Light Horse
SEPARATION	23 May 1862/Tupelo, MS/Discharge, unspecified

PERSONAL NARRATIVE

OCCUPATION	Farmer, grocer, newspaper publisher (*New-Orleans Times*)
GENEALOGY	Son of Thomas and Martha Eliza (Thomas) May, St. John the Baptist Parish, LA
	Married, ca. 1865, Louisiana, Mary Taylor (b. ca. 1845, Louisiana; d. after 1920, presumably Richmond, VA)
	Inherited the Irish title Sir Thomas May of Mayfield, Baronet, from his grandfather (1882)

RESIDENCES	1850, St. John the Baptist Parish, LA
	1860, St. John the Baptist Parish, LA
	1870, St. John the Baptist Parish, LA
	1880, New Orleans, LA
	1883, London, England

SOURCES

Border Watch (Mount Gambier, Australia), 2 Apr. 1887

Leicester Chronicle, 12 Feb. 1887

London Times, 23 and 26, May 1885, 1 Mar. 1887

NARA M320, reel 032

New Orleans, LA, Birth Records Index, 1790–1899

New-Orleans Times entry, on National Endowment for the Humanities and Library of Congress, *Chronicling America*, http://chroniclingamerica.loc.gov/lccn/sn83026550/

US Census 1850, 1860, 1870, 1880

McKNIGHT, John H.

| BIRTH | 1841/Mississippi |
| DEATH | Mar. 1865/Bentonville, NC |

RECORD OF SERVICE

| CSA ENLISTMENT | 22 Mar. 1862/New Orleans, LA/90 days |
| | 25 July 1862/Tupelo, MS/Duration of the war |

ORLEANS LIGHT HORSE TRANSFER DATA

| INBOUND | 22 Mar. 1862/Private |
| OUTBOUND | Mar. 1865/Private |

SERVICE RÉSUMÉ

22 Mar. 1862	New Orleans, LA/Mustered into service of CSA with the Orleans Light Horse
22 Mar.–25 May 1862	Present
6 June 1862	Camp Williamson, Tupelo, MS/Absent, sick
Sept.–Dec. 1862	Present
Jan.–June 1863	Present
July–Dec. 1863	Present
30 July 1863	Leave of absence for 12 days
May–June 1864	Present
24 June 1864	Received clothing issue
SEPARATION	Mar. 1865/Bentonville, NC/Killed in action

PERSONAL NARRATIVE

GENEALOGY	Son of Thomas Jefferson and Elizabeth (Hearn) McKnight, New Orleans, LA
RESIDENCES	1850, New Orleans, LA
	1860, New Orleans, LA

SOURCES

NARA M320, reel 032

US Census 1850, 1860

www.findagrave.com, 11713626

MITCHELL, Christophal C.

BIRTH	4 Jan. 1828/Hancock County, MS
DEATH	30 Dec. 1900/Hancock County, MS

RECORD OF SERVICE

CSA ENLISTMENT	22 Mar. 1862/New Orleans, LA/90 days
	25 July 1862/Tupelo, MS/Duration of the war

ORLEANS LIGHT HORSE TRANSFER DATA

INBOUND	22 Mar. 1862/Private
OUTBOUND	11 May 1865/Private

SERVICE RÉSUMÉ

22 Mar. 1862	New Orleans, LA/Mustered into service of CSA with the Orleans Light Horse
22 Mar.–25 May 1862	Present
6 June 1862	Camp Williamson, Tupelo, MS/Present
Sept.–Dec. 1862	Present
Jan.–June 1863	Present
July–Dec. 1863	Present
9 Aug. 1863	Detailed in charge of stock in pasture
May–June 1864	Present
29 June 1864	Received clothing issue
26 Apr. 1865	Durham Station, NC/Surrendered
SEPARATION	11 May 1865/New Bern, NC/Parole, released from military service

PERSONAL NARRATIVE

OCCUPATION	Farmer
GENEALOGY	Son of George Andrew and Phoebe Ann (Miller) Mitchell, Hancock County, MS
	Married, 5 June 1870, Hancock County, MS, Josephine E. McFadden (b. 1847, Mississippi)
RESIDENCES	1860, New Orleans, LA
	1870, Hancock County, MS
	1900, Hancock County, MS

SOURCES

Mississippi Marriages, 1776–1935
NARA M320, reel 032; M1781, reel 006
US Census 1860, 1870, 1900
www.findagrave.com, 32602672

MITCHELL, William C.

BIRTH   ca. 1836

RECORD OF SERVICE

CSA ENLISTMENT   22 Mar. 1862/New Orleans, LA/90 days

ORLEANS LIGHT HORSE TRANSFER DATA

    INBOUND   22 Mar. 1862/Private

    OUTBOUND   Apr. 1863/Private

SERVICE RÉSUMÉ

    22 Mar. 1862   New Orleans, LA/Mustered into service of CSA with the
                       Orleans Light Horse

    22 Mar.–25 May 1862 Present

    6 June 1862   Camp Williamson, Tupelo, MS/Absent, on leave

    Sept.–Dec. 1862   Absent without leave

    Jan.–Feb. 1863   Absent without leave

SEPARATION   Apr. 1863/Shelbyville, TN/Deserter, dropped from rolls

PERSONAL NARRATIVE

OCCUPATION   Printer (*New Orleans Times-Democrat*)

GENEALOGY   Arrived in New Orleans, LA, from Matamoros, Mexico,
                       17 June 1863

                       Married, 1 May 1889, New Orleans, LA, Rebecca L. McDowell

RESIDENCES   1865, New Orleans, LA

                       1890, New Orleans, LA

                       1891, New Orleans, LA

SOURCES

Louisiana Marriages, 1718–1925

NARA M320, reel 032

New Orleans, LA, Directories, 1890–1891

New Orleans Passenger Lists, 1813–1945

US IRS Tax Assessment Lists, 1862–1918

MONTY, F. P.

BIRTH   ca. 1823

RECORD OF SERVICE

CSA ENLISTMENT   22 Mar. 1862/New Orleans, LA/90 days

ORLEANS LIGHT HORSE TRANSFER DATA

    INBOUND   22 Mar. 1862/Private

    OUTBOUND   10 May 1862/Private

SERVICE RÉSUMÉ

    22 Mar. 1862   New Orleans, LA/Mustered into service of CSA with the
                       Orleans Light Horse

    22 Mar.–10 May 1862 Present

SEPARATION   10 May 1862/Corinth, MS/Honorable discharge, unspecified

PERSONAL NARRATIVE

GENEALOGY   Arrived in New Orleans, LA, from Havana, Cuba, 1 June 1868

ADDITIONAL INFORMATION   Alternate spelling: Monti, F. P.
SOURCES
NARA M320, reel 032
New Orleans Passenger Lists, 1813–1945

MOORE, James Bradner, Sr.

BIRTH   13 Aug. 1837/Orange County, NY
DEATH   29 Oct. 1903/New Orleans, LA

RECORD OF SERVICE
CSA ENLISTMENT   1 Aug. 1862/Chattanooga, TN/Duration of the war
ORLEANS LIGHT HORSE TRANSFER DATA
   INBOUND   1 Aug. 1862/Private
   OUTBOUND   27 May 1865/Private
SERVICE RÉSUMÉ
   1 Aug. 1862   Chattanooga, TN/Received into the Orleans Light Horse
   Sept.–Dec. 1862   Present
   Jan.–June 1863   Present
   July–Aug. 1863   Present
   9 July 1863   Detailed at Lt. Gen. Leonidas Polk's headquarters
   19 Aug. 1863   Detailed as clerk, quartermaster department
   Sept.–Dec. 1863   Mobile, AL/Absent, sick in hospital
   6 Feb. 1864   Receipt for pay due
   9 Feb. 1864   Meridian, MS/Medical reevaluation: unfit for field duty
   25 Mar. 1864   Received clothing issue
   May–June 1864   Absent, detailed in quartermaster department by order of
                        Lt. Gen. Polk
   4 May 1865   Montgomery, AL/Surrendered
SEPARATION   27 May 1865/Montgomery, AL/Parole, released from
                        military service

PERSONAL NARRATIVE
OCCUPATION   Hardware merchant
GENEALOGY   Son of Hector and Fanetta (Bailey) Moore, Middletown, NY
                        Married, 14 Dec. 1875, New Orleans, LA, Clemence
                           Ruthetta Folger (b. 1843, New Orleans, LA; d. 1934,
                           Jackson, MS)
RESIDENCES   1850, New York County, NY
                        1860, New Orleans, LA
                        1880, New Orleans, LA

SOURCES
Confederate Pension Applications Collection, Louisiana State Archives
NARA M320, reel 032
New Orleans, LA, Death Records Index, 1804–1949
New Orleans, LA, Marriage Records Index, 1831–1920
US Census 1850, 1860, 1880
www.findagrave.com, 70959116

MOREAU, Joseph Theophilus

BIRTH   ca. 1830/France
DEATH   9 Jan. 1891/New Orleans, LA

RECORD OF SERVICE

CSA ENLISTMENT   22 Mar. 1862/New Orleans, LA/90 days

ORLEANS LIGHT HORSE TRANSFER DATA
   INBOUND   22 Mar. 1862/Private
   OUTBOUND   Aug. 1862/Private

SERVICE RÉSUMÉ
   22 Mar. 1862   New Orleans, LA/Mustered into service of CSA with the Orleans Light Horse
   22 Mar.–25 May 1862   Present
   6 June 1862   Camp Williamson, Tupelo, MS/Absent, sick

PERSONAL NARRATIVE

OCCUPATION   Physician
GENEALOGY   Obtained US citizenship, 18 June 1851, New Orleans, LA
                        Married, 12 May 1877, New Orleans, LA, Henrietta Louise Witte (b. 30 Mar. 1859, New Orleans, LA; d. 10 May 1929, New Orleans, LA)
RESIDENCES   1850, New Orleans, LA
                        1880, New Orleans, LA
                        1890, New Orleans, LA

SOURCES

Louisiana Marriages, 1718–1925
NARA M320, reel 032
New Orleans, LA, Death Records Index, 1804–1949
New Orleans, LA, Directories, 1890–1891
New Orleans, LA, Marriage Records Index, 1831–1920
US Census 1880
US Naturalization Record Indexes, 1791–1992

MORIARTY, William Ambrose

BIRTH   1824/Batavia, OH
DEATH   3 Mar. 1877/New Orleans, LA

RECORD OF SERVICE

CSA ENLISTMENT   22 Mar. 1862/New Orleans, LA/90 days
                        25 July 1862/Tupelo, MS/Duration of the war

ORLEANS LIGHT HORSE TRANSFER DATA
   INBOUND   22 Mar. 1862/Private
   OUTBOUND   Feb. 1864/Private

SERVICE RÉSUMÉ
   22 Mar. 1862   New Orleans, LA/Mustered into service of CSA with the Orleans Light Horse
   Sept.–Dec. 1862   Present

Jan.–June 1863	Present
July–Oct. 1863	Present
9 Aug. 1863	Detailed to drive stock to Georgia
Nov.–Dec. 1863	Absent, furlough

PERSONAL NARRATIVE

OCCUPATION	Laborer, constable
GENEALOGY	Son of Gilbert Burling and Avey Ann (Ranson) Moriarty, Batavia, OH
	Married (1), 28 Feb. 1855, St. Landry Parish, LA, Aurore D'Avy (b. 30 Oct. 1834, Opelousas, LA; d. 8 Mar. 1864, Opelousas, LA)
	Married (2), 2 Mar. 1871, St. Mary Parish, LA, Emma Henriette Cuvillier (b. 24 Aug. 1849, Charenton, LA; d. 11 Nov. 1929, Alexandria, LA)
RESIDENCES	1830, Clermont County, OH
	1840, Clermont County, OH
	1855, Opelousas, LA
	1860, Opelousas, LA
	1871, Charenton, LA

SOURCES

Admissions and Dispositions Register, Charity Hospital, Louisiana Division, New Orleans Public Library

Louisiana Marriages, 1718–1925

Moriarty, pt. 2, 105–9

NARA M320, reel 032

US Census 1830, 1840, 1860

www.findagrave.com, 27785434

MORSE, Edward Malcolm

BIRTH	30 Dec. 1835/St. Martinsville, LA

RECORD OF SERVICE

CSA ENLISTMENT	22 Mar. 1862/New Orleans, LA/90 days
	25 July 1862/Tupelo, MS/Duration of the war

ORLEANS LIGHT HORSE TRANSFER DATA

INBOUND	22 Mar. 1862/Private
OUTBOUND	16 May 1865/Lieutenant

SERVICE RÉSUMÉ

22 Mar. 1862	New Orleans, LA/Mustered into service of CSA with the Orleans Light Horse
22 Mar.–24 May 1862	Present
25 May 1862	Tupelo, MS/In camp, sick, in rank of private
6 June 1862	Camp Williamson, Tupelo, MS/Absent, sick
Sept.–Oct. 1862	Present, detailed on duty
Nov.–Dec. 1862	Present, in rank of private
Jan.–June 1863	Present

20 Apr. 1863	Shelbyville, TN/Applied to the secretary of war for evaluation and appointment as a surgeon; necessary papers not on file; no further action
31 May 1863	Elected second lieutenant
July–Dec. 1863	Present, in position of second lieutenant
30 July, 9 Aug. 1863	Rome, GA/Absent, sick in hospital
May–June 1864	Present, in position of second lieutenant
4 May 1865	Meridian, MS/Surrendered
SEPARATION	16 May 1865/Meridian, MS/Parole, released from military service

PERSONAL NARRATIVE

OCCUPATION	Physician
GENEALOGY	Son of Isaac Edward and Margaretta (Wederstrandt) Morse, St. Martinville, LA
	Married, 1865, Louisiana, Angela Lewis Andrews (b. ca. 1844, Iberville, LA; d. 4 Mar. 1870, San Francisco, CA)
RESIDENCES	1850, Georgetown, DC
	1868, San Francisco, CA
	1871, San Luis Obispo County, CA

SOURCES

California Voter Registers, 1866–1898
Morse, 445
NARA M320, reel 032
Obituary: Mrs. E. M. Morse, *New Orleans Daily Picayune*, 8 and 13 Mar. 1870
US Census 1850

MULHOLLAND, John

RECORD OF SERVICE

CSA ENLISTMENT	1 July 1861/Memphis, TN/One year
	1 Sept. 1863/Chattanooga, TN/Duration of the war
ORLEANS LIGHT HORSE TRANSFER DATA	
INBOUND	1 Sept. 1863/Private
OUTBOUND	Aug. 1864/Private
SERVICE RÉSUMÉ	
1 Sept. 1863	Chattanooga, TN/Received into the Orleans Light Horse from the Twelfth Tennessee Regiment (dismounted)
Sept.–Dec. 1863	Present
May–June 1864	Present

SOURCES

NARA M320, reel 032

MURPHY, Con

BIRTH   ca. 1827, Ireland

RECORD OF SERVICE

CSA ENLISTMENT   22 Mar. 1862/New Orleans, LA/90 days
      25 July 1862/Tupelo, MS/Duration of the war

ORLEANS LIGHT HORSE TRANSFER DATA
     INBOUND   22 Mar. 1862/Private
     OUTBOUND   June 1862/Private

SERVICE RÉSUMÉ
     22 Mar. 1862   New Orleans, LA/Mustered into service of CSA with the Orleans Light Horse
     22 Mar.–25 May 1862   Present
     6 June 1862   Camp Williamson, Tupelo, MS/Approved for discharge

SEPARATION   10 June 1862/Tupelo, MS/Discharge, unspecified

PERSONAL NARRATIVE

OCCUPATION   Blacksmith

GENEALOGY   Arrived in New Orleans, LA, 18 Nov. 1852

SOURCES

Boston Passenger and Crew Lists, 1820–1954
NARA M320, reel 032
New Orleans Passenger Lists, 1813–1945
New York Passenger Lists, 1820–1957

NICHOLS, William Charles

BIRTH   ca. 1830

DEATH   31 Dec. 1871/New Orleans, LA

RECORD OF SERVICE

MILITIA SERVICE   23 Nov. 1861/Active

CSA ENLISTMENT   22 Mar. 1862/New Orleans, LA/90 days

ORLEANS LIGHT HORSE TRANSFER DATA
     INBOUND   1861/Surgeon
     OUTBOUND   25 May 1862/Surgeon

SERVICE RÉSUMÉ
     23 Nov. 1861   New Orleans, LA/Militia service with the Orleans Light Horse; present, in rank of surgeon
     22 Mar. 1862   New Orleans, LA/Mustered into service of CSA with the Orleans Light Horse
     22 Mar.–24 May 1862   Present, in rank of surgeon
     25 May 1862   Tupelo, MS/Detailed by Dr. Warren Stone, surgeon general of Louisiana

PERSONAL NARRATIVE

OCCUPATION   Physician

RESIDENCES   1859, New Orleans, LA
                               1860, New Orleans, LA
                               1862, Richmond, VA
                               1866, New Orleans, LA
                               1869, New Orleans, LA

SOURCES
Gardner's New Orleans Directory, 1866, 1869
NARA M320, reel 032; M331, reel 023
New Orleans Daily Picayune, 17 Feb. 1872
Olschner, 9
Waitt, 21

O'BRIEN, Patrick B.

BIRTH   1825/Ireland
DEATH   16 Oct. 1896/New Orleans, LA

RECORD OF SERVICE
MILITIA SERVICE   23 Nov. 1861/Resignation in progress
ORLEANS LIGHT HORSE TRANSFER DATA
   INBOUND   1861/Cornet
   OUTBOUND   1 Dec. 1861/Cornet
SERVICE RÉSUMÉ
   23 Nov. 1861   New Orleans, LA/Militia service with the Orleans Light
                               Horse; resignation received, not yet accepted
   1 Dec. 1861   New Orleans, LA/Transferred to Irish Regiment,
                               Louisiana Militia

PERSONAL NARRATIVE
OCCUPATION   Teamster
GENEALOGY   Married, 1856, Louisiana, Alice O'Sullivan (b. ca. 1831,
                               Ireland; d. 19 Nov. 1880, New Orleans, LA)
RESIDENCES   1850, New Orleans, LA
                               1860, New Orleans, LA
                               1863, New Orleans, LA
                               1880, St. Louis, MO
                               1890, New Orleans, LA

SOURCES
Booth, 3:5
NARA M320, reel 032
New Orleans, LA, Death Records Index, 1804–1949
New Orleans, LA, Directories, 1890–1891
US Census 1850, 1860, 1880
US IRS Tax Assessment Lists, 1862–1918
www.findagrave.com, 71466518

OPDENWEYER, William Charles

BIRTH	1835/Rheinland-Pfalz, Germany
DEATH	14 July 1883/Livingston Parish, LA

RECORD OF SERVICE

CSA ENLISTMENT	24 Feb. 1861/New Orleans, LA/90 days
	22 Mar. 1862/New Orleans, LA/90 days

ORLEANS LIGHT HORSE TRANSFER DATA

INBOUND	22 Mar. 1862/Private
OUTBOUND	Aug. 1862/Private

SERVICE RÉSUMÉ

22 Mar. 1862	New Orleans, LA/Received into the Orleans Light Horse from the First Chasseurs-à-Pied (disbanded)
25 May 1862	Memphis, TN/Sick, government hospital
6 June 1862	Camp Williamson, Tupelo, MS/Absent

PERSONAL NARRATIVE

OCCUPATION	Sawmill founder, postmaster, general store owner
GENEALOGY	Married, 1 Feb. 1864, New Orleans, LA, Mary Catherine Vugeley (b. Jan. 1844, Alsace-Lorraine, France; d. 26 Mar. 1924, New Orleans, LA)
RESIDENCES	1866, Bayou Barbara, LA
	1870, Livingston Parish, LA
	1880, Livingston Parish, LA
ADDITIONAL INFORMATION	The individual whose service is detailed in the compiled service records is listed by his family name only. Research on the Opdenweyer family revealed that Jean Joachim and Maria Opdenweyer (Opdenmeyer) emigrated from Rheinland-Pfalz, Germany, and settled in New Orleans, LA, ca. 1845. Only two sons, William Charles and Otto, were of military age. They enlisted in First Chasseurs-à-Pied, Louisiana Militia, 24 Feb. 1861, for a term of 90 days; that unit was disbanded with the fall of New Orleans, 28 Apr. 1862. Otto enlisted subsequently in Co. F, Thirtieth Louisiana Infantry, 11 Mar. 1862. The Opdenweyer who enlisted in the Light Horse is believed to be William.

SOURCES

Booth, 3:38
NARA M320, reel 032
US Census 1870, 1880
US IRS Tax Assessment Lists, 1862–1918

PARSONS, James Wellington

BIRTH	8 July 1839/New York
DEATH	5 Jan. 1873/Rochester, NY

RECORD OF SERVICE

CSA ENLISTMENT   22 Mar. 1862/New Orleans, LA/90 days

ORLEANS LIGHT HORSE TRANSFER DATA

    INBOUND   22 Mar. 1862/Private

    OUTBOUND   4 July 1862/Private

SERVICE RÉSUMÉ

    22 Mar. 1862   New Orleans, LA/Mustered into service of CSA with the Orleans Light Horse

    22 Mar.–25 May 1862   Present

    6 June 1862   Camp Williamson, Tupelo, MS/Present

SEPARATION   4 July 1862/Tupelo, MS/Discharge, physical disability

PERSONAL NARRATIVE

GENEALOGY   Son of Cyrus Wellington and Harriet (Withenbury) Parsons, Cazenovia, NY

    Married, ca. 1859, Amelia —— (b. ca. 1845, NY)

RESIDENCES   1850, Cazanovia, NY

    1870, Buffalo, NY

ADDITIONAL INFORMATION   Alternate spelling: J. M. Parsons

SOURCES

NARA M320, reel 032

US Census 1850, 1870

www.findagrave.com, 13507960

PATRICK, Josiah Clinton, Jr.

BIRTH	1839/West Baton Rouge Parish, LA
DEATH	24 May 1898/New Orleans, LA

RECORD OF SERVICE

CSA ENLISTMENT   22 Mar. 1862/New Orleans, LA/90 days

    25 July 1862/Tupelo, MS/Duration of the war

ORLEANS LIGHT HORSE TRANSFER DATA

    INBOUND   22 Mar. 1862/Private

    OUTBOUND   9 June 1863/Lieutenant

SERVICE RÉSUMÉ

    22 Mar. 1862   New Orleans, LA/Mustered into service of CSA with the Orleans Light Horse

    22 Mar.–25 May 1862   Present, in camp, sick, in rank of corporal

    6 June 1862   Camp Williamson, Tupelo, MS/Absent, sick, in rank of sergeant

    Nov.–Dec. 1862   Present, in position of second lieutenant

    Jan.–June 1863   Present, in position of second lieutenant

| 9 June 1863 | Furlough and transfer to Tensas Co., Major Harrison's Battalion, Louisiana Cavalry (later, Co. A, Third Louisiana Cavalry Regiment) |

PERSONAL NARRATIVE

OCCUPATION	Planter, notary public
GENEALOGY	Son of Josiah Clinton and Eliza (Connell) Patrick, West Baton Rouge Parish, LA
	Married, June 1863, Amelia Mumford Cooley (b. Mar. 1848, Pointe Coupée Parish, LA; d. Dec. 1917, New Orleans, LA)
RESIDENCES	1850, Wilkinson County, MS
	1860, West Baton Rouge Parish, LA
	1870, Pointe Coupée Parish, LA
	1880, Pointe Coupée Parish, LA

SOURCES

Louisiana Marriages, 1718–1925
NARA M320, reel 032
New Orleans, LA, Death Records Index, 1804–1949
US Census 1850, 1860, 1870, 1880
www.findagrave.com, 11894820

PAYAN, H.

| BIRTH | ca. 1838/New Orleans, LA |

RECORD OF SERVICE

| CSA ENLISTMENT | 15 Apr. 1862/New Orleans, LA/Duration of the war |

ORLEANS LIGHT HORSE TRANSFER DATA

| INBOUND | 6 June 1862/Private |
| OUTBOUND | 14 June 1862/Private |

SERVICE RÉSUMÉ

| 6 June 1862 | Camp Williamson, Tupelo, MS/Present with the Orleans Light Horse (reason unspecified), from Co. I, First Louisiana Cavalry Regiment |
| 14 June 1862 | Tupelo, MS/Returned to his own regiment (First Louisiana Cavalry Regiment) |

PERSONAL NARRATIVE

GENEALOGY	Son of Thomas Charles and Palmire (Maitrejean) Payan, New Orleans, LA
RESIDENCES	1840, New Orleans, LA
	1850, New Orleans, LA
	1860, New Orleans, LA
	1865, New Orleans, LA

SOURCES

Louisiana, Compiled Census and Census Substitutes Index, 1791–1890
NARA M320, reels 005, 032
US Census 1850, 1860
US IRS Tax Assessment Lists, 1862–1918

PENN, M. A.

RECORD OF SERVICE

CSA ENLISTMENT   27 Apr. 1864/Demopolis, AL/Duration of the war

ORLEANS LIGHT HORSE TRANSFER DATA

     INBOUND   27 Apr. 1864/Private

     OUTBOUND   Aug. 1864/Private

SERVICE RÉSUMÉ

     27 Apr. 1864   Demopolis, AL/Received into the Orleans Light Horse

     May–June 1864   Resaca, GA/Absent, sick

SOURCES

NARA M320, reel 032

PERKINS, John A.

BIRTH   Jan. 1838/Louisiana

DEATH   8 Jan. 1904/New Orleans, LA

RECORD OF SERVICE

CSA ENLISTMENT   6 Mar. 1862/New Orleans, LA/90 days

       1 June 1862/Tupelo, MS/Duration of the war

ORLEANS LIGHT HORSE TRANSFER DATA

     INBOUND   3 June 1862/Private

     OUTBOUND   17 May 1865/Private

SERVICE RÉSUMÉ

     3 June 1862   Tupelo, MS/Received into the Orleans Light Horse from the Crescent Regiment, Twenty-Fourth Louisiana Infantry

     Sept.–Oct. 1862   Present, detailed on duty

     Nov.–Dec. 1862   Present

     Jan.–Feb. 1863   Present, detailed at headquarters

     Mar.–June 1863   Present

     July–Dec. 1863   Present

     19 Sept. 1863   Chickamauga, GA/On duty as headquarters courier; involved in controversy that caused Lt. Gen. Leonidas Polk to be relieved of command

     May–June 1864   Present

     26 Apr. 1865   LaGrange, GA/Surrendered

SEPARATION   17 May 1865/LaGrange, GA/Parole, released from military service

PERSONAL NARRATIVE

OCCUPATION   Cotton weigher

GENEALOGY   Married, 3 Jan. 1866, New Orleans, LA, Emily Losene Norton (b. July 1839, Louisiana; d. 31 Jan. 1920, New Orleans, LA)

SOURCES
Confederate Pension Applications Collection, Louisiana State Archives
NARA M320, reel 032
New Orleans, LA, Death Records Index, 1804–1949
OR, ser. 1, vol. 30, pt. 2:60
US Census 1860, 1870, 1880, 1900

PERKINS, Louis William

BIRTH   14 Oct. 1842/Louisiana
DEATH   14 Feb. 1908/Washington, DC

RECORD OF SERVICE
CSA ENLISTMENT   27 Sept. 1863/Chickamauga, GA/Duration of the war
ORLEANS LIGHT HORSE TRANSFER DATA
   INBOUND   27 Sept. 1863/Private
   OUTBOUND   4 May 1865/Private
SERVICE RÉSUMÉ
   27 Sept. 1863   Chickamauga, GA/Received into the Orleans Light Horse,
                            in rank of private

   Sept.–Oct. 1863   Present
   Nov.–Dec. 1863   Detailed at headquarters, Lt. Gen. Leonidas Polk
   Feb. 1864   Receipt for extra-duty pay as a clerk
   May–June 1864   Absent, detailed at paymaster department by order of
                            Lt. Gen. Polk
   May 1864   Receipt for extra-duty pay as a clerk
   June 1864   Receipt for extra-duty pay as a clerk
   4 May 1865   Macon, GA/Surrendered
SEPARATION   4 May 1865/Macon, GA/Parole, released from military service

PERSONAL NARRATIVE
OCCUPATION   Commission merchant, clerk for a government agency
GENEALOGY   Son of John L. and Elvira Perkins
                           Married (1), 1868, New Orleans, LA, Anaîs Emelie Legeai
                            (b. 17 Aug. 1843, New Orleans, LA; d. 21 June 1900,
                            New Orleans, LA)
                           Married (2), 29 Aug. 1905, Loudoun County, VA, Martha
                            Alice Rollins (b. 22 Oct. 1860, Loudoun County, VA;
                            d. 21 Mar. 1945, Loudoun County, VA)
RESIDENCES   1850, St. Tammany Parish, LA
                           1860, St. Tammany Parish, LA
                           1870, New Orleans, LA
                           1880, New Orleans, LA
                           1900, Washington, DC

SOURCES
Confederate Pension Applications Collection, Louisiana State Archives
NARA M320, reel 032
US Census 1850, 1860, 1870, 1880, 1900
www.findagrave.com, 50184245

PETERS, Benjamin Franklin

BIRTH	Aug. 1831/New Orleans, LA
DEATH	20 June 1908/New Orleans, LA

RECORD OF SERVICE

MILITIA SERVICE	23 Nov. 1861/Active
CSA ENLISTMENT	22 Mar. 1862/New Orleans, LA/90 days
	25 July 1862/Tupelo, MS/Duration of the war

ORLEANS LIGHT HORSE TRANSFER DATA

INBOUND	1861/Private
OUTBOUND	Mar. 1865/Private

SERVICE RÉSUMÉ

23 Nov. 1861	New Orleans, LA/Militia service with the Orleans Light Horse; present, in rank of private
22 Mar. 1862	New Orleans, LA/Mustered into service of CSA
22 Mar.–24 May 1862	Present
25 May 1862	Tupelo, MS/Sick in camp
6 June 1862	Camp Williamson, Tupelo, MS/Present
Sept.–Dec. 1862	Present, in rank of private
Jan.–Aug. 1863	Present, in rank of private
1 Aug. 1863	Promoted to rank of corporal
Sept.–Oct. 1863	Present, in rank of corporal
Nov.–Dec. 1863	Absent, furlough
8 Jan. 1864	Madisonville, LA/Captured; transferred to military prison, New Orleans, LA
14 Aug. 1864	New Orleans, LA/Escaped prison; returned to CSA jurisdiction
28 Feb. 1865	Magnolia, MS/Medical review, recommended 60-day medical leave
4 May 1865	Magnolia, MS/Surrendered
SEPARATION	10 May 1865/McComb, MS/Parole, released from military service

PERSONAL NARRATIVE

OCCUPATION	Stockbroker
GENEALOGY	Son of Samuel Jarvis and Marianne (deSilly) Peters, New Orleans, LA
	Brother-in-law of Yves R. Le Monnier Jr.
	Uncle of Jules A. Blanc Jr.
	Married, ca. 1862, Marie Felicie Le Monnier (b. 1 Mar. 1841, New Orleans, LA; d. 22 Apr. 1919, New Orleans, LA)

SOURCES
Confederate Pension Applications Collection, Louisiana State Archives
NARA M320, reel 032
New Orleans, LA, Death Records Index, 1804–1949
US Census 1840, 1850, 1880, 1900
www.findagrave.com, 12150793

PHILLIPS, E. M.

RECORD OF SERVICE

CSA ENLISTMENT	1 July 1861/Memphis, TN/One year
	1 Sept. 1863/Chattanooga, TN/Duration of the war
ORLEANS LIGHT HORSE TRANSFER DATA	
INBOUND	1 Sept. 1863/Private
OUTBOUND	20 Dec. 1863/Private
SERVICE RÉSUMÉ	
1 Sept. 1863	Chattanooga, TN/Received into the Orleans Light Horse from the Twelfth Tennessee Regiment (dismounted)
Sept.–Dec. 1863	Present
18 Dec. 1863	Meridian, MS/Application approved for transfer to Co. K, Third Louisiana Infantry (Pelican Rifles)
ADDITIONAL INFORMATION	Alternate spelling: E. D. Phillips

SOURCES
NARA M320, reel 032

POLLOCK, John Fitz

BIRTH	Jan. 1836/New Orleans, LA
DEATH	13 Jan. 1909/New Orleans, LA

RECORD OF SERVICE

MILITIA SERVICE	23 Nov. 1861/Active
CSA ENLISTMENT	22 Mar. 1862/New Orleans, LA/90 days
ORLEANS LIGHT HORSE TRANSFER DATA	
INBOUND	1861/Corporal
OUTBOUND	14 June 1862/Sergeant
SERVICE RÉSUMÉ	
23 Nov. 1861	New Orleans, LA/Militia service with the Orleans Light Horse; present, in rank of corporal
22 Mar. 1862	New Orleans, LA/Mustered into service of CSA with the Orleans Light Horse
25 May 1862	Tupelo, MS/Present, in position of quartermaster sergeant
6 June 1862	Camp Williamson, Tupelo, MS/Absent, detailed

SEPARATION	14 June 1862/Tupelo, MS/Discharge, unspecified

PERSONAL NARRATIVE

OCCUPATION	Dealer in cotton and sugar
GENEALOGY	Son of George Auguste and Marie Augustine Elina (Miltenberger) Pollock Married, Dec. 1868, New Orleans, LA, Marie Louise Tuyes (b. 16 Dec. 1845, New Orleans, LA; d. 1 June 1921, New Orleans, LA)
RESIDENCES	1850, New Orleans, LA 1860, New Orleans, LA 1870, New Orleans, LA 1880, New Orleans, LA 1900, New Orleans, LA

SOURCES

NARA M320, reel 032
New Orleans, LA, Death Records Index, 1804–1949
Confederate Pension Applications Collection, Louisiana State Archives
US Census 1850, 1860, 1870, 1880, 1900

PRESSPRICH, Otto Hermann Julius

BIRTH	Sept. 1832/Saxony, Germany
DEATH	5 Sept. 1920/New York, NY

RECORD OF SERVICE

MILITIA SERVICE	23 Nov. 1861/Absent on leave

ORLEANS LIGHT HORSE TRANSFER DATA

INBOUND	1861/Private
OUTBOUND	22 Mar. 1862/Private

SERVICE RÉSUMÉ

23 Nov. 1861	New Orleans, LA/Militia service with the Orleans Light Horse; absent on leave (Prussian consul in New Orleans, LA)
SEPARATION	22 Mar. 1862/New Orleans, LA/Declined enlistment

PERSONAL NARRATIVE

OCCUPATION	Importer, commercial agent
GENEALOGY	Son of Gottfried and Juliana (Uhlemann) Pressprich, Saxony, Germany Arrived in New Orleans, LA, 1854; naturalized citizen, 11 Jan. 1861, New Orleans, LA Married, 1 Nov. 1862, New Orleans, LA, Marie Amelie Legendre Deize (b. 24 Jan. 1843, New Orleans, LA)
RESIDENCES	1854, New Orleans, LA 1861, New Orleans, LA 1880, New York, NY 1900, New York, NY 1910, New York, NY

SOURCES

NARA M320, reel 032
New Orleans, LA, Justices of the Peace Index to Marriage Records, 1846–1880
Obituary: *New York Times*, 6 Sept. 1920
US Census 1880, 1900, 1910
US Naturalization Record Indexes, 1791–1992
US Passport Applications, 1795–1925

RABBY, Jacob Mathew

BIRTH	ca. 1834/Mobile, AL
DEATH	ca. 1905/Mississippi

RECORD OF SERVICE

CSA ENLISTMENT	25 Apr. 1864/Demopolis, AL/Duration of the war

ORLEANS LIGHT HORSE TRANSFER DATA

INBOUND	25 Apr. 1864/Private
OUTBOUND	10 May 1865/Private

SERVICE RÉSUMÉ

25 Apr. 1864	Demopolis, AL/Received into the Orleans Light Horse
May–June 1864	Present
4 May 1865	Citronelle, AL/Surrendered
SEPARATION	10 May 1865/Meridian, MS/Parole, released from military service

PERSONAL NARRATIVE

OCCUPATION	Transportation getter
GENEALOGY	Son of Pierre and Sarah (Miller) Rabby, Mobile County, AL
	Married (1), 30 Aug. 1855, Mobile, AL, Adele Vidmer (b. ca. 1839, Mobile, AL)
	Married (2), 1875, Alabama, Ada A. —— (b. Nov. 1853, Alabama)
RESIDENCES	1850, Mobile, AL
	1860, Mobile, AL
	1880, Mobile, AL
	1900, Greene, MS

SOURCES

Alabama Homestead and Cash Entry Patents, Pre-1908
Civil War Prisoner of War Records, 1861–1865
Marriages of Mobile County, AL, 1813–1855
NARA M320, reel 032
US Census 1850, 1860, 1880, 1900

REYNOLDS, Thomas S.

BIRTH 25 Nov. 1822/Athens, GA
DEATH 6 Jan. 1891/Atlanta, GA

RECORD OF SERVICE

CSA ENLISTMENT 1 July 1861, Memphis, TN/One year
1 Sept. 1863, Chattanooga, TN/Duration of the war

ORLEANS LIGHT HORSE TRANSFER DATA
INBOUND 1 Sept. 1863/Private
OUTBOUND 1 May 1865/Private

SERVICE RÉSUMÉ
1 Sept. 1863 Chattanooga, TN/Received into the Orleans Light Horse from the Twelfth Tennessee Regiment (dismounted)
Sept.–Dec. 1863 Present
May–June 1864 Present
26 Apr. 1865 Durham Station, NC/Surrendered
SEPARATION 1 May 1865/Greensboro, NC/Parole, released from military service

PERSONAL NARRATIVE

OCCUPATION Printer, newspaper publisher
GENEALOGY Son of John A. and Elizabeth (Stephens) Reynolds, Oglethorpe, GA
Married, 27 Apr. 1852, Franklin County, GA, Mary King (b. ca. 1826, Franklin County, GA)
RESIDENCES 1840, Athens, GA
1850, Athens, GA
1860, Atlanta, GA
1870, Atlanta, GA
1880, Atlanta, GA
1890, Atlanta, GA

SOURCES

NARA M320, reel 032; M1781, reel 006
US Census 1840, 1850, 1860, 1870, 1880
www.findagrave.com, 41324530

RILEY, Bernard

BIRTH ca. 1831/Ireland
DEATH 13 Sept. 1915/New Orleans, LA

RECORD OF SERVICE

CSA ENLISTMENT 22 Mar. 1862/New Orleans, LA/90 days
25 July 1862/Tupelo, MS/Duration of the war

ORLEANS LIGHT HORSE TRANSFER DATA
INBOUND 22 Mar. 1862/Private
OUTBOUND 31 May 1865/Private

22 Mar. 1862	New Orleans, LA/Mustered into service of CSA with the Orleans Light Horse
22 Mar.–25 May 1862	Present
6 June 1862	Camp Williamson, Tupelo, MS/Present
Sept.–Dec. 1862	Present
Jan.–June 1863	Present
July–Dec. 1863	Present
May–June 1864	Present
20 May 1865	Atlanta, GA/Surrendered
SEPARATION	31 May 1865/Nashville, TN/Parole, released from military service

PERSONAL NARRATIVE

OCCUPATION	Laborer
GENEALOGY	Arrived in New York, NY, from Ireland, prior to 1850
	Married, ca. Feb. 1862, New Orleans, LA, Ellen —— (b. ca. 1833, Ireland)
RESIDENCES	1850, Brooklyn, NY
	1860, New Orleans, LA
	1870, New Orleans, LA
	1880, San Jose, CA

SOURCES

NARA M320, reel 032
New Orleans, LA, Death Records Index, 1804–1949
US Census 1850, 1860, 1870, 1880

ROBELOT, Emile L.

BIRTH	1841/Louisiana
DEATH	11 Oct. 1890/New Orleans, LA

RECORD OF SERVICE

MILITIA SERVICE	23 Nov. 1861/Absent without leave

ORLEANS LIGHT HORSE TRANSFER DATA

INBOUND	1861/Private
OUTBOUND	22 Mar. 1862/Private

SERVICE RÉSUMÉ

23 Nov. 1861	New Orleans, LA/Militia service with the Orleans Light Horse; absent without leave
SEPARATION	22 Mar. 1862/New Orleans, LA/Declined enlistment

PERSONAL NARRATIVE

OCCUPATION	Farmer
GENEALOGY	Son of Alfred and Louise (Verret) Robelot, New Orleans, LA
	Brother of Henry N. and Jules N. Robelot
	Married, ca. 1865, Louisiana, Marie Eulalie Georgianna Lauve (b. 11 July 1847, New Orleans, LA)

RESIDENCES	1850, Orleans Parish, LA
	1870, Iberville Parish, LA
	1880, New Orleans, LA
	1890, New Orleans, LA

SOURCES

NARA M320, reel 032

New Orleans, LA, Death Records Index, 1804–1949

New Orleans, LA, Directories, 1890–1891

US Census 1850, 1870, 1880

ROBELOT, Henry Nicholas

| BIRTH | 1837/Louisiana |
| DEATH | 4 Nov. 1869/New Orleans, LA |

RECORD OF SERVICE

| MILITIA SERVICE | 23 Nov. 1861/Absent, sick |

ORLEANS LIGHT HORSE TRANSFER DATA

| INBOUND | 1861/Private |
| OUTBOUND | 22 Mar. 1862/Private |

SERVICE RÉSUMÉ

| 23 Nov. 1861 | New Orleans, LA/Militia service with the Orleans Light Horse; absent, sick |
| SEPARATION | 22 Mar. 1862/New Orleans, LA/Medical discharge |

PERSONAL NARRATIVE

OCCUPATION	Clerk
GENEALOGY	Son of Alfred and Louise (Verret) Robelot, New Orleans, LA
	Brother of Jules N. and Emile L. Robelot
RESIDENCES	1840, Orleans Parish, LA
	1850, Orleans Parish, LA
	1866, St. James Parish, LA

SOURCES

NARA M320, reel 032

New Orleans, LA, Death Records Index, 1804–1949

US Census 1840, 1850, 1870

US Federal Census Mortality Schedules Index, 1850–1885

US IRS Tax Assessment Lists, 1862–1918

ROBELOT, Jules N.

| BIRTH | 1839/Louisiana |
| DEATH | 1 June 1889/New Orleans, LA |

RECORD OF SERVICE

MILITIA SERVICE	23 Nov. 1861/Active
CSA ENLISTMENT	22 Mar. 1862/New Orleans, LA/90 days
	25 July 1862/Tupelo, MS/Duration of the war

INBOUND	1861/Private
OUTBOUND	6 June 1862/Corporal

SERVICE RÉSUMÉ

23 Nov. 1861	New Orleans, LA/Militia service with the Orleans Light Horse; present, in rank of private
22 Mar. 1862	New Orleans, LA/Mustered into service of CSA with the Orleans Light Horse
25 May 1862	Tupelo, MS/In camp, sick, in rank of corporal
SEPARATION	6 June 1862/Tupelo, MS/Discharge, unspecified

PERSONAL NARRATIVE

OCCUPATION	Wholesale merchant
GENEALOGY	Son of Alfred and Louise (Verret) Robelot, New Orleans, LA
	Brother of Henry N. and Emile L. Robelot
	Married, 1864, Louisiana, Elizabeth Isabelle Rey
	(b. 27 Oct. 1842, New Orleans, LA; d. 18 Feb. 1924, New Orleans, LA)
RESIDENCES	1850, Orleans Parish, LA
	1860, Algiers, LA
	1870, New Orleans, LA
	1880, New Orleans, LA

SOURCES

NARA M320, reel 032
New Orleans, LA, Death Records Index, 1804–1949
US Census 1850, 1860, 1870, 1880
US IRS Tax Assessment Lists, 1862–1918

ROBINSON, Emanuel Thomas

BIRTH	22 Aug. 1843/Virginia
DEATH	3 Jan. 1924/Iberville Parish, LA

RECORD OF SERVICE

MILITIA SERVICE	23 Nov. 1861/Active
CSA ENLISTMENT	22 Mar. 1862/New Orleans, LA/90 days
	25 July 1862/Tupelo, MS/Duration of the war

ORLEANS LIGHT HORSE TRANSFER DATA

INBOUND	1861/Private
OUTBOUND	27 Oct. 1862/Private

SERVICE RÉSUMÉ

23 Nov. 1861	New Orleans, LA/Militia service with the Orleans Light Horse; present
22 Mar. 1862	New Orleans, LA/Mustered into service of CSA with the Orleans Light Horse
22 Mar.–25 May 1862	Present
6 June 1862	Camp Williamson, Tupelo, MS/Absent, sick
SEPARATION	27 Oct. 1862/Knoxville, TN/Discharge, unspecified

OCCUPATION   Rice farmer

GENEALOGY   Son of John Selser and Mary (Kendig) Robinson, Woodford County, IL

Married, 22 Aug. 1872, Woodford County, IL, Frances Susan Nofsinger (b. 11 Sept. 1853, Virginia; d. 16 Feb. 1929, Jefferson Davis Parish, LA)

RESIDENCES   1850, Woodford County, IL
1860, Woodford County, IL
1870, Woodford County, IL
1880, Woodford County, IL
1900, Calcasieu Parish, LA
1910, Calcasieu Parish, LA
1920, Jefferson Davis Parish, LA

ADDITIONAL INFORMATION   Alternate spellings: J. T. Robinson and Jos. T. Robinson

SOURCES

Louisiana Statewide Death Index, 1900–1949

NARA M320, reel 032

US Census 1850, 1860, 1870, 1880, 1900, 1910, 1920

US General Land Office Records, 1796–1907

Woodford County, IL, Prairie District Library, Obituaries, 1887 to Present

www.findagrave 69886445

ROGERS, William L.

BIRTH   1843/New Orleans, LA

DEATH   21 Oct. 1908/New Orleans, LA

RECORD OF SERVICE

CSA ENLISTMENT   1 July 1862/Tupelo, MS/Duration of the war

ORLEANS LIGHT HORSE TRANSFER DATA

    INBOUND   1 July 1862/Private

    OUTBOUND   16 July 1863/Private

SERVICE RÉSUMÉ

    1 July 1862   Tupelo, MS/Received into the Orleans Light Horse

    Sept.–Dec. 1862 Present

    Jan.–June 1863 Present

    16 July 1863   Chattanooga, TN/Transferred to the Confederate States Navy by order of the secretary of war

PERSONAL NARRATIVE

OCCUPATION   Machinist

GENEALOGY   Son of William and Catherine (McCrink) Rogers, New Orleans, LA

Married, 1878, New Orleans, LA, Mary Jane Green (b. ca. 1858, Wisconsin)

RESIDENCES	1850, New Orleans, LA
	1860, New Orleans, LA
	1880, New Orleans, LA
	1900, New Orleans, LA

SOURCES
NARA M320, reel 032
New Orleans, LA, Death Records Index, 1804–1949
US Census 1850, 1860, 1880, 1900

RONDEAU, William Arkinstall Sims

BIRTH	18 Aug. 1839/New Orleans, LA
DEATH	11 May 1904/Chatawa, MS

RECORD OF SERVICE

CSA ENLISTMENT	26 Dec. 1861/Columbus, KY/One year
	1 Sept. 1863/Chattanooga, TN/Duration of the war

ORLEANS LIGHT HORSE TRANSFER DATA

INBOUND	1 Sept. 1863/Private
OUTBOUND	Aug. 1864/Private

SERVICE RÉSUMÉ

1 Sept. 1863	Chattanooga, TN/Received into the Orleans Light Horse from Stanford's Battery, Mississippi Artillery
Sept.–Dec. 1863	Present
Mar–Apr. 1864	Marion, AL/Admitted to general hospital
May–June 1864	Present

PERSONAL NARRATIVE

OCCUPATION	Traveling clerk, furniture merchant
GENEALOGY	Son of William Henry and Ann (Paxton) Rondeau, New Orleans, LA
	Married, 10 Oct. 1867, Atlanta, GA, Alice Margaret Lightcap (b. ca. 1846, Louisville, KY; d. 8 Aug. 1884, Atlanta, GA)
RESIDENCES	1860, New Orleans, LA
	1870, Atlanta, GA
	1880 New Orleans, LA
	1900, St. Martin, LA

SOURCES
NARA M320, reel 032
US Census 1860, 1870, 1880, 1900

ROUNTREE, Austin W.

BIRTH	27 Mar. 1830/Augusta, GA
DEATH	14 Mar. 1893/New Orleans, LA

RECORD OF SERVICE

CSA ENLISTMENT	22 Mar. 1862/New Orleans, LA/90 days
	25 July 1862/Tupelo, MS/Duration of the war

ORLEANS LIGHT HORSE TRANSFER DATA
INBOUND	22 Mar. 1862/Private
OUTBOUND	Aug. 1864/Sergeant

SERVICE RÉSUMÉ

22 Mar. 1862	New Orleans, LA/Mustered into service of CSA with the Orleans Light Horse
22 Mar.–25 May 1862	Present
6 June 1862	Camp Williamson, Tupelo, MS/Absent, sick
Sept.–Oct. 1862	Present
Nov.–Dec. 1862	Present; detailed at Lt. Gen. Leonidas Polk's headquarters
Jan.–Feb. 1863	Present; detailed at headquarters
Mar.–June 1863	Shelbyville, TN/Absent, sick
July–Aug. 1863	Chattanooga, TN/Voucher for commissary sergeant
Nov. 1863	Meridian, MS/Receipt for pay as commissary sergeant
July–Dec. 1863	Present, in position of commissary sergeant
May–June 1864	Present

PERSONAL NARRATIVE

OCCUPATION	Wholesale grocer
GENEALOGY	Son of George R. and Pamela (Woolfork) Rountree, New Orleans, LA
RESIDENCES	1850, New Orleans, LA
	1860, Livingston Parish, LA
	1870, New Orleans, LA
	1880, Jefferson Parish, LA
	1890, New Orleans, LA

SOURCES

NARA M320, reel 032
New Orleans, LA, Death Records Index, 1804–1949
New Orleans, LA, Directories, 1890–1891
US Census 1850, 1860, 1870, 1880
www.findagrave.com, 12920442

RUSSELL, M.

BIRTH	ca. 1840

RECORD OF SERVICE

CSA ENLISTMENT	25 Dec. 1862/Murfreesboro, TN/Duration of the war

ORLEANS LIGHT HORSE TRANSFER DATA

INBOUND	25 Dec. 1863/Private
OUTBOUND	Feb. 1864/Private

SERVICE RÉSUMÉ

25 Dec. 1862	Murfreesboro, TN/Received into the Orleans Light Horse
Jan.–June 1863	Present
19 June 1863	Detailed as forage-master
July–Oct. 1863	Present
Nov.–Dec. 1863	Absent, detailed at headquarters of Lt. Gen. Leonidas Polk
ADDITIONAL INFORMATION	Alternate spelling: W. Russell

SOURCES
NARA M320, reel 032

RYALL, Henry Clay

BIRTH	19 Feb. 1845/Shelbyville, TN
DEATH	29 Nov. 1923/Shelbyville, TN

RECORD OF SERVICE

CSA ENLISTMENT	27 June 1863/Tullahoma, TN/Duration of the war

ORLEANS LIGHT HORSE TRANSFER DATA

INBOUND	27 June 1863/Private
OUTBOUND	20 Dec. 1864/Private

SERVICE RÉSUMÉ

27 July 1863	Tullahoma, TN/Received into the Orleans Light Horse
July–Dec. 1863	Present
May–June 1864	Present
20 Dec. 1864	Shelbyville, TN/Deserted; captured, placed on parole
27 Apr. 1865	Nashville, TN/Subscribed to US Oath of Allegiance
SEPARATION	27 Apr. 1865/Nashville, TN/Parole, released from military service

PERSONAL NARRATIVE

OCCUPATION	Grocer, lumber dealer
GENEALOGY	Son of Thomas Coleman and Elizabeth (Scudder) Ryall, Bedford County, TN
	Brother of Johnston S. Ryall
	Married, 17 Sept. 1868, Bedford County, TN, Frances J. "Fannie" Bomar (b. 25 May 1850, Wilson County, TN; d. 17 Aug. 1936, Richland Springs, TX)
RESIDENCES	1850, Bedford County, TN
	1870, Bedford County, TN
	1880, Shelbyville, TN
	1900, Shelbyville, TN
	1910, Shelbyville, TN
	1920, Shelbyville, TN

SOURCES
Civil War Prisoner of War Records, 1861–1865
NARA M320, reel 032
Tennessee State Marriages, 1780–2002
Tennessee Death Records, 1908–1951
Tennessee Deaths and Burials Index, 1874–1955
US Census 1850, 1870, 1880, 1900, 1910, 1920
www.findagrave.com, 84422541

RYALL, Johnston Scudder

BIRTH	31 Oct. 1838/Shelbyville, TN
DEATH	5 Dec. 1917/Marengo County, AL

RECORD OF SERVICE

CSA ENLISTMENT	15 Mar. 1864/Demopolis, AL/Duration of the war

ORLEANS LIGHT HORSE TRANSFER DATA

INBOUND	15 Mar. 1864/Private
OUTBOUND	Aug. 1864/Private

SERVICE RÉSUMÉ

15 Mar. 1864	Demopolis, AL/Received into the Orleans Light Horse, from Capt. Jackson's Co. Tennessee Cavalry
May–June 1864	Absent without leave

PERSONAL NARRATIVE

OCCUPATION	Farmer
GENEALOGY	Son of Thomas Coleman and Elizabeth (Scudder) Ryall, Bedford County, TN
	Brother of Henry C. Ryall
RESIDENCES	1850, Bedford County, TN
	1870, Marengo County, AL
	1880, Marengo County, AL
	1900, Marengo County, AL
	1910, Marengo County, AL

SOURCES

Alabama Census of Confederate Soldiers, 1907
Alabama Deaths, 1908–1959
NARA M320, reel 032
US Census 1850, 1870, 1880, 1900, 1910
www.findagrave.com, 84422260

SAFFORD, Henry, Jr.

BIRTH	9 Dec. 1824/South Carolina
DEATH	5 Mar. 1884/Natchitoches, LA

RECORD OF SERVICE

CSA ENLISTMENT	27 Apr. 1863/Shelbyville, TN/Duration of the war

ORLEANS LIGHT HORSE TRANSFER DATA

INBOUND	27 Apr. 1863/Private
OUTBOUND	Apr. 1864/Private

SERVICE RÉSUMÉ

27 Apr. 1863	Shelbyville, TN/Received into the Orleans Light Horse
Mar.–June 1863	Absent, detached at headquarters of Lt. Gen. Leonidas Polk, effective 4 May 1863
July–Dec. 1863	Absent, detailed at headquarters of Lt. Gen. Polk
14 Jan. 1864	Shreveport, LA/Courier between Lt. Gen. Polk and Lt. Gen. E. Kirby Smith

4 Feb. 1864	Received clothing issue
8 Feb. 1864	Executed receipt for pay due
14 Jan.–1 Feb. 1864	Executed receipt for expenses to Shreveport, LA
SEPARATION	28 May 1865/Shreveport, LA/Parole, released from military service

PERSONAL NARRATIVE

OCCUPATION	Attorney
GENEALOGY	Son of Henry and Eliza (Burr) Safford, Greene County, GA
	Married, ca. 1858, Natchitoches Parish, LA, Harriett Eliza Airey (b. 8 Jan. 1836, Natchitoches, LA; d. 30 June 1873, Natchitoches, LA)
RESIDENCES	1850, De Soto Parish, LA
	1860, Natchitoches Parish, LA
	1880, Natchitoches Parish, LA

SOURCES

Louisiana, Compiled Census and Census Substitutes Index, 1791–1890
NARA M320, reel 032
US Census 1850, 1860, 1880
US General Land Office Records, 1796–1907
www.findagrave.com, 30052617

SAUNDERS, Robert William

| BIRTH | 1827/New Orleans, LA |
| DEATH | 30 Apr. 1866/New Orleans, LA |

RECORD OF SERVICE

| MILITIA SERVICE | 23 Nov. 1861/Absent without leave |

ORLEANS LIGHT HORSE TRANSFER DATA

| INBOUND | 1861/Private |
| OUTBOUND | 22 Mar. 1862/Private |

SERVICE RÉSUMÉ

| 23 Nov. 1861 | New Orleans, LA/Militia service with the Orleans Light Horse; absent without leave |
| SEPARATION | 22 Mar. 1862/New Orleans, LA/Declined enlistment |

PERSONAL NARRATIVE

OCCUPATION	Clerk
GENEALOGY	Married, 1858, New Orleans, LA, Amanda —— (b. ca. 1830, Massachusetts)
RESIDENCES	1860, New Orleans, LA

SOURCES

Louisiana, Compiled Census and Census Substitutes Index, 1791–1890
NARA M320, reel 032
US Census 1860

SCOTT, Samuel R.

BIRTH   ca. 1825/England

RECORD OF SERVICE

MILITIA SERVICE   23 Nov. 1861/Absent with leave

ORLEANS LIGHT HORSE TRANSFER DATA

     INBOUND   1861/Private

     OUTBOUND   22 Mar. 1862/Private

SERVICE RÉSUMÉ

     23 Nov. 1861   New Orleans, LA/Militia service with the Orleans Light Horse; absent with leave in Europe

SEPARATION   22 Mar. 1862/New Orleans, LA/Declined enlistment

PERSONAL NARRATIVE

OCCUPATION   Merchant

GENEALOGY   Arrived in New Orleans, LA, from England, 8 Feb. 1848

RESIDENCES   1860, New Orleans, LA

SOURCES

NARA M320, reel 032

New Orleans Passenger Lists, 1813–1945

US Census 1860

SEILER, Friederick W.

BIRTH   1834/Germany

DEATH   1 Dec. 1911/New Orleans, LA

RECORD OF SERVICE

CSA ENLISTMENT   22 Mar. 1862/New Orleans, LA/90 days

     25 July 1862/Tupelo, MS/Duration of the war

ORLEANS LIGHT HORSE TRANSFER DATA

     INBOUND   22 Mar. 1862/Private

     OUTBOUND   Aug. 1864/Private

SERVICE RÉSUMÉ

     22 Mar. 1862   New Orleans, LA/Mustered into service of CSA with the Orleans Light Horse

     25 May 1862   Corinth, MS/Absent, sick in hospital

     6 June 1862   Camp Williamson, Tupelo, MS/Absent, sick

     Sept.–Oct. 1862   Absent without leave

     Nov.–Dec. 1862   Present

     Jan.–June 1863   Present

     July–Dec. 1863   Present

     May–June 1864   Present

PERSONAL NARRATIVE

OCCUPATION   Accountant, commercial broker

GENEALOGY   Married, 18 Apr. 1866, Leake County, MS, Mary Susan (Wideman) Harris (b. 2 Jan. 1832)

RESIDENCES 1861, New Orleans, LA
1866, New Orleans, LA
1868, New Orleans, LA
1873, New Orleans, LA
1877, New Orleans, LA

SOURCES

Edwards' Annual Director, 1873
Gardner's New Orleans Directory, 1866, 1868
Mississippi Marriages, 1776–1935
NARA M320, reel 032
New Orleans, LA, Death Records Index, 1804–1949
Soards' New Orleans City Directory, 1877
www.findagrave.com, 70785862

SHALLY, Charles Edwin

BIRTH 1826/Ohio
DEATH 26 Mar. 1880/New Orleans, LA

RECORD OF SERVICE

CSA ENLISTMENT 22 Mar. 1862/New Orleans, LA/90 days
ORLEANS LIGHT HORSE TRANSFER DATA
    INBOUND 22 Mar. 1862/Private
    OUTBOUND 16 July 1862/Private
SERVICE RÉSUMÉ
    22 Mar. 1862 New Orleans, LA/Mustered into service of CSA with the Orleans Light Horse
    22 Mar.–25 May 1862 Present
    6 June 1862 Camp Williamson, Tupelo, MS/Present
SEPARATION 16 July 1862/Tupelo, MS/Discharge, over age

PERSONAL NARRATIVE

OCCUPATION Railroad clerk
GENEALOGY Married, ca. 1867, Louisiana, Euphemia Baysset (b. 1846, Louisiana; d. 23 Jan. 1931, New Orleans, LA)
RESIDENCES 1860, New Orleans, LA
1870, New Orleans, LA

SOURCES

Louisiana, Compiled Census and Census Substitutes Index, 1791–1890
NARA M320, reel 032
New Orleans, LA, Death Records Index, 1804–1949
New Orleans, LA, Directories, 1890–1891
US Census 1860, 1870, 1880
US Federal Census Mortality Schedules, 1850–1885

SHAW, William N.

BIRTH	ca. 1825/Louisiana
DEATH	31 May 1863/Shelbyville, TN

RECORD OF SERVICE

CSA ENLISTMENT	22 Mar. 1862/New Orleans, LA/90 days
	25 July 1862/Tupelo, MS/Duration of the war

ORLEANS LIGHT HORSE TRANSFER DATA

INBOUND	22 Mar. 1862/Private
OUTBOUND	31 May 1863/Private

SERVICE RÉSUMÉ

22 Mar. 1862	New Orleans, LA/Mustered into service of CSA with the Orleans Light Horse
25 May 1862	Tupelo, MS/Sick in camp
6 June 1862	Camp Williamson, Tupelo, MS/Absent, sick
Sept.–Oct. 1862	Present, detailed on duty
Nov.–Dec. 1862	Present, detailed at Lt. Gen. Leonidas Polk's headquarters
Jan.–Apr. 1863	Present, detailed at headquarters
SEPARATION	31 May 1863/Shelbyville, TN/Death

PERSONAL NARRATIVE

OCCUPATION	Planter
GENEALOGY	Married, ca. 1845, Louisiana, Eliza Garberent (b. ca. 1826, Kentucky; d. 19 Sept. 1861, New Orleans, LA)
RESIDENCES	1850, Claiborne Parish, LA

SOURCES

NARA M320, reel 032
US Census 1850

SHEPHERD, Henry H.

BIRTH	ca. 1842/Virginia

RECORD OF SERVICE

MILITIA SERVICE	23 Nov. 1861/Active
CSA ENLISTMENT	7 Feb. 1864/Meridian, MS/Duration of the war

ORLEANS LIGHT HORSE TRANSFER DATA

INBOUND	7 Feb. 1864/Private
OUTBOUND	Aug. 1864/Private

SERVICE RÉSUMÉ

23 Nov. 1861	New Orleans, LA/Militia service with the Orleans Light Horse; present
22 Mar. 1862	New Orleans, LA/Dropped from rolls prior to muster (declined enlistment)
7 Feb. 1864	Meridian, MS/Received into the Orleans Light Horse
May–June 1864	Present

PERSONAL NARRATIVE

OCCUPATION	Farmer

GENEALOGY	Son of Henry and Nancy Shepherd, Bedford County, VA
	Married, ca. 1865, Virginia, M. E. —— (b. ca. 1846, Virginia)
RESIDENCES	1850, Bedford County, VA
	1860, St. James Parish, LA
	1880, Blacksburg, VA

SOURCES
NARA M320, reel 032
US Census 1850, 1860, 1880

SIMMONS, Jackson W.

| BIRTH | July 1834/Pike County, MS |
| DEATH | 1917/Washington Parish, LA |

RECORD OF SERVICE

MILITIA SERVICE	23 Nov. 1861/Active
CSA ENLISTMENT	6 Mar. 1862/New Orleans, LA/90 days
	25 July 1862/Tupelo, MS/Duration of the war

ORLEANS LIGHT HORSE TRANSFER DATA

| INBOUND | 1861/Private |
| OUTBOUND | 14 May 1865/First sergeant |

SERVICE RÉSUMÉ

23 Nov. 1861	New Orleans, LA/Militia service with the Orleans Light Horse; present, in rank of private
22 Mar. 1862	New Orleans, LA/Mustered into service of CSA
22 Mar.–25 May 1862	Present, in rank of private
6 June 1862	Camp Williamson, Tupelo, MS/Present, in rank of private
Sept.–Oct. 1862	Present, in rank of corporal
Nov.–Dec. 1862	Present, in rank of sergeant
Jan.–June 1863	Present, in rank of sergeant
July–Oct. 1863	Present, in rank of sergeant
Nov.–Dec. 1863	Absent, furlough
May–June 1864	Present, in rank of sergeant
14 May 1865	Citronelle, MS/Surrendered
SEPARATION	19 May 1865/Jackson, MS/Parole, released from military service

PERSONAL NARRATIVE

| RESIDENCES | 1870, Lee County, MS |

SOURCES
Booth, 3:569
Civil War Prisoner of War Records, 1861–1865
NARA M320, reel 032
New Orleans Passenger Lists, 1820–1945
US Census 1870
www.findagrave.com, 26201465

SIMMONS, Robert Winston

BIRTH   1830/Bullitt County, KY
DEATH   28 Jan. 1909/New Orleans, LA
RECORD OF SERVICE
CSA ENLISTMENT   6 Mar. 1862/New Orleans, LA/90 days
                            5 July 1862/Tupelo, MS/Duration of the war
ORLEANS LIGHT HORSE TRANSFER DATA
     INBOUND   5 July 1862/Private
     OUTBOUND   Oct. 1862/Private
SERVICE RÉSUMÉ
     5 July 1862   Tupelo, MS/Received into the Orleans Light Horse from the
                            Fifth Co., Washington Artillery (possibly an exchange
                            with William A. Freret II, transferred to Washington
                            Artillery)

PERSONAL NARRATIVE
OCCUPATION   Cotton weigher
RESIDENCES   1860, New Orleans, LA
                            1878, New Orleans, LA
                            1895, New Orleans, LA
                            1900, New Orleans, LA
SOURCES
NARA M320, reel 032
New Orleans, LA, Death Records Index, 1804–1949
Soards' New Orleans City Directory, 1878, 1895, 1900
US Census 1860
US Passport Applications, 1795–1925
www.findagrave.com, 70785879

SMITH, E.

BIRTH   1825
RECORD OF SERVICE
CSA ENLISTMENT   22 Mar. 1862/New Orleans, LA/90 days
                            25 July 1862/Tupelo, MS/Duration of the war
ORLEANS LIGHT HORSE TRANSFER DATA
     INBOUND   22 Mar. 1862/Private
     OUTBOUND   16 July 1862/Private
SERVICE RÉSUMÉ
     22 Mar. 1862   New Orleans, LA/Mustered into service of CSA with the
                            Orleans Light Horse
     22 Mar.–25 May 1862   Present, in position of farrier
     6 June 1862   Camp Williamson, Tupelo, MS/Approved for discharge
SEPARATION   16 July 1862/Tupelo, MS/Discharge, over age
SOURCES
NARA M320, reel 032

SPRATT, Robert Barnett

BIRTH | 18 Feb. 1847/Sumter County, AL
DEATH | 24 Apr. 1864/Marietta, GA

RECORD OF SERVICE

CSA ENLISTMENT | 17 Apr. 1864/Demopolis, AL/Duration of the war

ORLEANS LIGHT HORSE TRANSFER DATA

INBOUND | 17 Apr. 1864/Private
OUTBOUND | 24 Apr. 1864/Private

SERVICE RÉSUMÉ

17 Apr. 1864 | Demopolis, AL/Received into the Orleans Light Horse

SEPARATION | 24 Apr. 1864/Marietta, GA/Death

PERSONAL NARRATIVE

GENEALOGY | Son of Robert Davie and Lillas (Barnett) Spratt, Livingston, AL

RESIDENCES | 1850, Livingston, AL
1860, Livingston, AL

SOURCES

NARA M320, reel 032
US Census 1850, 1860
www.findagrave.com, 118454686

SPRIGG, Horatio Stevenson, Jr.

BIRTH | 22 Nov. 1840/Indiana
DEATH | Oct. 1867/Rapides Parish, LA

RECORD OF SERVICE

CSA ENLISTMENT | 22 Mar. 1862/New Orleans, LA/90 days
25 July 1862/Tupelo, MS/Duration of the war

ORLEANS LIGHT HORSE TRANSFER DATA

INBOUND | 22 Mar. 1862/Private
OUTBOUND | June 1863/Private

SERVICE RÉSUMÉ

22 Mar. 1862 | New Orleans, LA/Mustered into service of CSA with the Orleans Light Horse

22 Mar.–25 May 1862 | Present
6 June 1862 | Camp Williamson, Tupelo, MS/Present
Sept.–Oct. 1862 | Knoxville, TN/Absent, detached
17 Mar. 1863 | Shelbyville, TN/Executed receipt for pay due

PERSONAL NARRATIVE

OCCUPATION | Planter

GENEALOGY	Son of Horatio Stevenson and Frances (Jones) Sprigg, Rapides Parish, LA
	Married, ca. 1861, Louisiana, Judith Ann Hyams (b. 24 Feb. 1843, Alexandria, LA; d. Dec. 1866, Alexandria, LA), daughter of Henry M. Hyams, lieutenant governor of Louisiana
RESIDENCES	1850, Rapides Parish, LA
	1860, Alexandria, LA
	1865, Rapides Parish, LA

SOURCES

Louisiana, Compiled Census and Census Substitutes Index, 1791–1890

NARA M320, reel 032; M769, reel 008

US Census 1850, 1860

US IRS Tax Assessment Lists, 1862–1918

STEWART, James John

BIRTH	14 Nov. 1837/New Orleans, LA
DEATH	19 June 1888/New Orleans, LA

RECORD OF SERVICE

CSA ENLISTMENT	22 Mar. 1862/New Orleans, LA/90 days
	25 July 1862/Tupelo, MS/Duration of the war

ORLEANS LIGHT HORSE TRANSFER DATA

INBOUND	22 Mar. 1862/Private
OUTBOUND	9 May 1865/Private

SERVICE RÉSUMÉ

22 Mar. 1862	New Orleans, LA/Mustered into service of CSA with the Orleans Light Horse, in rank of private
26 Mar. 1862	Resigned commission as captain of Co. B, Fourth Regiment, Third Brigade, Louisiana Militia, by reason of having enlisted in the Orleans Light Horse
22 Mar.–25 May 1862	Present
6 June 1862	Camp Williamson, Tupelo, MS/Absent, sick
Sept.–Dec. 1862	Present
Jan.–Feb. 1863	Present
Mar.–June 1863	Chattanooga, TN/Absent, detailed at headquarters of Lt. Gen. Leonidas Polk
July–Dec. 1863	Absent, detailed at headquarters of Lt. Gen. Polk
May–June 1864	Absent, detailed at headquarters of Army of Mississippi by order of Lt. Gen. Polk
4 May 1865	Citronelle, AL/Surrendered
SEPARATION	9 May 1865/Meridian, MS/Parole, released from military service

PERSONAL NARRATIVE

OCCUPATION	Cotton broker

Son of Samuel and Marie Marguerite Nisidia (Giquel)
                        Stewart, New Orleans, LA
                      Brother of Samuel R. Stewart Jr.; brother-in-law of
                        Thomas W. P. Foley
                      Married, 1870, Mary Gertrude Goodwin (b. 17 May 1840,
                        Bibb County, AL; d. 18 Aug. 1916, Selma, AL)
RESIDENCES   1850, New Orleans, LA
                      1860, New Orleans, LA
                      1870, New Orleans, LA
                      1880, New Orleans, LA

SOURCES
NARA M320, reel 032
New Orleans, LA, Death Records Index, 1804–1949
US Census 1850, 1860, 1870, 1880

STEWART, Reuben C.

BIRTH   1 July 1825/Fayette County, AL
DEATH   21 Nov. 1926/St. Landry, LA

RECORD OF SERVICE
ORLEANS LIGHT HORSE TRANSFER DATA
     INBOUND   Unknown
     OUTBOUND   1 May 1865/Lieutenant
SERVICE RÉSUMÉ
     26 Apr. 1865   On a list of individuals paroled at Greensboro, NC, under
                        the terms of the Sherman-Johnston agreement
SEPARATION   1 May 1865/Greensboro, NC/Parole, released from
                        military service

PERSONAL NARRATIVE
OCCUPATION   Farmer
GENEALOGY   Son of Benjamin and Nancy (Pullum) Stewart, Fayette
                        County, AL
                      Married, 1858, Mississippi, Elizabeth Biggs (b. 17 Mar. 1836,
                        Kosciusko, MS; d. 12 Dec. 1923, St. Landry, LA)
RESIDENCES   1860, Fayette County, AL
                      1880, Attala County, MS
                      1900, St. Landry Parish, LA
                      1920, St. Landry Parish, LA

SOURCES
Confederate Pension Applications Collection, Louisiana State Archives
NARA M320, reel 032
US Census 1860, 1880, 1900, 1910, 1920
www.findagrave.com, 16173146

STEWART, Samuel Robert, Jr.

BIRTH   25 July 1843/New Orleans, LA
DEATH   5 Mar. 1885/Havana, Cuba

RECORD OF SERVICE

CSA ENLISTMENT   7 Mar. 1861/New Orleans, LA/One year
                                   20 Apr. 1862/Chattanooga, TN/Duration of the war

ORLEANS LIGHT HORSE TRANSFER DATA
    INBOUND   20 Apr. 1862/Private
    OUTBOUND   Aug. 1864/Private

SERVICE RÉSUMÉ
    20 Apr. 1862   Chattanooga, TN/Received into the Orleans Light Horse
                                   from the Louisiana Guards, Co. C, First Louisiana
                                   Infantry
    Sept.–Dec. 1862   Present
    Jan.–Feb. 1863   Present
    Mar.–Apr. 1863   Shelbyville, TN/Detached at headquarters of
                                   Lt. Gen. Leonidas Polk
    May–June 1863   Shelbyville, TN/Absent, sick
    July–Dec. 1863   Present
    May–June 1864   Present

PERSONAL NARRATIVE

OCCUPATION   Assayer at US Mint
GENEALOGY   Son of Samuel and Marie Marguerite (Giquel) Stewart,
                                   New Orleans, LA
                                   Brother of James J. Stewart; brother-in-law of
                                   Thomas W. P. Foley
                                   Married, 7 Dec. 1871, New Orleans, LA, Sarah Smith Harvey
                                   (b. 26 Dec. 1847, Jefferson Parish, LA; d. 14 Apr. 1920,
                                   New Orleans, LA)
RESIDENCES   1850, New Orleans, LA
                                   1860, New Orleans, LA
                                   1880, New Orleans, LA

SOURCES

Louisiana Marriages, 1718–1925
NARA M320, reels 032, 099
US Census 1850, 1860, 1880
US Passport Applications, 1795–1925
US Sons of the American Revolution Membership Applications, 1889–1979

ST. PHAR, Alexander H.

RECORD OF SERVICE

MILITIA SERVICE | 23 Nov. 1861/Active
CSA ENLISTMENT | 22 Mar. 1862/New Orleans, LA/90 days
ORLEANS LIGHT HORSE TRANSFER DATA
    INBOUND | 1861/Musician
    OUTBOUND | 30 Apr. 1863/Musician
SERVICE RÉSUMÉ

23 Nov. 1861	New Orleans, LA/Militia service with the Orleans Light Horse; present, detailed as trumpeter
22 Mar. 1862	New Orleans, LA/Mustered into service of CSA with the Orleans Light Horse
29 Mar. 1862	New Orleans, LA/Missed movement; absent without leave
6 June 1862	Camp Williamson, Tupelo, MS/Absent without leave
Jan.–Feb. 1863	Shelbyville, TN/Absent without leave

SEPARATION | 30 Apr. 1863/Shelbyville, TN/Deserter, dropped from rolls

SOURCES

NARA M320, reel 032

SUTHERLAND, P. F.

BIRTH | ca. 1836/France

RECORD OF SERVICE

CSA ENLISTMENT | 18 Sept. 1862/Munfordville, KY/Duration of the war
ORLEANS LIGHT HORSE TRANSFER DATA
    INBOUND | 18 Sept. 1862/Private
    OUTBOUND | Feb. 1864/Private
SERVICE RÉSUMÉ

18 Sept. 1862	Munfordville, KY/Received into the Orleans Light Horse
Nov.–Dec. 1862	Present
Jan.–June 1863	Present
July–Oct. 1863	Present
28 Nov. 1863	Enterprise, MS/Application approved for 30-day furlough
Nov.–Dec. 1863	Absent, furlough

PERSONAL NARRATIVE

OCCUPATION | Bookkeeper
GENEALOGY | Married, 25 Oct. 1871, New Orleans, LA, Mrs. C. M. Brown (b. ca. 1839, Louisiana)
RESIDENCES | 1860, New Orleans, LA
| 1871, New Orleans, LA
ADDITIONAL INFORMATION | Alternate spelling: P. Southerland

SOURCES

Louisiana Marriages, 1718–1925
NARA M320, reel 032
US Census 1860

TAYLOR, John McDonald

BIRTH	ca. 1799/Inverness, Scotland
DEATH	19 Nov. 1883/New Orleans, LA

RECORD OF SERVICE

MILITIA SERVICE	1 Feb.–31 May 1861

ORLEANS LIGHT HORSE TRANSFER DATA

INBOUND	1 Feb. 1861/Captain
OUTBOUND	31 May 1861/Captain

SERVICE RÉSUMÉ

1 Feb. 1861	New Orleans, LA/Militia service with the Orleans Light Horse; present, elected captain at formation of unit
SEPARATION	31 May 1861/New Orleans, LA/Resignation, competing pressures of personal business

PERSONAL NARRATIVE

OCCUPATION	Merchant (B. Toledano and Taylor, New Orleans, LA)
GENEALOGY	Arrived in New Orleans, LA, prior to 1835
	Married, ca. 1835, New Orleans, LA, Basilice Toledano (b. 1810, New Orleans, LA; d. 11 Jan. 1857, New Orleans, LA)
RESIDENCES	1840, New Orleans, LA
	1850, New Orleans, LA
	1860, New Orleans, LA
	1866, New Orleans, LA
	1876, New Orleans, LA
	1880, New Orleans, LA

SOURCES

Bartlett, sec. 2:31
Gardner's New Orleans Directory, 1861, 1866
Louisiana, Compiled Census and Census Substitutes Index, 1791–1890
NARA M320, reel 032
Obituary: *New Orleans Daily Picayune*, 20 and 25 Nov. 1883
Soards' New Orleans City Directory, 1876
US Census 1840, 1850, 1860, 1880
www.findagrave.com, 11758920

TENNISON, William Harrison

BIRTH	15 Apr. 1840/Washington County, MO
DEATH	7 Aug. 1914/Washington County, MO

RECORD OF SERVICE

CSA ENLISTMENT	27 Apr. 1864/Demopolis, AL/Duration of the war

ORLEANS LIGHT HORSE TRANSFER DATA

INBOUND	27 Apr. 1864/Private
OUTBOUND	Aug. 1864/Private

27 Apr. 1864	Demopolis, AL/Received into the Orleans Light Horse
May–June 1864	Present

PERSONAL NARRATIVE

OCCUPATION	Farmer
GENEALOGY	Son of Archibald and Ruth (Jones) Tennison, Washington County, MO
	Married (1), 20 Nov. 1863, St. Claire County, MO, Mary Jane Bressie (b. 15 Dec. 1844, Indiana; d. 28 Dec. 1897, Salem, IN)
	Married (2), 23 Aug. 1899, Washington County, MO, Elmira Fortune (b. 15 Sept. 1853, Virginia; d. 15 Nov. 1921, Belgrade, MO)
RESIDENCES	1850, Belleview, MO
	1860, Belleview, MO
	1870, Belleview, MO
	1880, Belgrade, MO
	1900, Belgrade, MO
	1910, Belgrade, MO

SOURCES

Missouri Marriage Records, 1805–2002
Missouri Marriages, 1766–1983
NARA M320, reel 032
US Census 1850, 1860, 1870, 1880, 1900, 1910
www.findagrave.com, 5282968

THORNHILL, Henry M.

BIRTH	1824/Fauquier County, VA
DEATH	11 Nov. 1870/New Orleans, LA

RECORD OF SERVICE

MILITIA SERVICE	23 Nov. 1861/Active
CSA ENLISTMENT	22 Mar. 1862/New Orleans, LA/90 days
	25 July 1862/Tupelo, MS/Duration of the war

ORLEANS LIGHT HORSE TRANSFER DATA

INBOUND	1861/Private
OUTBOUND	1 June 1863/Lieutenant

SERVICE RÉSUMÉ

23 Nov. 1861	New Orleans, LA/Militia service with the Orleans Light Horse; present, in rank of private
22 Mar. 1862	New Orleans, LA/Mustered into service of CSA, in position of fourth sergeant
25 May 1862	Camp Leeds, Corinth, MS/Present, in position of fourth sergeant
1 July 1862	Tupelo, MS/Elected second lieutenant
1 June 1863	Shelbyville, TN/Reassigned to other duty (unspecified)

OCCUPATION   Commission merchant

GENEALOGY   Son of Elijah and Nancy (Fisher) Thornhill, Fauquier County, VA

Married, 16 May 1859, New Orleans, LA, Mary C. Covington (b. 1840, Rankin County, MS; d. 19 Oct. 1914, New Orleans, LA)

RESIDENCES   1830, Fauquier County, VA

1850, Boone County, MO

1860, New Orleans, LA

1870, New Orleans, LA

SOURCES

Confederate Pension Applications Collection, Louisiana State Archives

Louisiana, Compiled Census and Census Substitutes Index, 1791–1890

NARA M320, reel 032; M769, reel 005

New Orleans, LA, Death Records Index, 1804–1949

Obituary: *New Orleans Daily Picayune*, 12 Nov. 1870

US Census 1830, 1850, 1860, 1870

US IRS Tax Assessment Lists, 1862–1918

www.findagrave.com, 94631935

THUER, John, Jr.

BIRTH   1841/Switzerland

DEATH   16 Mar. 1893/New Orleans, LA

RECORD OF SERVICE

CSA ENLISTMENT   1 July 1862/Tupelo, MS/Duration of the war

ORLEANS LIGHT HORSE TRANSFER DATA

     INBOUND   1 July 1862/Private

     OUTBOUND   1 May 1865/Private

SERVICE RÉSUMÉ

     1 July 1862   Tupelo, MS/Received into the Orleans Light Horse

     Sept.–Oct. 1862   Present, detailed on duty

     Nov.–Dec. 1862   Present

     Jan.–June 1863   Present

     July–Aug. 1863   Chattanooga, TN/Present, detailed at headquarters of Lt. Gen. Leonidas Polk

     30 July 1863   Detailed at headquarters stables

     9 Aug. 1863   Detailed at stables, Lt. Gen. Polk and staff

     Sept.–Dec. 1863   Present

     9 Dec. 1863   Enterprise, MS/Receipt for expenses incurred for eight-day cattle drive

     May–June 1864   Dalton, GA/Absent, detailed at headquarters of Lt. Gen. Polk

     26 Apr. 1865   Durham Station, NC/Surrendered

SEPARATION   1 May 1865/Greensboro, NC/Parole, released from military service

PERSONAL NARRATIVE

OCCUPATION   Clerk in retail store
GENEALOGY   Son of John Thuer, Switzerland
                       Married, ca. 1869, Louisiana, Rosalee Magdelena
                           Freudenstein (b. June 1850, Louisiana; d. Mar. 1942,
                           New Orleans, LA)
RESIDENCES   1860, Jefferson County, MS
                       1870, Ascension Parish, LA
                       1880, New Orleans, LA
                       1890, New Orleans, LA

SOURCES

NARA M320, reel 032; M1781, reel 006
New Orleans, LA, Death Records Index, 1804–1949
New Orleans, LA, Directories, 1890–1891
Obituary: *New Orleans Daily Picayune*, 17, 18, 19, and 30 Mar. 1893
US Census 1860, 1870, 1880
US and Canada, Passenger and Immigration Lists Index, 1500s–1900s

TOURTAREL, Jean Baptiste, Jr.

BIRTH   ca. 1839/Louisiana
DEATH   20 July 1875/New Orleans, LA

RECORD OF SERVICE

CSA ENLISTMENT   6 Mar. 1862/New Orleans, LA/90 days
                       29 May 1863/Mobile, AL/Duration of the war

ORLEANS LIGHT HORSE TRANSFER DATA
   INBOUND   29 May 1863/Private
   OUTBOUND   29 Jan. 1864/Private
SERVICE RÉSUMÉ
   29 May 1863   Mobile, AL/Received into the Orleans Light Horse from
                           Co. D, Orleans Guards Regiment, Louisiana Militia;
                           enlistment bounty, $50

   May–June 1863   Present
   July–Aug. 1863   Absent, sick
   Aug. 1863   Chattanooga, TN/Sent to hospital at Rome, GA
   Sept.–Oct. 1863   Cassville, GA/Absent, sick in hospital
   Nov.–Dec. 1863   Cassville, GA/Absent, sick
   29 Jan. 1864   Cassville, GA/Detailed to duty in Flewellen Hospital, by
                           reason of being medically unfit for field duty
   May–June 1864   Absent, detailed in hospital by order of secretary of war

PERSONAL NARRATIVE

OCCUPATION   Clerk in cotton exchange
GENEALOGY   Married, ca. 1864, Ada Marguerite Delpuech (b. Jan. 1837,
                           Louisiana; d. 18 Feb. 1921, New Orleans, LA)

        1860, New Orleans, LA
1870, New Orleans, LA
1873, New Orleans, LA
1874, New Orleans, LA
1875, New Orleans, LA

SOURCES

Edwards' Annual Director, 1873
Louisiana, Compiled Census and Census Substitutes Index, 1791–1890
NARA M320, reels 032, 0400
New Orleans, LA, Death Records Index, 1804–1949
Soards' New Orleans Directory, 1874–75
US Census 1860, 1870

TRELLUE, Marcus George

BIRTH   1841/Harrison, IN

RECORD OF SERVICE

CSA ENLISTMENT   1 July 1861/Memphis, TN/One year
1 Sept. 1863/Chattanooga, TN/Duration of the war

ORLEANS LIGHT HORSE TRANSFER DATA

    INBOUND   1 Sept. 1863/Private
    OUTBOUND   1 May 1865/Private

SERVICE RÉSUMÉ

    1 Sept. 1863   Chattanooga, TN/Received into the Orleans Light Horse
from the Twelfth Tennessee Regiment
    Sept.–Dec. 1863   Present
    May–June 1864   Present
    26 Apr. 1865   Durham Station, NC/Surrendered
SEPARATION   1 May 1865/Greensboro, NC/Parole, released from
military service

PERSONAL NARRATIVE

OCCUPATION   Farmer
GENEALOGY   Son of John and Sara (Matheny) Trellue, Louisville, KY
Brother of Napoleon B. Trellue
Married, ca. 1865, Tennessee, Linnie —— (b. ca. 1849,
Tennessee)
RESIDENCES   1860, Louisville, KY
1870, Gibson County, TN

SOURCES

NARA M320, reel 032
US Census 1860, 1870

TRELLUE, Napoleon Bonaparte

BIRTH   Apr. 1843/Louisville, KY
DEATH   1920/Patterson, LA

RECORD OF SERVICE

CSA ENLISTMENT   1 July 1861/Memphis, TN/One year
    1 Sept. 1863/Chattanooga, TN/Duration of the war

ORLEANS LIGHT HORSE TRANSFER DATA
    INBOUND   1 Sept. 1863/Private
    OUTBOUND   1 May 1865/Private

SERVICE RÉSUMÉ
    1 Sept. 1863   Chattanooga, TN/Received into the Orleans Light Horse from the Twelfth Tennessee Regiment

    Sept.–Dec. 1863   Present
    May–June 1864   Present
    16 Apr. 1865   West Point, GA/Captured
    23 Apr. 1865   Transferred to US military prison, Macon, GA
SEPARATION   1 May 1865/Macon, GA/Parole, released from military service

PERSONAL NARRATIVE

OCCUPATION   Retail merchant
GENEALOGY   Son of John and Sara (Matheny) Trellue, Louisville, KY
    Brother of Marcus G. Trellue
    Married, 18 May 1879, St. Mary Parish, LA, Sophia Grout
      (b. Jan. 1851, Patterson, LA; d. 23 Jan. 1919, Patterson, LA)

RESIDENCES   1860, Louisville, KY
    1880, Patterson, LA
    1900, St. Mary Parish, LA
    1910, St. Mary Parish, LA
    1920, St. Mary Parish, LA

SOURCES

NARA M320, reel 032
US Census 1860, 1880, 1900, 1910, 1920
www.findagrave.com, 53778529

TREPAGNIER, François Edmond

BIRTH   27 Feb. 1835/Convent, LA
DEATH   13 June 1895/New Orleans, LA

RECORD OF SERVICE

CSA ENLISTMENT   22 Mar. 1862/New Orleans, LA/90 days
    25 July 1862/Tupelo, MS/Duration of the war

ORLEANS LIGHT HORSE TRANSFER DATA
    INBOUND   22 Mar. 1862/Private
    OUTBOUND   25 June 1862/Private

SERVICE RÉSUMÉ
22 Mar. 1862   New Orleans, LA/Mustered into service of CSA with the
                      Orleans Light Horse
25 May 1862   Tupelo, MS/Sick in camp
6 June 1862   Camp Williamson, Tupelo, MS/Approved for discharge
SEPARATION   25 June 1862/Tupelo, MS/Discharge, acceptable substitute

PERSONAL NARRATIVE
OCCUPATION   Planter, manager of a sugar refinery
GENEALOGY   Son of Louis Edmond and Zillia (Roman) Trepagnier,
                      St. James Parish, LA
                      Married, 23 Nov. 1858, St. James Parish, LA, Eulalie
                      Humphries (b. 24 Mar. 1841, Louisiana; d. 17 Mar. 1883,
                      New Orleans, LA)
RESIDENCES   1850, St. James Parish, LA
                      1860, New Orleans, LA
                      1870, Plaquemines, LA
                      1880, New Orleans, LA

SOURCES
Louisiana Marriages, 1718–1925
NARA M320, reel 032
New Orleans, LA, Death Records Index, 1804–1949
US Census 1850, 1860, 1870, 1880

TRIST, Nicholas Philip, Sr.

BIRTH   25 Sept. 1843/Ascension Parish, LA
DEATH   22 Feb. 1913/New Orleans, LA

RECORD OF SERVICE
CSA ENLISTMENT   6 Mar. 1862/New Orleans, LA/90 days
                      1 July 1862/Tupelo, MS/Duration of the war
ORLEANS LIGHT HORSE TRANSFER DATA
    INBOUND   1 July 1862/Private
    OUTBOUND   5 June 1864/Lieutenant
SERVICE RÉSUMÉ
1 July 1862   Tupelo, MS/Received into the Orleans Light Horse from
                      Co. B, Crescent Regiment, Twenty-Fourth Louisiana
                      Infantry
Sept.–Dec. 1862   Present
Jan.–June 1863   Present
July–Oct. 1863   Present
9 Aug. 1863   Chattanooga, TN/Detailed in charge of stock in pasture
Nov.–Dec. 1863   Absent, furlough
May–June 1864   Present
5 June 1864   Resaca, GA/Commissioned lieutenant; ordered transferred
                      to Trans-Mississippi Department by secretary of war

PERSONAL NARRATIVE
OCCUPATION   Planter

GENEALOGY	Son of Hore Browse and Elizabeth (Bringier) Trist, Pointe Coupée Parish, LA
	Married (1), 3 Jan. 1867, New Orleans, LA, Marie Emilie Felice Tureaud (b. 17 Jan. 1845, New Orleans, LA; d. 10 Dec. 1885, Lake Harris, FL)
	Married (2), 19 Mar. 1887, New Orleans, LA, Alice Tureaud (b. Aug. 1850, Mississippi; d. 24 Apr. 1928, New Orleans, LA)
RESIDENCES	1860, New York, NY
	1870, St. James Parish, LA
	1880, St. James Parish, LA
	1885, Lake Harris, FL
	1900, New Orleans, LA
	1910, New Orleans, LA

SOURCES

Florida State Census, 1885
Louisiana Marriages, 1718–1925
NARA M320, reel 032
New Orleans, LA, Death Records Index, 1804–1949
New Orleans, LA, Marriage Records Index, 1831–1920
New York Passenger Lists, 1820–1957
OR, ser. 1, vol. 7:325
US Census 1860, 1870, 1880, 1900, 1910
www.findagrave.com, 88113908

TUREMAN, Thomas Young Payne

| BIRTH | ca. 1829/Alabama |
| DEATH | before 1880/New Orleans, LA |

RECORD OF SERVICE

| CSA ENLISTMENT | 15 June 1863/Shelbyville, TN/Duration of the war |

ORLEANS LIGHT HORSE TRANSFER DATA

| INBOUND | 15 June 1863/Private |
| OUTBOUND | 20 May 1865/Private |

SERVICE RÉSUMÉ

June 1863	Shelbyville, TN/Received into the Orleans Light Horse
July–Oct. 1863	Present
19 July 1863	Shelbyville, TN/Detailed at Lt. Gen. Leonidas Polk's stable
Nov.–Dec. 1863	Absent, sick
19 Jan. 1864	Meridian, MS/Received clothing issue
May–June 1864	Dalton, GA/Absent, detailed to commissary department by order of Lt. Gen. Polk
12 July 1864	Griffin, GA/Medical determination: unfit for field service by reason of epilepsy; detailed to commissary department
20 May 1865	Greensboro, AL/Surrendered
SEPARATION	25 May 1865/Selma, AL/Parole, released from military service

OCCUPATION   Pharmacist
GENEALOGY   Son of Zachary Tureman, Gainesville, AL
                      Married, 11 July 1869, New Orleans, LA, Margaret Anna
                          Cooper (b. 15 June 1848, New Orleans, LA;
                          d. 2 Dec. 1902, New Orleans, LA)
RESIDENCES   1850, Gainesville, AL
                      1866, New Orleans, LA
                      1868, New Orleans, LA
                      1869, New Orleans, LA
                      1871, New Orleans, LA
                      1872, New Orleans, LA
                      1874, New Orleans, LA
                      1875, New Orleans, LA
ADDITIONAL INFORMATION Alternate spellings: T. Z. P. Tureman, T. W. Turennam,
                          T. Y. P. Turennam, and T. Z. P. Turennan

SOURCES

Edwards' Annual Director, 1871–72
Gardner's New Orleans Directory, 1866, 1868–69
NARA M320, reel 032
Soards' New Orleans City Directory, 1874–75
US Census 1850, 1880
www.findagrave.com, 12326667

URQUHART, Robert P.

BIRTH   ca. 1843/Louisiana

RECORD OF SERVICE

CSA ENLISTMENT   22 Mar. 1862/New Orleans, LA/90 days
ORLEANS LIGHT HORSE TRANSFER DATA
   INBOUND   22 Mar. 1862/Private
   OUTBOUND   25 June 1862/Private
SERVICE RÉSUMÉ
   22 Mar. 1862   New Orleans, LA/Mustered into service of CSA with the
                          Orleans Light Horse
   22 Mar.–25 May 1862 Present
   25 May 1862   Tupelo, MS/Detailed to duty
   6 June 1862   Camp Williamson, Tupelo, MS/Absent, detailed
SEPARATION   25 June 1862/Tupelo, MS/Discharge, unspecified

PERSONAL NARRATIVE

GENEALOGY   Son of James and Amanda Urquhart
                      Nephew of Lt. Col. David Urquhart, aide-de-camp to
                          Gen. Braxton Bragg
RESIDENCES   1850, Orleans Parish, LA
                      1870, New Orleans, LA
                      1880, Hinds County, MS

SOURCES
Edwards' Annual Director, 1870–72
Gardner's New Orleans Directory, 1866
NARA M320, reel 032
US Census 1850, 1880

VIAVANT, Auguste, Jr.

BIRTH	1835/New Orleans, LA
DEATH	26 Dec. 1896/New Orleans, LA

RECORD OF SERVICE

CSA ENLISTMENT	22 Mar. 1862/New Orleans, LA/90 days
	25 July 1862/Tupelo, MS/Duration of the war

ORLEANS LIGHT HORSE TRANSFER DATA

INBOUND	22 Mar. 1862/Private
OUTBOUND	1 May 1865/Sergeant

SERVICE RÉSUMÉ

22 Mar. 1862	New Orleans, LA/Mustered into service of CSA with the Orleans Light Horse
22 Mar.–25 May 1862	Present, in rank of private
6 June 1862	Camp Williamson, Tupelo, MS/Present, in rank of private
Sept.–Oct. 1862	Knoxville, TN/Present, in rank of sergeant
Nov.–Dec. 1862	Absent on leave, in position of fourth sergeant
Jan.–June 1863	Absent, on duty in rank of sergeant
9 Jan. 1863	Shelbyville, TN/Ordered to apprehend deserters in Louisiana
July–Aug. 1863	Absent, under orders, in rank of sergeant
Sept.–Oct. 1863	Absent with leave, in rank of sergeant
Nov.–Dec. 1863	Absent, under orders, in rank of sergeant
May–June 1864	Absent, sick, in rank of sergeant
26 Apr. 1865	Durham Station, NC/Surrendered
SEPARATION	1 May 1865/Greensboro, NC/Parole, released from military service

PERSONAL NARRATIVE

OCCUPATION	Accountant
GENEALOGY	Son of François Augustin and Charlotte (Bienvenu) Viavant, Dominican Republic
	Married, 28 Aug. 1867, New Orleans, LA, Emma Marie Matthey (b. 14 Aug. 1842, Louisiana; d. 19 Oct. 1900, New Orleans, LA)
RESIDENCES	1850, Orleans Parish, LA
	1860, New Orleans, LA
	1861, New Orleans, LA
	1869, New Orleans, LA
	1870, New Orleans, LA
	1871, New Orleans, LA
	1880, New Orleans, LA

SOURCES

Edwards' Annual Director, 1871
Gardner's New Orleans Directory, 1861, 1869
NARA M320, reel 032; M1781, reel 006
New Orleans, LA, Birth Records Index, 1790–1899
New Orleans, LA, Death Records Index, 1804–1949
US Census 1850, 1860, 1870, 1880

WALKER, James Campbell

BIRTH	14 Jan. 1837/Louisiana
DEATH	8 July 1898/New Orleans, LA

RECORD OF SERVICE

CSA ENLISTMENT	22 Mar. 1862/New Orleans, LA/90 days
	25 July 1862/Tupelo, MS/Duration of the war

ORLEANS LIGHT HORSE TRANSFER DATA

INBOUND	22 Mar. 1862/Private
OUTBOUND	17 May 1865/Corporal

SERVICE RÉSUMÉ

22 Mar. 1862	New Orleans, LA/Mustered into service of CSA with the Orleans Light Horse
22 Mar.–25 May 1862	Present, in rank of private
6 June 1862	Camp Williamson, Tupelo, MS/Absent, sick
Sept.–Oct. 1862	Present, in rank of private
Nov.–Dec. 1862	Murfreesboro, TN/Present, in rank of corporal
Jan.–Apr. 1863	Present, in rank of corporal
May–June 1863	Shelbyville, TN/Absent, sick, in rank of corporal
July–Aug. 1863	Present, in rank of corporal
Sept.–Dec. 1863	Meridian, MS/Present, in rank of corporal
May–June 1864	Present, in rank of corporal
26 Apr. 1865	LaGrange, GA/Surrendered
SEPARATION	17 May 1865/LaGrange, GA/Parole, released from military service

PERSONAL NARRATIVE

OCCUPATION	Attorney
GENEALOGY	Son of John and Catherine (Livingston) Walker, New Orleans, LA
	Married, 19 June 1876, New Orleans, LA, Corrine Louise Fabré (b. 1 Oct. 1851, Louisiana; d. 28 Aug. 1930, New Orleans, LA)
RESIDENCES	1850, New Orleans, LA
	1860, New Orleans, LA
	1880, New Orleans, LA
	1891, New Orleans, LA

SOURCES

Confederate Pension Applications Collection, Louisiana State Archives
NARA M320, reel 032

New Orleans, LA, Death Records Index, 1804–1949
New Orleans, LA, Directories, 1890–1891
New Orleans, LA, Marriage Records Index, 1831–1920
US Census 1850, 1880

WALLER, William Mikell

BIRTH	30 Dec. 1846/Lawrence County, MS
DEATH	28 Nov. 1931/Silver Creek, MS

RECORD OF SERVICE

CSA ENLISTMENT	27 Apr. 1864/Demopolis, AL/Duration of the war
ORLEANS LIGHT HORSE TRANSFER DATA	
INBOUND	27 Apr. 1864/Private
OUTBOUND	Aug. 1864/Private
SERVICE RÉSUMÉ	
27 Apr. 1864	Demopolis, AL/Received into the Orleans Light Horse
May–June 1864	Dalton, GA/Present

PERSONAL NARRATIVE

OCCUPATION	Farmer
GENEALOGY	Son of Benjamin and Nancy (Mikell) Waller, Silver Creek, MS
	Married, 15 Oct. 1868, Mississippi, Clarinda Cordelia
	Longino (b. 14 Feb. 1850, Silver Creek, MS;
	d. 4 May 1954, Silver Creek, MS)
RESIDENCES	1850, Hinds County, MS
	1860, Covington County, MS
	1870, Lawrence County, MS
	1880, Lawrence County, MS
	1920, Silver Creek, MS
	1930, Silver Creek, MS

SOURCES
NARA M320, reel 032
US Census 1850, 1860, 1870, 1880, 1920, 1930
US and International Marriage Records, 1560–1900
www.findagrave.com, 40487393

WATT, Andrew John

BIRTH	1835/Mississippi
DEATH	21 Mar. 1866/Paris, France

RECORD OF SERVICE

MILITIA SERVICE	Feb.–Nov. 1861
ORLEANS LIGHT HORSE TRANSFER DATA	
INBOUND	Feb. 1861/Private
OUTBOUND	30 Nov. 1861/Private

SERVICE RÉSUMÉ

23 Nov. 1861	New Orleans, LA/Militia service with the Orleans Light Horse; absent with leave
30 Nov. 1861	New Orleans, LA/Transferred, effective 19 Nov. 1861; accepted appointment as junior second lieutenant, Co. H, Eighteenth Louisiana Infantry Regiment

PERSONAL NARRATIVE

OCCUPATION — Cotton factor

GENEALOGY — Son of John and Harriet Louise (Hobbes) Watt, New Orleans, LA

RESIDENCES — 1860, New Orleans, LA

SOURCES

Gardner's New Orleans Directory, 1861, 1866

NARA M320, reel 032

US Census 1860

www.findagrave.com, 70830664

WATTERS, Samuel Paxon

BIRTH — 2 Nov. 1833/North Carolina

DEATH — 23 Nov. 1912/Charlottesville, VA

RECORD OF SERVICE

CSA ENLISTMENT — 1 May 1863/Shelbyville, TN/Duration of the war

ORLEANS LIGHT HORSE TRANSFER DATA

INBOUND — 1 May 1863/Private

OUTBOUND — 22 Oct. 1863/Private

SERVICE RÉSUMÉ

1 May 1863	Shelbyville, TN/Received into the Orleans Light Horse
May–June 1863	Present
Jul–Aug. 1863	Absent, sick
9 Aug. 1863	Rome, GA/Sick in hospital
Sept.–Oct. 1863	Present
22 Oct. 1863	Chickamauga, GA/Discharged by reason of having been offered a commission as lieutenant in the department of conscripts for the State of North Carolina

PERSONAL NARRATIVE

OCCUPATION — Episcopal clergy

GENEALOGY — Son of John and Mary Etta (Black) Watters, Wilmington, NC
Married Lydia Gates (b. 1851, Virginia; d. 2 Jan. 1918, Washington, DC)

RESIDENCES — 1850, Wilmington, NC
1860, New Hanover County, NC
1870, Madison, MS
1880, Newport, RI
1900, Hillsboro, NC

ADDITIONAL INFORMATION — Alternate spelling: S. P. Waters

SOURCES
Genealogical and Historical Notes on Culpeper County, Virginia
NARA M320, reel 032
Protestant Episcopal Church Clerical Directory, 1898
US Census 1850, 1860, 1870, 1900
www.findagrave.com, 67964214

WEATHERSBY, A. D.

RECORD OF SERVICE

CSA ENLISTMENT	27 Apr. 1864/Demopolis, AL/Duration of the war

ORLEANS LIGHT HORSE TRANSFER DATA

INBOUND	27 Apr. 1864/Private
OUTBOUND	Aug. 1864/Private

SERVICE RÉSUMÉ

27 Apr. 1864	Demopolis, AL/Received into the Orleans Light Horse
May–June 1864	Absent, furlough
29 June 1864	Atlanta, GA/Received clothing issue

SOURCES
NARA M320, reel 032

WHITE, ——

RECORD OF SERVICE

ORLEANS LIGHT HORSE TRANSFER DATA

INBOUND	June 1862/Private
OUTBOUND	6 June 1862/Private

SERVICE RÉSUMÉ

6 June 1862	Camp Williamson, Tupelo, MS/Approved for discharge
SEPARATION	6 June 1862/Tupelo, MS/Discharge, unspecified

SOURCES
NARA M320, reel 032

WILLIAMS, Joseph Minnick

BIRTH	7 Sept. 1833/Nashville, TN
DEATH	8 Dec. 1899/Nashville, TN

RECORD OF SERVICE

CSA ENLISTMENT	23 June 1863/Shelbyville, TN/Duration of the war

ORLEANS LIGHT HORSE TRANSFER DATA

INBOUND	23 June 1863/Private
OUTBOUND	1 May 1865/Private

SERVICE RÉSUMÉ

23 June 1863	Shelbyville, TN/Received into the Orleans Light Horse
July–Dec. 1863	Chattanooga, TN/Present, detailed at headquarters of Lt. Gen. Leonidas Polk

9 July 1863	Chattanooga, TN/Detailed with Maj. Arthur M. Rutledge, chief of ordnance
19 Sept. 1863	Chickamauga, GA/On duty as headquarters courier; involved in controversy that caused Lt. Gen. Leonidas Polk to be relieved of command; his sworn statement is included in military record
2 Mar. 1864	Receipt for pay due, Jan.–Feb. 1864
May–June 1864	Atlanta, GA/Absent, detailed to inspector general's office by order of Lt. Gen. Polk
2 May 1864	Dalton, GA/Receipt for pay due, Mar.–Apr. 1864
31 Oct. 1864	Franklin, TN/Present, detailed to inspector general department, Stewart's Corps
12 Jan. 1865	Commended in dispatches by Lieut. Gen. Alexander P. Stewart for operations at Atlanta, GA, 18 June–29 Sept. 1864
26 Apr. 1865	Durham Station, NC/Surrendered
SEPARATION	1 May 1865/Greensboro, NC/Parole, released from military service

PERSONAL NARRATIVE

OCCUPATION	Real estate
GENEALOGY	Son of David and Priscilla (Shelby) Williams, Davidson County, TN
	Married, 13 Nov. 1860, Maury County, TN, Emily Donelson Polk (b. 29 Mar. 1837, Maury County, TN; d. 22 Dec. 1892, Nashville, TN), niece of Lt. Gen. Polk
RESIDENCES	1860, Maury County, TN
	1880, Maury County, TN
ADDITIONAL INFORMATION	Alternate spelling: J. N. Williams

SOURCES

NARA M320, reel 032; M1781, reel 006

Nashville City Directory, 1900

OR, ser. 1, vol. 30, pt. 2:60, 61; *OR*, ser. 1, vol. 38, pt. 3:872

Tennessee Deaths and Burials Index, 1874–1955

Tennessee State Marriages, 1780–2002

US Census 1880

www.findagrave.com, 93197210

WILLIAMS, T. H.

| BIRTH | 1840 |

RECORD OF SERVICE

CSA ENLISTMENT	22 Mar. 1862/New Orleans, LA/90 days
ORLEANS LIGHT HORSE TRANSFER DATA	
INBOUND	22 Mar. 1862/Private
OUTBOUND	5 July 1862/Private

SERVICE RÉSUMÉ
22 Mar. 1862   New Orleans, LA/Mustered into service of CSA with the
                          Orleans Light Horse
22 Mar.–25 May 1862 Present
6 June 1862   Camp Williamson, Tupelo, MS/Present
SEPARATION   5 July 1862/Tupelo, MS/Discharge, physical disability
SOURCES
NARA M320, reel 032

WINDSOR, Nathaniel Anderson

BIRTH   12 Oct. 1840/Webster County, GA
DEATH   25 Oct. 1918/Richmond, VA

RECORD OF SERVICE
CSA ENLISTMENT   1 July 1861/Memphis, TN/One year
                     1 Sept. 1863/Chattanooga, TN/Duration of the war

ORLEANS LIGHT HORSE TRANSFER DATA
INBOUND   1 Sept. 1863/Private
OUTBOUND   1 May 1865/Private
SERVICE RÉSUMÉ
1 Sept. 1863   Chattanooga, TN/Received into the Orleans Light Horse
                          from the Twelfth Tennessee Regiment (dismounted)
Sept.–Dec. 1863   Present
May–June 1864   Present
26 Apr. 1865   Durham Station, NC/Surrendered
SEPARATION   1 May 1865/Greensboro, NC/Parole, released from
                          military service

PERSONAL NARRATIVE
OCCUPATION   Farmer
GENEALOGY   Son of Alexander S. and Harriett (Terry) Windsor, Webster
                         County, GA
                     Married, 2 Jan. 1868, Webster, GA, Martha Amarintha Peel
                         (b. 2 Sept. 1847, Webster, GA; d. 10 May 1912,
                         Atlanta, GA)
RESIDENCES   1850, Stewart, GA
                     1860, Webster, GA
                     1870, Webster, GA
                     1880, Webster, GA
                     1900, Villa Rica, GA
                     1910, Atlanta, GA
                     1915, Atlanta, GA

SOURCES
Atlanta City Directory, 1915
NARA M320, reel 032; M1781, reel 006
Obituary: *Atlanta Constitution*, 27 Oct. 1918
US Census 1850, 1860, 1870, 1880, 1900, 1910
US and International Marriage Records, 1560–1900

WINN, J.

RECORD OF SERVICE
CSA ENLISTMENT   1 July 1861/Memphis, TN/One year

                                 1 Sept. 1863/Chattanooga, TN/Duration of the war

ORLEANS LIGHT HORSE TRANSFER DATA

   INBOUND   1 Sept. 1863/Private

   OUTBOUND   30 June 1865/Private

SERVICE RÉSUMÉ

   1 Sept. 1863   Chattanooga, TN/Received into the Orleans Light Horse from the Twelfth Tennessee Regiment

   Sept.–Dec. 1863   Present

   May–June 1864   Absent, sick

   14 Feb. 1865   Meridian, MS/Admitted to hospital; transferred to Montgomery, AL

   4 May 1865   Citronelle, AL/Surrendered

SEPARATION   30 June 1865/Gainesville, AL/Parole, released from military service

SOURCES
NARA M320, reel 032

WOODLIEF, Peter William, Sr.

BIRTH   July 1808/Petersburg, VA

DEATH   13 Mar. 1883/New Orleans, LA

RECORD OF SERVICE
MILITIA SERVICE   23 Nov. 1861/Active

ORLEANS LIGHT HORSE TRANSFER DATA

   INBOUND   1861/Private

   OUTBOUND   22 Mar. 1862/Private

SERVICE RÉSUMÉ

   23 Nov. 1861   New Orleans, LA/Militia service with the Orleans Light Horse; present

SEPARATION   22 Mar. 1862/New Orleans, LA/Declined enlistment

PERSONAL NARRATIVE
OCCUPATION   Mortgage broker

GENEALOGY   Son of Thomas and Elizabeth (Claiborne) Woodlief, New Orleans, LA

                                 Married, 1835, New Orleans, LA, Louisa Modeste Bouligny (b. 12 Aug. 1810, New Orleans, LA; d. 12 Jan. 1892, New Orleans, LA)

RESIDENCES   1840, New Orleans, LA

                                   1850, New Orleans, LA

                                   1870, New Orleans, LA

                                   1880, New Orleans, LA

SOURCES
NARA M320, reel 032
New Orleans, LA, Death Records Index, 1804–1949
US Census 1840, 1850, 1870, 1880
www.findagrave.com, 58426750

WOODS, Arthur V.

RECORD OF SERVICE

MILITIA SERVICE	23 Nov. 1861/Active
ORLEANS LIGHT HORSE TRANSFER DATA	
INBOUND	1861/Private
OUTBOUND	22 Mar. 1862/Private
SERVICE RÉSUMÉ	
23 Nov. 1861	New Orleans, LA/Militia service with the Orleans Light Horse; present
SEPARATION	22 Mar. 1862/New Orleans, LA/Declined enlistment

PERSONAL NARRATIVE

OCCUPATION	Painter
GENEALOGY	Married, 8 Mar. 1871, New Orleans, LA, Jane Sherman (b. 1848)

SOURCES
Louisiana Marriages, 1718–1925
NARA M320, reel 032

WRESTER, J.

RECORD OF SERVICE

CSA ENLISTMENT	27 Apr. 1864/Demopolis, AL/Duration of the war
ORLEANS LIGHT HORSE TRANSFER DATA	
INBOUND	27 Apr. 1864/Private
OUTBOUND	Aug. 1864/Private
SERVICE RÉSUMÉ	
27 Apr. 1864	Demopolis, AL/Received into the Orleans Light Horse
May–June 1864	Present

SOURCES
NARA M320, reel 032

ORLEANS LIGHT HORSE.

APPENDIX A

◄ • • ►

CONSTITUTION AND BYLAWS

This transcription preserves the punctuation, capitalization, and spelling of the original document, which is in the holdings of The Historic New Orleans Collection (2014.0271), thanks to the generous donation of Bonnie Lee Corban.

CONSTITUTION.

OF THE

ORLEANS LIGHT HORSE.

ARTICLE 1.

SECTION 1.　In conformity to the Articles of War, or Military Regulations, the Company or Troop shall be composed of one Captain, one Lieutenant, two Sergeants, two Corporals and at least thirty members.

SEC. 2.　In the event of the Company increasing its members to the number of sixty privates, then and in that case, in conformity with the above mentioned laws for the regulation of the militia of Louisiana, there shall be elected one First Lieutenant, two Sergeants and two Corporals, in addition to the officers and non-commissioned officers elected or appointed for the first thirty members.

The company may have two trumpeters, but for the present, one will suffice.

ARTICLE 2.

SECTION 1.　Every member of the Orleans Light Horse shall be called upon to provide himself with the following necessaries and equipments:—

1.— Kepi, sky blue cloth, same as pantaloons; dark blue cloth band.

2.—One short single-breasted dark blue frock coat, regulation length of skirt, pelican buttons.

3.—One pair sky blue pantaloons, to be worn inside the boots, with a dark blue cloth stripe down the outside seam, two inches wide.

4.—A pair of long boots to come up to the knees, calf-skin, with enamelled leather legs.

5.—One horse, at least fifteen hands high.

6.—An english saddle, holsters, breast-plate, crupper, and pad at cantle of saddle to carry portmanteau on, and a portmanteau,—steel stirrups.

7.—Bit and bridoon, black leather reins.

8.—One or two blue blankets, halter and strap, sursingle, pair of steel spurs with straps.

9.—A pair of buckskin riding gloves, with gauntletts.

10.—A cartouch box, with shoulder straps in black varnished leather, two and a half inches wide.

SEC. 2.   The style and cut of the uniform, color, etc. shall be settled by the Committee on Administration and Discipline. The same as regards the other equipments and necessaries.

SEC. 3.   The arms of the company for the present shall be a light cavalry sabre and one or two pistols, as furnished by the State.

ARTICLE 3.

The officers and non-commissioned officers shall be elected by the members of the company assembled in meeting, by a majority of votes.

ARTICLE 4.

SECTION 1.   The Company will mount for instruction whenever the commanding officer shall judge necessary. The day, the time, and the place, shall be determined by him. The order for the meetings shall be given by him to the first sergeant, who shall inform the corporals, who shall apprise the other members.

SEC. 2.   A book for "orders of the day," and "General orders," shall be kept by the Commandant. Orders issuing from the Brigade or Division to which the Company may belong, shall be regularly entered as well as their own, and read at least once a week in the presence of the Company.

ARTICLE 5.

SECTION 1.   A permanent Council of Discipline and Administration shall be composed as follows:

1. Captain or Commanding Officer,
2. Lieutenant,
3. First Sergeant.
4. First Corporal.
5. One Private.

The Commanding officer shall be the permanent President, and shall appoint a Secretary.

SEC. 2.   Vote by proxy shall not be permitted.

Sec. 3.   This Committee shall be charged with watching over the enforcement of the rules and by-laws of the Company and the maintainance of discipline, the acceptance or rejection of demands for admission, and over the fines imposed for neglect of duty.

Sec. 4.   While under arms, or during any exercise, the members of the Company owe the most absolute subordination to their Chief. In the ranks, when not at a rest, they must obstain from speaking, laughing, smoking, chewing, and everything that may cause confusion or disorder. It is forbidden to make the least observation to the Commandant when at drill.

Sec. 5.   Punishments shall be, according to the slightness or gravity of the offense: censure at order of the day; fine; degrading to the ranks; expulsion from the company.

ARTICLE 6.

Section 1.   Every officer, non-commissioned officer, or private who shall neglect to attend drill, or parade, or any duty ordered by the Commanding officer, shall be fined from one dollar to ten, ($1 to $10), which sum shall be paid into the treasury of the Company.

Any one prevented from attendance, will give his excuses in writing to the Captain; if they are reasonable, he shall remit said fine. The Captain is sole judge, but may refer to the Committee on Discipline, if he thinks proper.

ARTICLE 7.

Section 1.   When the Company shall be mounted by order of the Commandant, every member shall assemble at the place of meeting at least a quarter of an hour before the appointed time. The Lieutenant, or Sergeant acting for him, shall report to the Captain the number of men under arms and the reason for absence of those not present.

ARTICLE 8.

Section 1.   One month after the formation of the Company, a general meeting shall be held for the revision of the present Constitution and additions of such By-Laws as experience may show to be desirable.

Sec. 2   The Company shall be duly organized, as soon as thirty-five members shall have signed this Constitution.

BY-LAWS

ORLEANS LIGHT HORSE.

ARTICLE 1.

MEMBERSHIP.

Any person desirous of joining the Orleans Light Horse, shall cause himself to be proposed in writing, stating his name, occupation and address, in full. Upon being notified of his election, it shall be his duty within three days to report himself at head quarters, sign the Constitution, and State Roll, and pay to the Treasurer ten dollars ($10) Fee of Initiation.

ART. 2.

MEMBERS.

Members are divided into two classes: 1st—Active. 2d—Members on the reserved list.

Honorary members may from time to time be elected as such, if they, from their distinguished services to the Company or the State, be deemed worthy of the honor.

ART. 3.

RESERVED LIST.

Such members as from ill health, press of business or occupations incompatible with their constant attendance at drill, may, when they are considered as competent by the Captain to perform their duties effectually when on active service, on application to the Committee on Discipline and Administration, be transferred to the reserved list.

It shall be the duty of members on the reserved list, to keep their arms and equipments at all times ready for active service; to turn out at all full dress parades, and whenever especially ordered by the Captain. It shall be their right to attend all drills and meetings of the Company and vote at the same, but they shall be exempt from fines for non-attendance at ordinary drills, etc., except when, as before stated, they may be especially ordered by the Captain.

They shall pay their dues semi-annually, in advance.

ART. 4.

CAPTAIN.

The duty of the Captain, besides the ordinary duties of his office, and those prescribed by the Constitution, shall be to call together the Committee on discipline and Administration at least once in every two weeks, and to see that orders from either Division, Brigade or Company head quarters are read at least once every week, and to preside at all meetings.

ART. 5.

LIEUTENANT.

The duty of the Lieutenant, besides taking the place of the Captain during his absence or disability to serve, shall be to act as Treasurer, and as such to keep an exact account of the receipts and disbursements of the Company. He shall enter all fines, assessments and dues against each member, and at each monthly meeting exhibit a tableaux of the same.

He shall have the right to call upon the Corporals for assistance in collecting from delinquent members.

ART. 6.

FIRST SERGEANT.

Shall call the roll at all drills and meetings, and hand to the Treasurer a list of members amenable to fines. He shall be ex-officio Secretary of all meetings. He shall keep a list of all members of the troop, with their residences or address. He shall divide the Company into the squads among the Corporals, so that any order from head-quarters may be communicated to each member with the shortest delay. He shall be the party through whom all applicants for leave of absence or excuse from drill shall be made, and all applications for membership, and generally, all applications from members to the Committee on Discipline and Administration.

ART. 7.

SECOND SERGEANT.

Shall keep duplicate rolls and lists of the members, and be at all times ready and prepared to take the place of the Orderly Sergeant when he may be absent or disqualified for serving.

ART. 8.

CORPORALS.

The Corporals must at all times keep a list of the members composing their own squad, with their addresses. They must be qualified to act as sub-instructors, and in the absence of the Sergeants, to act as drill masters of squads.

ART. 9.

ASSESSMENTS.

A monthly assessment of three dollars on each member must be paid at the regular monthly meetings. Any member asking for leave of absence for more than thirty days, must pay the assessment accruing in the time of his proposed absence in advance.

ART. 10.

The regular fines for non-attendance at drill, etc., shall be:

For a Private, ... $1 00
For a Non-Commissioned Officer, 1 50
For a Commissioned Officer, ... 2 00

They must be paid at each monthly meeting.

The Captain shall have the right to fine for any misconduct, or continued absence from drill, any amount not to exceed ten dollars, for each offense, subject to appeal to the Committee on Discipline and Administration.

ART. 11.

RESIGNATIONS.

All resignations shall be in writing, addressed to the Captain, and shall be accompanied by the payment to the Treasurer of the sum of twenty dollars, before it shall be accepted, as the proportion of the liabilities incurred by the Company in the lease of a riding hall, etc., besides all fines and dues that may be charged against him.

ART. 12.

MEETINGS.

The regular monthly meetings of the Company, unless otherwise ordered, shall take place on the first Wednesday of each month, at 7, P. M., at the Headquarters. The Annual meeting shall be the regular monthly meeting of the month of February; at which all accounts of the Treasurer shall be examined, audited, etc.

ART. 13.

ORDER OF BUSINESS.

The Order of Business at the regular Monthly meeting shall be:

1st.—Roll Call.
2d.—Reading of minutes of previous meeting.
3d.—Collection of fines and dues.
4th.—Report of Treasurer.
5th.—Report of Committees.
6th.—Elections.
7th.—Business laid over from previous meetings
8th.—New Business.

ART. 14.

COMMITTEE ON DISCIPLINE AND ADMINSTRATION.

This Committee shall be called by the Captain at least once in two weeks, and pass upon all applications for membership, hear all appeals, settle all difficulties that may arise between members of the corps, etc. Pass upon all questions of Uniform, equipments, finance and other matters that may be brought before them by the Captain.

HONORARY MEMBER.

J. McD. TAYLOR.

OFFICERS AND MEMBERS.

THOS. L. LEEDS,.................... CAPTAIN.
W. ALEX. GORDON, ... LIEUTENANT.
GEO. FOSTER,.................... 1st SERGEANT.
LEEDS GREENLEAF............,.... 2d SERGEANT.
P. B. O'BRIEN,...................... COLOR SERGEANT.
J. F. POLLOCK,.................... 1st CORPORAL.
NORMAN STORY,.................. 2d CORPORAL.
L. A. WELTON,.................... 3d CORPORAL.
ADOLPHE FAURE,................ 4th CORPORAL.

Henry Denis,
Will A. Bell,
B. F. Peters,
James Blanc,
James Miltenberger,
Edgar Boisblanc,
Aristide Hopkins,
Jos. T. Robinson,
Jas. Gallier, jr.,
S. P. Duncan,
Thos. L. Clarke,
H. Thornhill,
Chas. Andrew Johnson,
A. Freriche,
Arthur Woods,
Andrew J. Watt,
Thos. M. Simmons,
W. Wallace,

R. W. Saunders,
Otto Pressprich,
Fitz Londale,
Geo. J. Olivier,
Sam'l R. Scott,
C. B. Broadwell,
E. L. Robelot,
Adolphe Boudousquie,
Chas. D. Lallande,
E. K. Converse,
Will. A. Freret,
J. P. Broadwell,
H. N. Robelot,
J. B. Lallande,
H. de Mahy,
Edward Hobart,
M. J. Brenan,
J. L. Gubernator,

A. B. Griswold.

VETERINARY SURGEON.

DR. L. R. DELRIEU.

HEAD-QUARTERS AND RIDING HALL.

Nos. 99 & 101 CIRCUS STREET.

Trumpeter,................ Alexander St. Phar.

APPENDIX B

◆ ◆ ◆ ◆

KNOWN BURIAL SITES OF THE ORLEANS LIGHT HORSE CAVALRYMEN AND THEIR GENERALS

NAME	LOCATION	DATES	FINDAGRAVE.COM
THE GENERALS			
Polk, Leonidas	Christ Church Cathedral New Orleans, LA	b. 10 Apr. 1806 d. 14 June 1864	4419
Stewart, Alexander P.	Bellefontaine Cemetery St. Louis, MO	b. 2 Oct. 1821 d. 30 Aug. 1908	11084
THE CAVALRYMEN			
Armstrong, Christian D.	Cypress Grove Cemetery New Orleans, LA	b. 30 Jan. 1843 d. 21 May 1908	90110923
Armstrong, Henry A.	Metairie Cemetery New Orleans, LA	b. 20 Aug. 1844 d. 28 Dec. 1919	70466416
Bein, Hagart	Washington Cemetery Houston, TX	b. 26 May 1843 d. 1 Mar. 1902	64407741
Belknap, Morris S.	Cave Hill Cemetery Louisville, KY	b. 12 Aug. 1845 d. 19 July 1890	74635069
Bergeron, Octave J.	Immaculate Conception Cemetery Assumption Parish, LA	b. 17 Dec. 1842 d. 8 Oct. 1921	94569223
Blanc, Jules A., Jr.	Lafayette Cemetery No. 1 New Orleans, LA	b. 12 Oct. 1846 d. 1 Oct. 1867	11811162
Carré, Walter W.	Greenwood Cemetery New Orleans, LA	b. 6 June 1829 d. 31 Jan. 1877	89704881
Cenas, Edgar H.	St. Louis Cemetery No. 1 New Orleans, LA	b. 13 Apr. 1844 d. 30 July 1866	39830162
Chaillé, Stanford E.	Lafayette Cemetery No. 1 New Orleans, LA	b. 9 July 1830 d. 27 May 1911	11713493
Christian, Paul J.	Jackson Cemetery Jackson, LA	b. Apr. 1829 d. 15 Dec. 1913	78227228
Clarke, Thomas L.	Lafayette Cemetery No. 1 New Orleans, LA	b. 1830 d. 18 Feb. 1874	11893910
Clough, John A.	Sharkey Cemetery Amite, LA	b. ca. 1840 d. 9 Nov. 1897	64965435
Delgado, Alexander	Glenwood Cemetery Houston, TX	b. 8 Mar. 1844 d. 21 Jan. 1920	39160403
Denis, Henri W.	Live Oak Cemetery Pass Christian, MS	b. 12 Jan. 1828 d. Aug. 1916	50789346

Dowsing, Jonathan W.	Oak Hill Cemetery Birmingham, AL	b. 9 Mar. 1830 d. 29 May 1895	15296988
Egelly, Charles R.	Lake Providence Cemetery Lake Providence, LA	b. 25 Apr. 1845 d. 23 Feb. 1903	43664679
Fazende, Leon Jacques	St. Louis Cemetery No. 1 New Orleans, LA	b. Oct. 1827 d. 26 Mar. 1907	103052044
Fisher, John H.	Greenville Cemetery Greenville, MS	b. 26 June 1841 d. 1 Mar. 1892	31873163
Foley, Thomas W. P.	Metairie Cemetery New Orleans, LA	b. 5 Apr. 1837 d. 10 Feb. 1866	94569836
Freret, Frederick G.	Lafayette Cemetery No. 1 New Orleans, LA	b. Dec. 1839 d. 14 Mar. 1904	11894153
Freret, William A., II	Metairie Cemetery New Orleans, LA	b. 19 Jan. 1833 d. 5 Dec. 1911	70632843
Gallier, James, Jr.	St. Louis Cemetery No. 3 New Orleans, LA	b. 25 Sept. 1827 d. 16 May 1868	94570013
Gardner, Livingston H., Sr.	Greenwood Cemetery New Orleans, LA	b. 7 Nov. 1836 d. 23 Nov. 1910	77926395
Glynn, Michael	Franklin Cemetery Franklin, LA	b. 6 Nov. 1838 d. 24 Apr. 1918	61292303
Gordon, William A.	Saint Mary Cemetery Chatawa, MS	b. 1828 d. 1 Mar. 1885	26065033
Gribble, William C.	Asbury Cemetery Warren County, TN	b. Jan. 1831 d. 7 Nov. 1910	37543873
Griswold, Arthur B.	Lafayette Cemetery No. 1 New Orleans, LA	b. 9 Sept. 1829 d. 30 May 1877	6589311
Gubernator, John L.	Lafayette Cemetery No. 1 New Orleans, LA	b. 17 June 1821 d. 6 Feb. 1895	11894561
Gunnison, Amos B.	Lafayette Cemetery No. 1 New Orleans, LA	b. 10 May 1839 d. 8 Mar. 1885	11894570
Haney, Martin	Saint Vincent de Paul No. 2 New Orleans, LA	b. July 1842 d. 1 Aug. 1906	94670501
Hardin, James O.	Spring Hill Cemetery Spring Hill, TN	b. 18 May 1837 d. 24 Apr. 1924	14327995
Hébert, Jules A.	Metairie Cemetery New Orleans, LA	b. Apr. 1840 d. 9 Feb. 1905	70632921
Hite, Cadwalader M.	Glenwood Cemetery Houston, TX	b. 11 June 1836 d. 22 Apr. 1882	83905638
Hobart, Edward	Central Cemetery Plymouth, MA	b. 26 June 1825 d. 18 Feb. 1885	108699275
Hopkins, Aristide R.	Metairie Cemetery New Orleans, LA	b. 10 Nov. 1839 d. 27 June 1925	8584395
Huntington, Benjamin W.	Natchez City Cemetery Natchez, MS	b. 16 July 1822 d. 9 Jan. 1887	102355749
Jonas, Julian J.	Dispersed of Judah Cemetery New Orleans, LA	b. 12 Aug. 1836 d. 27 Feb. 1872	71341439

Keeble, Richard C.	Live Oak Cemetery Selma, AL	b. 12 Dec. 1840 d. 14 July 1885	76996724
Kennedy, Thomas S.	St. Louis Cemetery No. 1 New Orleans, LA	b. 1 Mar. 1844 d. 20 Oct. 1917	105643915
Lawler, John W.	Evergreen Memorial Park Riverside, CA	b. Dec. 1836 d. 1910	7129066
Le Sassier, George	Metairie Cemetery New Orleans, LA	b. 1 July 1839 d. 11 Mar. 1908	70785786
Lonsdale, Fitzwilliam	Lafayette Cemetery No. 1 New Orleans, LA	b. 1832 d. 12 Aug. 1875	12326515
Lotspeich, James T.	Oakwood Cemetery Corsicana, TX	b. Dec. 1830 d. 11 Dec. 1907	104362920
Mansfield, Richard	Magnolia Cemetery Mobile, AL	b. ca. 1832 d. 2 Dec. 1863	70944272
Martindale, Fenelon B.	Covington Cemetery Covington, LA	b. Sept. 1828 d. 10 Feb. 1906	86565118
McKnight, John H.	Lafayette Cemetery No. 1 New Orleans, LA	b. 1841 d. Mar. 1865	11713626
Mitchell, Christophal C.	Old Palestine Cemetery Pearl River County, MS	b. 4 Jan. 1828 d. 30 Dec. 1900	32602672
Moore, James B., Sr.	St. Louis Cemetery No. 1 New Orleans, LA	b. 13 Aug. 1837 d. 29 Oct. 1903	70959116
Moriarty, William A.	Charity Hospital Cemetery New Orleans, LA	b. 1824 d. 3 Mar. 1877	27785434
O'Brien, Patrick B.	Metairie Cemetery New Orleans, LA	b. 1825 d. 16 Oct. 1896	71466518
Parsons, James W.	Mount Hope Cemetery Rochester, NY	b. 8 July 1839 d. 5 Jan. 1873	13507960
Patrick, Josiah C., Jr.	Lafayette Cemetery No. 1 New Orleans, LA	b. 1839 d. 24 May 1898	11894820
Perkins, John A.	Lafayette Cemetery No. 1 New Orleans, LA	b. Jan. 1838 d. 8 Jan. 1904	—
Perkins, Louis W.	Union Cemetery Leesburg, VA	b. 14 Oct. 1842 d. 14 Feb. 1908	50184245
Peters, Benjamin F.	Lafayette Cemetery No. 1 New Orleans, LA	b. Aug. 1831 d. 20 June 1908	12150793
Reynolds, Thomas S.	Oakland Cemetery Atlanta, GA	b. 25 Nov. 1822 d. 6 Jan. 1891	41324530
Robinson, Emanuel T.	Oaklawn Cemetery Welsh, LA	b. 22 Aug. 1843 d. 3 Jan. 1924	69886445
Rountree, Austin W.	Lafayette Cemetery No. 1 New Orleans, LA	b. 27 Mar. 1830 d. 14 Mar. 1893	12920442
Ryall, Henry C.	Willow Mount Cemetery Shelbyville, TN	b. 19 Feb. 1845 d. 29 Nov. 1923	84422541
Ryall, Johnston S.	Willow Mount Cemetery Shelbyville, TN	b. 31 Oct. 1838 d. 5 Dec. 1917	84422260

Safford, Henry, Jr.	American Cemetery Natchitoches, LA	b. 9 Dec. 1824 d. 5 Mar. 1884	30052617
Seiler, Frederick W.	Metairie Cemetery New Orleans, LA	b. 1834 d. 1 Dec. 1911	70785862
Simmons, Jackson W.	Simmons Family Cemetery Washington Parish, LA	b. July 1834 d. 1917	26201465
Simmons, Robert W.	Metairie Cemetery New Orleans, LA	b. 1830 d. 28 Jan. 1909	70785879
Spratt, Robert B.	Myrtlewood Cemetery Livingston, AL	b. 18 Feb. 1847 d. 24 Apr. 1864	118454686
Stewart, Reuben C.	Whipp Cemetery St. Landry Parish, LA	b. 1 July 1825 d. 21 Nov. 1926	16173146
Taylor, John M.	Lafayette Cemetery No. 1 New Orleans, LA	b. ca. 1799 d. 19 Nov. 1883	11758920
Tennison, William H.	Sunlight Cemetery Belgrade, MO	b. 15 Apr. 1840 d. 7 Aug. 1914	5282968
Thornhill, Henry M.	Cypress Grove Cemetery New Orleans, LA	b. 1824 d. 11 Nov. 1870	94631935
Trellue, Napoleon B.	Patterson Protestant Cemetery Patterson, LA	b. Apr. 1843 d. 1920	53778529
Trist, Nicholas P., Sr.	Saint Michael Cemetery Convent, LA	b. 25 Sept. 1843 d. 22 Feb. 1913	88113908
Tureman, Thomas Y. P.	Lafayette Cemetery No. 1 New Orleans, LA	b. ca. 1829 d. before 1880	12326667
Waller, William M.	Calvary Baptist Cemetery Silver Creek, MS	b. 30 Dec. 1846 d. 28 Nov. 1931	40487393
Watt, Andrew J.	Metairie Cemetery New Orleans, LA	b. 1835 d. 21 Mar. 1866	70830664
Watters, Samuel P.	Oakdale Cemetery Wilmington, NC	b. 2 Nov. 1833 d. 23 Nov. 1912	67964214
Williams, Joseph M.	Mount Olivet Cemetery Nashville, TN	b. 7 Sept. 1833 d. 8 Dec. 1899	93197210
Woodlief, Peter W., Sr.	Lafayette Cemetery No. 1 New Orleans, LA	b. July 1808 d. 13 Mar. 1883	58426750

❖ BIBLIOGRAPHY ❖

GOVERNMENT AND MILITARY RECORDS

NARA M231 *Index to Compiled Service Records of Confederate Soldiers Who Served in Organizations from the State of Tennessee.* National Archives Microfilm Publication M231. War Department Collection of Confederate Records, Record Group 109. Washington, DC: National Archives and Records Service, 1957.

NARA M237 *Passenger Lists of Vessels Arriving at New York, 1820–1897.* National Archives Microfilm Publication M237. Records of the US Customs Service, Record Group 36. Washington, DC: National Archives and Records Service, 1962.

NARA M320 *Compiled Service Records of Confederate Soldiers Who Served in Organizations from the State of Louisiana.* National Archives Microfilm Publication M320. War Department Collection of Confederate Records, Record Group 109. Washington, DC: National Archives and Records Service, 1961.

NARA M331 *Compiled Service Records of Confederate General and Staff Officers, and Nonregimental Enlisted Men.* National Archives Microfilm Publication M331. War Department Collection of Confederate Records, Record Group 109. Washington, DC: National Archives and Records Service, 1962.

NARA M347 *Unfiled Papers and Slips Belonging in Confederate Compiled Service Records.* National Archives Microfilm Publication M347. War Department Collection of Confederate Records, Record Group 109. Washington, DC: National Archives and Records Service, 1962.

NARA M359 *Records of the Louisiana State Government, 1850–1888.* National Archives Microfilm Publication M359. War Department Collection of Confederate Records, Record Group 109. Washington, DC: National Archives and Records Service, 1962.

NARA M378 *Index to Compiled Service Records of Confederate Soldiers Who Served in Organizations from the State of Louisiana.* National Archives Microfilm Publication M378. War Department Collection of Confederate Records, Record Group 109. Washington, DC: National Archives and Records Service, 1962.

NARA M598 *Selected Records of the War Department Relating to Confederate Prisoners of War, 1861–1865.* National Archives Microfilm Publication M598. War Department Collection of Confederate Records, Record Group 109. Washington, DC: National Archives and Records Service, 1966.

NARA M603 *Internal Revenue Assessment Lists for New York and New Jersey, 1862–1866.* National Archives Microfilm Publication M603. Records of the Internal Revenue Service, Record Group 58. Washington, DC: National Archives and Records Service, n.d.

NARA M711 *Registers of Letters Received by the Office of the Adjutant General, 1812–1889.* National Archives Microfilm Publication M711. Records of the Adjutant General's Office, 1780s–1917, Record Group 94. Washington, DC: National Archives and Records Service, 1968.

NARA M754 *Internal Revenue Assessment Lists for Alabama, 1865–1866.* National Archives Microfilm Publication M754. Records of the Internal Revenue Service, Record Group 58. Washington, DC: National Archives and Records Service, 1969.

NARA M769 *Internal Revenue Assessment Lists for Louisiana, 1863–1866.* National Archives Microfilm Publication M769. Records of the Internal Revenue Service, Record Group 58. Washington, DC: National Archives and Records Service, 1972.

NARA M818 *Index to Compiled Service Records of Confederate Soldiers Who Served in Organizations Raised Directly by the Confederate Government and of General and Staff Officers and Nonregimental*

Enlisted Men. National Archives Microfilm Publication M818. War Department Collection of Confederate Records, Record Group 109. Washington, DC: National Archives and Records Service, 1970.

NARA M861   *Compiled Records Showing Service of Military Units in Confederate Organizations.* National Archives Microfilm Publication M861. War Department Collection of Confederate Records, Record Group 109. Washington, DC: National Archives and Records Service, 1973.

NARA M1781   *Muster Rolls and Lists of Confederate Troops Paroled in North Carolina.* National Archives Microfilm Publication M1781. War Department Collection of Confederate Records, Record Group 109. Washington, DC: National Archives and Records Service, 1994.

OR   United States War Department. *The War of the Rebellion: A Compilation of the Official Records of the Union and Confederate Armies.* Edited by Robert N. Scott, H. M. Lazelle, George B. Davis, Leslie J. Perry, Joseph W. Kirkley, Fred C. Ainsworth, John S. Moodey, and Calvin D. Cowles. 4 ser. 70 vols. Washington, DC: Government Printing Office, 1880–1901.

ARCHIVAL REPOSITORIES

The Historic New Orleans Collection, New Orleans, LA

Louisiana State Archives, Baton Rouge, LA

Louisiana Division, New Orleans Public Library, New Orleans, LA

Rosenbach Collection, Philadelphia, PA

Special Collections, Howard-Tilton Memorial Library, Tulane University, New Orleans, LA

Tennessee State Library and Archives, Nashville, TN

UNPUBLISHED SOURCES

Ancestry.com
> *Following are the databases and records accessed on Ancestry.com. The site compiled these databases and records through a variety of archiving bodies, including courthouses; genealogical, medical, military, and religious organizations; libraries; the National Archives and Records Administration (NARA); and state archives.*
> 1881 England Census
> Alabama Census of Confederate Soldiers, 1907
> Alabama Deaths, 1908–1959
> Alabama, Deaths and Burials Index, 1881–1974
> Alabama Homestead and Cash Entry Patents, Pre-1908
> Alabama Marriage Collection, 1800–1969
> Alabama Marriages, 1809–1920 (Selected Counties)
> Alabama State Census, 1820–1866
> Birmingham, AL, Directories, 1888–1890
> Boston, 1821–1850, Passenger and Immigration Lists
> Boston Passenger and Crew Lists, 1820–1954
> California Death Index, 1940–1997
> California Voter Registers, 1866–1898
> Civil War Prisoner of War Records, 1861–1865
> Confederate Applications for Presidential Pardons, 1865–1867
> Directory of Deceased American Physicians, 1804–1929
> Florida State Census, 1718–1925
> Genealogical and Historical Notes on Culpeper County, Virginia

Louisiana, Compiled Census and Census Substitutes Index, 1791–1890

Louisiana Marriages, 1718–1925

Louisiana Statewide Death Index, 1900–1949

Marriages of Mobile County, AL, 1813–1855

Massachusetts, Town Birth Records, 1620–1850

Massachusetts, Town and Vital Records, 1620–1988

Mississippi Marriages, 1776–1935

Missouri Marriage Records, 1805–2002

Missouri Marriages, 1766–1983

New Hampshire Births and Christenings Index, 1714–1904

New Orleans City Directory, 1892–1895

New Orleans, LA, Birth Records Index, 1790–1899

New Orleans, LA, Death Records Index, 1804–1949

New Orleans, LA, Directories, 1890–1891

New Orleans, LA, Justices of the Peace Index to Marriage Records, 1846–1880

New Orleans, LA, Marriage Records Index, 1831–1920

New Orleans, LA, Marriage Records Index, 1831–1925

New Orleans Passenger List Quarterly Abstracts, 1820–1875

New Orleans Passenger Lists, 1813–1945

New Orleans Passenger Lists, 1820–1945

New York, Death Newspaper Extracts, 1801–1890 (Barber Collection)

New York Passenger Lists, 1820–1957

New York Passenger and Immigration Lists, 1820–1850

Protestant Episcopal Church Clerical Directory, 1898

Sons of the American Revolution Membership Applications, 1889–1970

Tennessee Civil War Confederate Pension Applications Index

Tennessee Death Records, 1908–1951

Tennessee Deaths and Burials Index, 1874–1955

Tennessee Marriages, 1851–1900

Tennessee State Marriages, 1780–2002

Texas Death Index, 1903–2000

US and Canada, Passenger and Immigration Lists Index, 1500s–1900s

US Confederate Pensions, 1884–1958

US Federal Census Mortality Schedules Index, 1850–1885

US Federal Censuses

US General Land Office Records, 1796–1907

US and International Marriage Records, 1560–1900

US IRS Tax Assessment Lists, 1862–1918

US Military and Naval Academies Cadet Records and Applications, 1805–1908

US Naturalization Record Indexes, 1791–1992

US Passport Applications, 1795–1925

US Sons of the American Revolution Membership Applications, 1889–1979

Warren County, MS, Marriage Records

Woodford County, IL, Prairie District Library, Obituaries, 1887 to Present

Burnam, Catherine Barrett Robertson. "The Death and Funerals of Bishop-General Leonidas Polk." St. Paul's Church, Augusta, GA. http://www.saintpauls.org/history/polk-funeral/death-and -funerals-of-leonidas-polk-burnam/.

Crego, Arthur Van Voorhis. "The Organization and Function of the Staff of the Confederate Army of Tennessee." Master's thesis, Louisiana State University, 1965.

Findagrave.com.

JewishGen Online Worldwide Burial Registry. http://www.jewishgen.org/databases/cemetery.

Johnson, Robert Lewis. "Confederate Staff Work at Chickamauga: An Analysis of the Staff of the Army of Tennessee." Master's thesis, US Army Command and General Staff College, 1992.

Maki, Terence W., Jr., USAF. "Daniel Harvey Hill and His Contribution to the Battle of Chickamauga." Master's thesis, US Army Command and General Staff College, 2001.

National Endowment for the Humanities and Library of Congress. *Chronicling America: Historic American Newspapers*. http://chroniclingamerica.loc.gov.

PUBLISHED SOURCES

CITY DIRECTORIES

Atlanta City Directory, 1915. Atlanta: Atlanta City Directory Co., 1915.

Directory of the City of Mobile for the Year 1866. Mobile, AL: Farrow and Dennett Job Printers, 1866.

Edwards' Annual Director to the Inhabitants, Institutions, Incorporated Companies, Manufacturing Establishments, Business, Business Firms, etc., in the City of New Orleans. New Orleans: Southern Publishing Co., 1870–73.

Gardner's New Orleans Directory. New Orleans: Charles Gardner, 1861, 1866–69.

Morrison and Fourmy's General Directory of the City of Galveston, 1896–97… Galveston, TX: Morrison and Fourmy, 1896.

Nashville City Directory, 1900… Nashville: Marshall and Bruce Co., 1900.

Soards' New Orleans City Directory. New Orleans: L. Soards and Co., 1874–79, 1890–91, 1895, 1900, 1903.

BOOKS AND PERIODICALS

Alexander, Edward Porter. *Military Memoirs of a Confederate.* 1907. Reprinted with introduction and notes by T. Harry Williams. Bloomington: Indiana University Press, 1962.

Amann, William Frayne, ed. *Personnel of the Civil War.* Vol. 1, *The Confederate Armies.* New York: Thomas Yoseloff, 1961.

Antunes de Oliveira, Betty. "Some North Americans Naturalized as Brazilians, 1866–1889." *South Carolina Magazine of Ancestral Research* 25, no. 4 (Fall 1997): 183–90.

Arceneaux, Pamela D. "Library Acquisitions." *The Historic New Orleans Collection Quarterly* 30, no. 4 (Fall 2013): 18–19.

Bartlett, Napier. *Military Record of Louisiana.* 5 sec. 1875. Reprint, Baton Rouge: Louisiana State University Press, 1964.

Bennett, William W. *A Narrative of the Great Revival which Prevailed in the Southern Armies.* 1877. Reprint, Harrisonburg, VA: Sprinkle Publications, 1976.

Bergeron, Arthur W., Jr., ed. *The Civil War Reminiscences of Major Silas T. Grisamore, C. S. A.* Baton Rouge: Louisiana State University Press, 1993.

———. *Confederate Mobile.* Jackson: University Press of Mississippi, 1991.

———. *Guide to Louisiana Confederate Military Units, 1861–1865.* Baton Rouge: Louisiana State University Press, 1989.

Biographical and Historical Memoirs of Louisiana… 2 vols. Goodspeed Publishing, 1892.

Blair, Jayne E. *The Essential Civil War: A Handbook to the Battles, Armies, Navies and Commanders.* Jefferson, NC: McFarland, 2006.

Bonds, Russell S. *War Like the Thunderbolt: The Battle and Burning of Atlanta.* Yardley, PA: Westholme, 2009.

Booth, Andrew B., comp. *Records of Louisiana Confederate Soldiers and Louisiana Confederate Commands.* 3 vols. Spartanburg, SC: Reprint Co., 1984.

Bradley, Mark L. *Last Stand in the Carolinas: The Battle of Bentonville.* Campbell, CA: Savas Woodbury, 1996.

Cameron, Robert S. *Staff Ride Handbook for the Battle of Perryville, 8 October 1862*. Fort Leavenworth, KS: Combat Studies Institute Press, US Army Command and General Staff College, 2005.

Carter, Hodding, and Betty Werlein Carter. *So Great a Good: A History of the Episcopal Church in Louisiana and of Christ Church Cathedral, 1805–1955*. Sewanee, TN: University Press, 1955.

Castel, Albert E. *Decision in the West: The Atlanta Campaign of 1864*. Lawrence: University Press of Kansas, 1992.

Catton, Bruce. *The Coming Fury*. Vol. 1 of *The Centennial History of the Civil War*. New York: Doubleday, 1961.

———. *Never Call Retreat*. Vol. 3 of *The Centennial History of the Civil War*. New York: Doubleday, 1965.

———. *Terrible Swift Sword*. Vol. 2 of *The Centennial History of the Civil War*. New York: Doubleday, 1963.

Confederate States of America War Department. *Regulations for the Army of the Confederate States, 1864*. 3rd ed. Richmond, VA: J. W. Randolph, 1864.

Connelly, Thomas Lawrence. *Army of the Heartland: The Army of Tennessee, 1861–1862*. Baton Rouge: Louisiana State University Press, 1967.

———. *Autumn of Glory: The Army of Tennessee, 1862–1865*. Baton Rouge: Louisiana State University Press, 1971.

Conservation Fund. *The Civil War Battlefield Guide*. 2nd ed. Edited by Frances H. Kennedy. Boston: Houghton Mifflin, 1998.

Cozzens, Peter. *The Darkest Days of the War: The Battles of Iuka and Corinth*. Chapel Hill: University of North Carolina Press, 1997.

Cunningham, O. Edward. *Shiloh and the Western Campaign of 1862*. Edited by Gary D. Joiner and Timothy B. Smith. New York: Savas Beatie, 2007.

Daniel, Larry J. *Soldiering in the Army of Tennessee: A Portrait of Life in a Confederate Army*. Chapel Hill: University of North Carolina Press, 1991.

Dyer, John P. "Some Aspects of Cavalry Operations in the Army of Tennessee." *Journal of Southern History* 8, no. 2 (May 1942): 210–25.

Eicher, David J. *The Civil War in Books: An Analytical Bibliography*. Urbana: University of Illinois Press, 1997.

Eicher, John H., and David J. Eicher. *Civil War High Commands*. Stanford, CA: Stanford University Press, 2001.

Elliott, Sam Davis. *Soldier of Tennessee: General Alexander P. Stewart and the Civil War in the West*. Baton Rouge: Louisiana State University Press, 1999.

Emerson, W. Eric. *Sons of Privilege: The Charleston Light Dragoons in the Civil War*. Columbia: University of South Carolina Press, 2005.

Engle, Stephen Douglas. *Struggle for the Heartland: The Campaigns from Fort Henry to Corinth*. Lincoln: University of Nebraska Press, 2001.

Esposito, Vincent J., ed. *The West Point Atlas of War*. Vol. 1, *The Civil War*. Compiled by the Department of Military Art and Engineering, The United States Military Academy. New York: Tess Press, 1995.

Evans, Clement A., ed. *Confederate Military History, Extended Edition*. 17 vols. 1899. Reprinted with a 2-volume cumulative index edited by Robert S. Bridgers. Wilmington, NC: Broadfoot, 1987.

Field, Ron. *The Confederate Army, 1861–65 (3): Louisiana and Texas*. Men-At-Arms. Oxford, UK: Osprey Publishing, 2006.

Fleming, Thomas. *A Disease in the Public Mind: A New Understanding of Why We Fought the Civil War*. New York: Da Capo, 2013.

Flood, Charles Bracelen. *Grant and Sherman: The Friendship That Won the Civil War*. New York: Farrar, Straus and Giroux, 2005.

Foreman, Amanda. *A World on Fire: The Epic History of the British in the American Civil War*. London: Allen Lane, 2010.

Foster, Buckley Thomas. *Sherman's Mississippi Campaign*. Tuscaloosa: University of Alabama Press, 2006.

Freeman, Douglas Southall, ed. *Lee's Dispatches*. New York: Putnam, 1957.

———. *Lee's Lieutenants: A Study in Command*. 3 vols. New York: Charles Scribner's Sons, 1950.

French, Samuel G. *Two Wars: An Autobiography of General Samuel G. French*. Nashville: Confederate Veteran, 1901.

Gabel, Christopher R. *Rails to Oblivion: The Decline of Confederate Railroads in the Civil War*. Leavenworth, KS: Combat Studies Institute Press, US Army Command and General Staff College, 2002.

Gallier, James. *Autobiography of James Gallier, Architect*. 1864. Reprinted with an introduction by Samuel Wilson Jr. New York, NY: Da Capo Press, 1973.

Greenleaf, James Edward, comp. *Genealogy of the Greenleaf Family*. Boston: F. Wood, 1896.

Groom, Winston. *Shrouds of Glory: From Atlanta to Nashville—The Last Great Campaign of the Civil War*. New York: Atlantic Monthly Press, 1995.

Gudmens, Jeffrey J., and the Staff Ride Team, Combat Studies Institute. *Staff Ride Handbook for the Battle of Shiloh, 6–7 April 1862*. Leavenworth, KS: Combat Studies Institute Press, US Army Command and General Staff College, 2005.

Hallock, Judith Lee. *Braxton Bragg and Confederate Defeat*. Vol. 2. Tuscaloosa: University of Alabama Press, 1991.

Henry, Robert Selph, ed. *As They Saw Forrest*. Monographs, Sources and Reprints in Southern History 3. Jackson, TN: McCowat-Mercer, 1956.

Hess, Earl J. *The Civil War in the West: Victory and Defeat from the Appalachians to the Mississippi*. Chapel Hill: University of North Carolina Press, 2012.

———. *Kennesaw Mountain: Sherman, Johnston, and the Atlanta Campaign*. Chapel Hill: University of North Carolina Press, 2013.

Hewitt, Lawrence L., and Arthur W. Bergeron Jr., eds. *Confederate Generals in the Western Theater: Essays on America's Civil War*. 3 vols. Knoxville: University of Tennessee Press, 2010–11.

Hill, Daniel Harvey. "Chickamauga." In *Battles and Leaders of the Civil War*, edited by Robert U. Johnson and Clarence C. Buel, 3:638–61. New York: Thomas Yoseloff, 1956.

Hood, Stephen M. *John Bell Hood: The Rise, Fall, and Resurrection of a Confederate General*. El Dorado Hills, CA: Savas Beatie, 2013.

Horn, Stanley F. *The Army of Tennessee*. Norman: University of Oklahoma Press, 1941.

Hughes, Nathaniel Cheairs, Jr. *Bentonville: The Final Battle of Sherman and Johnston*. Chapel Hill: University of North Carolina Press, 1996.

Johnson, Robert Underwood, and Clarence Clough Buel, eds. *Battles and Leaders of the Civil War*. 4 vols. 1887. Reprint, Norwalk, CT: Easton, 2002.

Johnston, Joseph E. *Narrative of Military Operations Directed during the Late War Between the States*. New York: D. Appleton, 1874.

Le Monnier, Yves R. "Gen. Leonidas Polk at Chickamauga." *Confederate Veteran* 24, no. 1 (Jan. 1916): 17–19.

Long, E. B., with Barbara Long. *The Civil War Day by Day: An Almanac, 1861–1865*. With a foreword by Bruce Catton. Garden City, NY: Doubleday, 1971.

McCardell, John. *The Idea of a Southern Nation: Southern Nationalists and Southern Nationalism, 1830–1860*. New York: Norton and Company, 1979.

McDonough, James L., and Thomas Lawrence Connolly. *Five Tragic Hours: The Battle of Franklin*. Knoxville: University of Tennessee Press, 1983.

McMurry, Richard M. *John Bell Hood and the War for Southern Independence*. Lexington: University Press of Kentucky, 1982.

———. *Two Great Rebel Armies: An Essay in Confederate Military History*. Chapel Hill: University of North Carolina Press, 1989.

McWhiney, Grady. *Braxton Bragg and Confederate Defeat*. Vol. 1. 1969. Reprint, Tuscaloosa: University of Alabama Press, 1991.

Military Historical Society of Massachusetts. *Papers of the Military Historical Society of Massachusetts*. Vol. 7, *Campaigns in Kentucky and Tennessee Including the Battle of Chickamauga, 1862–1864*. Boston, 1908.

Moriarty, Donald P. "William Ambrose Moriarty of Louisiana: An Historical Genealogy." Pts. 1 and 2. *Louisiana Genealogical Register* 38, no. 1 (Mar. 1991): 1–24; no. 2 (June 1991): 105–19.

Morse, Edward C. "The Morse Family in Louisiana." *Louisiana Historical Quarterly* 7, no. 3 (July 1924): 445.

Nichols-Belt, Traci, and Gordon Belt. *Onward Southern Soldiers: Religion and the Army of Tennessee in the Civil War*. Charleston, SC: History Press, 2011.

Nolan, Louis Edward. *Cavalry: Its History and Tactics*. 1853. Reprinted with an introduction by Jon Coulston. Yardley, PA: Westholme, 2007.

Olschner, Kay. "Medical Journals in Louisiana before the Civil War." *Bulletin of the Medical Library Association* 60, no. 1 (Jan. 1972): 1–13.

Parks, Joseph Howard. *General Leonidas Polk, C. S. A.: The Fighting Bishop*. Baton Rouge: Louisiana State University Press, 1962.

Polk, William Mecklenburg. *Leonidas Polk, Bishop and General*. 2 vols. 1893. Rev. ed. New York: Longmans, Green, 1915.

Ridley, Bromfield Lewis. *Battles and Sketches of the Army of Tennessee*. Mexico, MO: Missouri Printing and Publishing, 1906.

———. "Coming Home from Greensboro, N. C." *Confederate Veteran* 3, no. 10 (Oct. 1895): 308–9.

———. "The Last Night of Sixty-Four." *Confederate Veteran* 8, no. 12 (Dec. 1900): 539.

Rightor, Henry. *Standard History of New Orleans, Louisiana*. Chicago: Lewis, 1900.

Robertson, William Glenn, Edward P. Shanahan, John I. Boxberger, and George E. Knapp. *Staff Ride Handbook for the Battle of Chickamauga, 18–20 September 1863*. Leavenworth, KS: Combat Studies Institute Press, US Army Command and General Staff College, 1992.

Robins, Glenn. *The Bishop of the Old South: The Ministry and Civil War Legacy of Leonidas Polk*. Macon, GA: Mercer University Press, 2006.

Rodenbough, Theophilus F., ed. *The Cavalry*. Vol. 4 of *The Photographic History of the Civil War in Ten Volumes*. New York: Review of Reviews, 1911.

Rutstein, Robert P., and Kent M. Daum. *Anomalies of Binocular Vision: Diagnosis and Management*. St. Louis: C. V. Mosby, 1998.

Seitz, Don Carlos. *Braxton Bragg, General of the Confederacy*. Columbia, SC: State Co., 1924.

Sherman, William T. *Memoirs of General William T. Sherman*. 2 vols. New York: Appleton, 1875.

Sifakis, Stewart. *Compendium of the Confederate Armies: Louisiana*. New York: Facts on File, 1995.

Smith, Timothy B. *The Untold Story of Shiloh: The Battle and the Battlefield*. Knoxville: University of Tennessee Press, 2006.

Snow, William Parker. *Southern Generals: Who They Are and What They Have Done*. New York: Charles B. Richardson, 1865.

Spence, Philip B. "Campaigning in Kentucky." *Confederate Veteran* 9, no. 3 (Mar. 1901): 121–23.

———. "General Polk and His Staff." *Confederate Veteran* 9, no. 1 (Jan. 1901): 22–23.

———. "Services in the Confederacy." *Confederate Veteran* 8, no. 11 (Nov. 1900): 500–501.

Steiner, Paul E. *Disease in the Civil War: Natural Biological Warfare in 1861–1865*. Springfield, IL: Charles C. Thomas, 1968.

Stephens, Alexander H. *A Constitutional View of the Late War Between the States*. 2 vols. Philadelphia: National Publishing Co., 1868–70.

Stiles, Kenneth L. *4th Virginia Cavalry*. The Virginia Regimental Histories Series. Lynchburg, VA: H. E. Howard, 1985.

Stoddard, Brooke C., and Daniel P. Murphy. *The Everything Civil War Book*. Avon, MA: Adams Media, 2009.

Sword, Wiley. *Embrace an Angry Wind: The Confederacy's Last Hurrah: Spring Hill, Franklin, and Nashville*. New York: HarperCollins, 1992.

———. *Mountains Touched with Fire: Chattanooga Besieged, 1863*. New York: St. Martins, 1995.

Taylor, F. Jay, ed. *Reluctant Rebel: The Secret Diary of Robert Patrick, 1861–1865*. Baton Rouge: Louisiana State University Press, 1959.

Taylor, Richard. *Destruction and Reconstruction: Personal Experiences of the Late War*. New York: Appleton, 1879.

Van Zante, Gary. "James Gallier Sr." *KnowLA Encyclopedia of Louisiana* (October 1, 2012). http://www.knowla.org/entry/815.

Vandiver, Frank E. *Rebel Brass: The Confederate Command System*. Baton Rouge: Louisiana State University Press, 1956.

Wagner, Margaret E., Gary W. Gallagher, and Paul Finkelman, eds. *The Library of Congress Civil War Desk Reference*. New York: Simon and Schuster, 2002.

Waitt, Robert W. *Confederate Military Hospitals in Richmond*. Richmond, VA: Civil War Centennial Committee, 1964.

Walker, Scott. *Hell's Broke Loose in Georgia: Survival in a Civil War Regiment*. Athens: University of Georgia Press, 2005.

Warner, Ezra J. *Generals in Gray: Lives of the Confederate Commanders*. Baton Rouge: Louisiana State University Press, 1959.

Watkins, Samuel R. *Company Aytch, Maury Grays, First Tennessee Regiment; or, A Side Show of the Big Show*. Chattanooga: The Chattanooga Times, 1900.

Welsh, Jack. *Two Confederate Hospitals and Their Patients: Atlanta to Opelika*. Macon, GA: Mercer University Press, 2005.

Wert, Jeffry D. *General James Longstreet: The Confederacy's Most Controversial Soldier: A Biography*. New York: Simon and Schuster, 1993.

Wharton, Thomas K. *Queen of the South: New Orleans, 1853–1862, the Journal of Thomas K. Wharton*. Edited by Samuel Wilson Jr., Patricia Brady, and Lynn D. Adams. New Orleans: The Historic New Orleans Collection and the New York Public Library, 1999.

Wildey, Anna Chesebrough. *Genealogy of the Descendants of William Chesebrough of Boston, Rehoboth, Mass*. New York: T. A. Wright, 1903.

Wiley, Bell Irvin. *The Life of Johnny Reb*. 1943. Updated ed. Baton Rouge: Louisiana State University Press, 2008.

Williams, G. A. "Aristide Hopkins." *Confederate Veteran* 33, no. 9 (Sept. 1925): 346.

Williams, T. Harry, and A. Otis Hébert Jr. *The Civil War in Louisiana: A Chronology*. Baton Rouge: Louisiana Civil War Centennial Commission, 1961.

Winters, John D. *The Civil War in Louisiana*. Baton Rouge: Louisiana State University Press, 1963.

Wise, John S. *The End of an Era*. Boston: Houghton, Mifflin, 1902.

Woodworth, Steven E. *The American Civil War: A Handbook of Literature and Research*. Westport, CT: Greenwood, 1996.

———. *Decision in the Heartland: The Civil War in the West*. Westport, CT: Praeger, 2008.

———. *Jefferson Davis and His Generals: The Failure of Confederate Command in the West*. Lawrence: University Press of Kansas, 1990.

———. *Six Armies in Tennessee: The Chickamauga and Chattanooga Campaigns*. Lincoln: University of Nebraska Press, 1998.

Wortman, Marc. *The Bonfire: The Siege and Burning of Atlanta*. New York, Public Affairs, 2009.

❧ INDEX ❧

Note: Page numbers in italics refer to illustrations. The letter t *following a page number denotes a table.*

Bryan, Courtland A., 25t, 64t, 133
Bryan, T., 25t, 64t, 133–34
Bryan, William Hardy, Jr., 25t, 42t, 134
Bryantsville, Kentucky, *48* (map), 51, 52
Buell, Don Carlos, 26, 50–52
Buford, Abraham, 70t
Buord, Louis A., 25t, 96t, 134–35
Burnside, Ambrose E., 59–60
bushwhackers, 112
Butler, James M., 72t, 110, 135–36
Butler, William B., 100t
Byrd, John Grayson, 64t, 96t, 136
Byrne, Thomas K., 25t, 42t, 137

Cammack, Thomas Dixon, 110, 137–38
Campbell, James, 47t, 96t, 138
Campbell, Martin Gordon, 25t, 47t, 138
Cantey, James W., 75, 76t, 77, 82n3
Canton, Mississippi, *68* (map), 71
Carey, Henry Shields, 25t, 47t, 139
Carey, R. S., 64t, 72t, 139
Carré, Walter William, 18t, 25t, 140, appendix B
Cassady, B., 64t, 104t, 110, 140–41
Cassville, Georgia, 77, *85* (map)
Cavalry: Its History and Tactics (Nolan), 14
Cenas, Edgar Henry, 47t, 110, 141, appendix B
Chaillé, Stanford Emerson, 17, 18t, 142, appendix B
Chalaron, Joseph A., 11n3, 62, 67n28
Chalmers, James R., 50, 50t, 56t, 70t
Charleston, South Carolina, 13, 36n16, 73n8, 102, *107* (map)
Charvet, Lucien, 63, 64t, 110, 143
Chattahoochee River, 81, *85* (map), 87, 90, 92
Chattanooga, Tennessee, 8t, 46, *48* (map), 49, 58–60, 62, *65* (map), 71, 77, 112
Cheatham, Benjamin Franklin, 83n17
        as corps commander, Army of Tennessee, 81, 89, 93, 97n12, 100–101, 105n11
        as division commander, Army of Mississippi, 40t, 49, 50t
        as division commander, Army of Tennessee, 56t, 61t, 88
Chester, South Carolina, *107* (map), 111
Chew, ——, 42t, 47t, 144
Chickamauga, Georgia, 8t, *65* (map)
        Battle of, 60–63, 66n14, 67n23, 83n6, 83n11, 83n17
chief commissary of subsistence, role of, 31–32
chief of artillery, role of, 32
chief of staff, role of, 30
Choppin, Samuel, 39, *41*
Christian, Paul John, 25t, 64t, 144–45, appendix B
Citronelle, Alabama, 105n2, 109, 113n2
Claiborne, Archibald Junius, 25t, 72t, 145–46
Clark, Charles, 40t
Clarke, Thomas L., 18t, 25t, 146, appendix A, appendix B
Clauden, Edmon, 18t, 25t, 146–47
Cleburne, Patrick R., 61t
Clough, John Adolphus, 25t, 96t, 147, appendix B
Cockrell, Francis M., 70t, 76t, 88t
Colquitt, Peyton H., 61t
Columbia, South Carolina, 102, *107* (map)
Columbia, Tennessee, *84* (map), 92, 93
Columbus, Georgia, *106* (map), 112

Columbus, Mississippi, 46, *68* (map), 70, 71, 101
 garrison, 45, 46t
Confederate States Army (CSA)
 and command structure, 35–36n6
 and corps structure, 9, 28–32
 and the end of the war, 113n2
 and field rations, 32–33, 37n40
 and force structure, 19
 and medical services, 34
 and Orleans Light Horse mustering into, 9, 19–20, 23
 and unit structure, 28t
 See also specific armies and departments, battles, campaigns, and commanders
Confederate States Congress, 19, 36n7
 and conscription acts, 35n3, 46, 47n6
Confederate States war department, 55–57, 63, 69, 76, 78, 81, 82, 91, 99, 100
Connelly, Thomas L., 34
conscription acts, 35n3, 46, 47n6
Converse, Ephraim Kingsbury, 17, 18t, 23, 25t, 47t, 148, appendix A
Conyers Station, Georgia, 97n5
Coonley, Jacob F., photograph by, *95*
Cooper, Samuel, 81
Corinth, Mississippi, 8t, 23, 24, 26, 40, *43*, 50
Cosby, George B., 70t
Cowan, Tennessee, 58, *65* (map)
Cowarden, Samuel Lynch, 72t, 110, 149
Crain, Peter Wood, 53t, 64t, 149–50
Crain, Robert A., 25t, 64t, 150
Crumhorn, Harvey Nicholas, 9, 25t, 110, 150–51
Cumberland River, *48* (map), 50, *65* (map)

Dallas, Georgia, 77, *85* (map)
Dalton, Georgia, 60, *65* (map), 75, 77, *85* (map)
D'Aquin, Thomas Albert, 53t, 96t, 151–52
Davis, Jefferson, 66–67n14, 69, 97n5, 109
 and Atlanta Campaign, 90
 and Franklin-Nashville Campaign, 92
 and the Great Revival, 59, 67n16
 and Polk suspension, 63
 and review of Army of Tennessee, 57
Davis, R. H., 25t, 42t, 152–53
Delgado, Alexander, 53t, 110, 153–54, appendix B
Delrieu, Leon Raymond, 17, 18t, 23, 25t, 154, appendix A
De Mahy, Henry J., 18t, 25t, 154–55, appendix A
Demopolis, Alabama, *68* (map), 75, *84* (map)
Denis, Henri William, 18t, 25t, 155, appendix A, appendix B
Department of Alabama, Mississippi, and East Louisiana, 67n23, 69–74, 70t, 82n5, 100, 105n2, 109, 113n2
Department of East Tennessee, 45, 55, 56, 57
Department of Florida and South Georgia, 113n2
Department of Louisiana, 35–36n6
Department of Mississippi, 35–36n6
Department of Mississippi and East Louisiana, 35–36n6, 57, 59, 63, 66n6, 69, 73n8
Department No. 1, 16, 17, 36n6
Department No. 2, 8t, 19, 28, 36n16, 45–47, 46t, 83n11
 and Army of Mississippi, 23, 39–42, 45
 supplanted by the Department of the West, 57
Department of North Carolina, 66n14, 102, 105n11
Department of North Carolina and Southern Virginia, 113n2

pelican buckle, *35*
pelican button, *10*, 16
secession of, 13, 35n1
See also Natchitoches, New Orleans, Port Hudson, Shreveport
Louisiana Militia, 16, 36n7, 36n9, 115
First Division, 8t, 14, 17
See also Orleans Guards, Washington Artillery of New Orleans
Louisville, Kentucky, *48* (map), 50–51
Love, William Dickson, 64t, 110, 206–7
Lovejoy's Station, Georgia, *85* (map), 90
Lovell, Mansfield, 17, 36n10
Lovie, Henri, sketch by, *43*
Lowry, Robert, 100t
Lynd, Sav., 53t, 96t, 207

Mabry, Hinche P., 70t
Mackall, William W., 70t
Macon, Georgia, *85* (map), 90, *106* (map), 110, 112
Macready, John, 64t, 96t, 208
Macready, René, 47t, 110, 208–9
Mallen, J. B., 64t, 96t, 209
Manassas, First Battle of, 16, 36n16, 66n5, 105n2
Manchester, Tennessee, 56, 58, *65* (map)
Mandeville, T., 47t, 64t, 209–10
Maney, George E., 40t, 50t, 56t, 61t
Manigault, Arthur M., 50t, 56t
Mansfield, Richard, 64t, 72t, 210, appendix B
Marietta, Georgia, 10, 77, 78, *85* (map)
Martindale, Fenelon Beardsly, 53t, 110, 210–11, appendix B
Maury, Dabney H., 109, 113n2
May, Thomas Paine, 25t, 42t, 211–12
McCook, Edward M., 89, 113n2
McCulloch, Robert, 70t
McKnight, John H., 25t, 104t, 110, 212, appendix B
McNair, Evander, 70t
McPherson, James B., 88, 89
medical director, role of, 32
Memphis, Tennessee, 23, 26, *68* (map), 70, 71, 110
Menlo, Georgia. *See* Alpine, Georgia
Meridian, Mississippi, 8t, 9, *68* (map), 69, 70–71, *84* (map), 100, 110
mess furniture, 33
Military Record of Louisiana (Bartlett), 39–40
military service acts, 46, 47n6
militias and militia acts, 14, 35n3
See also Louisiana Militia
Milledgeville, Georgia, 100, 106 (map)
Miltenberger, James, 115, appendix A
Mississippi, 13, 16, 22, 36n16, 63, 67n23, 67n28, *68* (map), 71, 75, *84* (map), 90, 93, 100, 101, 109
See also Canton, Columbus, Corinth, Enterprise, Grenada, Iuka, Meridian, Okolona, Tupelo, Vicksburg, West Point
Mitchell, Christophal C., 25t, 110, 213, appendix B
Mitchell, William C., 25t, 64t, 214
Mobile, Alabama, 35n6, 46, 70, 71, 77, 101, 105n2, 109, 113n2
Montevallo, Alabama, 76, *84* (map)
Montgomery, Alabama, 13, 46, 110
Monty, F. P., 25t, 42t, 214–15
Moore, James Bradner, Sr., 47t, 110, 215, appendix B
Moore, Thomas O., 17